The Country Life Book of
Britain's
Offshore Islands

The Country Life Book of
Britain's
Offshore Islands

Michael Shea

Country Life Books

Frontispiece
*The St Kilda Group: the wild magnificence of high Stacs, boiling
seas and wheeling seabirds.*

Published by Country Life Books
Holman House, 95 Sheen Road,
Richmond upon Thames, Surrey, TW9 1YJ
and distributed for them by
The Hamlyn Publishing Group Limited
London . New York . Sydney . Toronto
Astronaut House, Feltham, Middlesex, England

First published 1981

ISBN 0 600 36766 5

Set in 10pt Palatino

Printed in England by
Fakenham Press Limited, Fakenham

Contents

Preface   9

Introduction   11

1. The Channel Islands   17

2. The Islands of the South Coast of England   30

3. The Isles of Scilly   45

4. The Islands of North Devon and Cornwall and the Bristol Channel   61

5. The Islands of Wales   68

6. The Isle of Man and the Islands of North-West England   81

7. The Islands of Northern Ireland   88

8. The Islands of South-West Scotland and the Firth of Clyde   96

9. The Inner Hebrides   108

10. The Outer Hebrides   149

11. The Far Isles   169

12. The Islands of the North-West and North
    Coasts of Scotland   181

13. The Orkney Islands   184

14. The Shetland Isles   194

15. The Islands of the East Coast of Scotland   210

16. The Islands of the East Coast of England   221

Afterthought   232

Additional Islands   234

A Note on Island Wildlife by Patrick Roper   236

Index   266

Illustration Acknowledgements   272

List of Colour Illustrations

View from Herm	41
The Asparagus Islands	42
Tresco Gardens	43
Bardsey	44
The Calf of Man	109
The remains of Bruce's Castle, Rathlin	110–11
Portree Harbour, Skye	112
The Storr Rock, Skye	112
Tràigh Seilebost, Harris	177
Callanish standing stones, Lewis	178–9
North Ronaldsay lighthouse	180
Italian Chapel, Lamb Holm	180
Papa Stour	213
The Bass Rock	213
Foula	214–15
Lindisfarne Castle	216

Preface

There are books in print about many of the more popular and accessible islands and island groups around the British mainland. But there is, at the time of writing, no single, comprehensive book that describes and illustrates the bulk of the more important islands, great and small, which together make a very significant contribution to what are called 'The British Isles'. This book aims to fill some of the gap, but, with an estimate of four thousand or more islands around the coastline (depending on how one defines an island), the selection process is a difficult one.

People who like islands will each have his or her favourite, since that is a symptom of what Lawrence Durrell has called 'islomania'; it will, in consequence, be surprising if some do not object to theirs being left out of the selection or to what they consider is the wrong emphasis or attributes being given to some aspect of their particular choice. To give a basic example: at a very early stage in the preparation of this book I was stridently taken to task by someone who argued that such and such an island was inhabited. I had stated the contrary. The point was one of definition – whether the absentee landlord of a remote Scottish isle, who perhaps spent a few holiday weeks in a cottage there each year, gave it the status of being inhabited or not. The reader can make up his own mind on the issue and on the many other points of stress, opinion and definition that he will find.

Seventy thousand words – the length of this book – seemed to offer vast scope when the venture was begun: in the end it has been much too small even for the vagaries of this unashamedly partial and eclectic approach. Judgements on the subject are, in consequence, often abbreviated and points of fact omitted by reason of lack of space rather than as a result of author's whim or by accident. Major suggestions raised by readers will however be welcomed and carefully noted. I should point out that for the sake of simplicity and consistency I have throughout the book adopted the spellings used on the Ordnance Survey metric maps of Great Britain.

The sources of the material in this book are legion, but personal investigation and the experience of friends and contacts have been of primary importance. Books, brochures, pamphlets, newspapers, magazines, all have added their own considerable supplement, but no particular book has been used to an extent which requires acknowledgement here, and to incorporate a bibliography would give an unbalanced impression of source and method. Many people have looked at parts of the manuscript and have offered helpful suggestions for improvement. It would be invidious to single them out but I would particularly like to thank Patrick Roper who has contributed an appendix on aspects of the natural history of islands, an area of expertise over which I have no substantial claim.

Finally, I would like to thank M.D.D.S. for all her most valuable research, and my wife for suggesting the idea and developing it with me.

Introduction

There are consistent but disparate fascinations about the growing sense of isolation, of remoteness, of leaving cares behind as one crosses the water away from the mainland. For many, the smaller the island goal and the more distant it is, the better. For others, even the larger islands, many with substantial climatic differences from the mainland, have equal attraction. Most of the major islands and groups of islands in the British archipelago are familiar to large numbers of people: The Isles of Man and Wight, the Scillies, the Orkneys, Shetland and the Channel Islands are relatively well populated or are popular holiday centres. Other islands, such as St Kilda and Staffa, are well known by name, but visited by few. Then there are a host of others, some populated, some deserted, some visitable and some privately owned, even the names of which are known only to a tiny proportion of the nation's population. How many have heard of Pladda, or Coquet Island, the Shiants or St Tudwal's Islands?

The geography and physical characteristics of these islands vary from the inhospitable remoteness of Rockall, the grandeur of the Bass Rock and the variety of Caldey, to the subtle gentleness of some of the flat green islands of the south. Their history is sometimes unimportant and sometimes crucial in the pattern of the past. Some were settled and are no longer; some support life easily; some are devoid of conditions that can sustain reasonable agricultural life; some have plant and animal populations that are peculiar to them alone.

It is a statement that offers little for dispute to say that the lure of any given island is radically different for different people. To a member of the National Trust for Scotland the remote island of St Kilda is, for example, an intrinsic part of the heritage of the country; for the ornithologist or naturalist it has its specific individualities of bird life, flora and fauna; to the historian or social anthropologist it offers the study of a society in microcosm, a society that declined to tragic extinction; to the geologist or geographer the rock formations and physical remoteness are of peculiar and exciting significance; to a child it is a black dot to the right-hand side of a blue-coloured Atlantic, conjuring up, perhaps, a picture of an even, green lump, sticking out of the sea, complete with sparkling lighthouse and wheeling seagulls; to the escapist (provided that permissions were forthcoming) it offers the supreme remoteness from the pressures of modern society, or it would do, were it not for the Defence Chiefs in Whitehall to whom St Kilda is an advance base and rocket-range tracking station of major strategic importance.

To the kings and queens of history and to their law officers islands have offered, in their turn, convenient places of banishment or imprisonment; but they offer refuge for the godly as well as the ungodly, free as they are from the temptations of the wider world. For these reasons of remoteness and difficulty of access, they became places of escape from political or religious persecution and chosen goals for the solitary monk or hermit. Equally, many writers and poets have had their output inspired by island living, imbued, like W. B. Yeats, with that peace of mind that comes from the natural and the remote.

Throughout the centuries, diplomats and statesmen have been beset by problems created by the geographical location of certain islands: they entice every question of international law, from problems of sovereignty through to those most modern considerations of oil, mineral and fishing rights. Politicians and economic planners, worried by the harsh and far from romantic realities of life in these remoter parts of the United Kingdom, call for reforms and produce blueprints; landlords depopulate to turn them into conveniently boundaried grouse moors, deer forests or sheep farms; crofters croft; fishermen fish and, with yachtsmen, seek safe shelter in their lee; weavers weave; ministers and priests preach to their tiny, dedicated flocks; distillers and brewers produce, and rich oil men and tourists help drink their output.

During the researching and writing of this book certain other strong historical and sociological factors presented themselves again and again as being part of a traditional condition of islands. One such common theme was violence-based: Vikings, pirates and smugglers naturally homed in on them. With the development of boats that held sufficient warriors, islands were easy to capture, since their populations tended to be small and poor. They then became easily defended bases for hit-and-run raids or forays to pillage and plunder the mainland. Equally, to privateers, they offered safe yet secretly convenient havens; and for smugglers of casks of brandy and bales of silk they provided discreet staging posts and hide-outs away from the excisemen.

A second factor is an even more obvious one, and a common-place of islands the world over: they offer danger of another kind, the physical risk to the mariner. Wrecks of galleys and coracles, longboats, brigantines and three-masters, tramp steamers, tankers and yachts litter the rock-strewn barriers to the British mainland. (At a rough count, if all the individual reports of Armada galleons having foundered round these islands were justified, then the Spaniards had a massive fleet indeed.) The consequence of this geographical fact was man's desire, from the earliest centuries, to try to prevent such disasters. And the lighthouses which now offer an almost unbroken chain of warning around our islands were the result. The history of lighthouse construction, from a primitive fire on a rocky promontory to the modern, thousand-candlepower-strong beam atop an invincible white tower, is a long and exciting story. While lighthouses are not by any means the monopoly of islands, the most famous of them – Longstone, Needles, Farne, Flannan – are island-based.

A third common denominator, one that in some ways is related to the varied dangers listed above, is that population figures, particularly of the smaller and remoter islands, have, almost without exception, reached their lowest in this century. Specifically excepting the large and prosperous islands – Wight, Jersey and Man, for example – the migration across the centuries has been in one direction only. Evidence is widespread of there having been, in centuries back to the Bronze Age and before, relatively large populations on many of the now uninhabited islands around the coast. For islands, in very primitive societies, offered better protection from hostile neighbouring tribes than any brushwood or earthwork fortification could ever do. Deliberate depopulation and the Clearances apart, the reasons for the later migrations are straightforward: as standards of life and expectations increased away from the subsistence level, people were drawn towards the more prosperous, more secure, less elemental, and away from famine and seaborne dangers.

Two other phenomena which recur again and again on islands round the British mainland have strong religious or mystical significance. The first is the surprising number of burial grounds, dating from early and primitive times, and found particularly in the west. One reason for this is certainly to do with the old Celtic tradition that the further west one was buried, the nearer to heaven and the better for one's soul. A second reason, more speculatively, was that the bodies of the dead, even if death was not caused by some disease or plague, were considered, by some primitive awareness of hygiene and the dangers of cross-infection, to be better buried and allowed to decompose at the other side of a sanitising cordon of water. The remoter the better, as was and is the case with siting graveyards away from human habitation, even in inland areas. Equally, the souls of the dead could not cross water, so there was less likelihood of the spirits of the past coming back to haunt the living.

An additional factor leading on to a further strong bond between so many of Britain's little islands is that large numbers of them were, to a greater or lesser degree, sanctified by the presence on them of religious communities of one form or another. Traces of monasteries, priories, even of lone hermit caves (many of their occupants through their austerity and sanctity ending up as saints), are found on a vast number of islands, so much so that in some areas, for example off the coast of Wales, nearly every one of them has had a religious foundation of some sort on it in its past. Why so? Undoubtedly it was in part due to a wish to seek peace and seclusion in a troubled world, a degree of safety for a community forbidden military disciplines, and a sense of unity and communality of purpose which isolated living brings even today. After all, where no islands were available, religious orders tended to build high walls to create their own islands of defendable and temptation-free peace wherever they went. From there they could, armed with the Word, sally forth to proselytise and convert, before returning to the fold to recharge themselves.

The number and frequency of monastic and other ancient sites on islands has however to be seen in perspective. By contrast with the situation on the mainland, much archaeological evidence has survived, simply because, where there was a decreasing population, there was less of a tendency or need to destroy the evidence of the past and pillage its ancient stones. How many castles and other monuments have been pulled asunder not so much by war but by the short-sighted requirement of successive generations to use what dressed stone was easily available for new homes and ways of life?

Finally in this brief list, two modern phenomena, tourism and oil, perhaps more than any other individual factor, have had their effect, and will continue to change what are often the highly puritanical life styles and economies of a large number of the offshore islands with which this book is concerned. Both offer great wealth and prosperity; yet, at the same time, all the risks and dangers of social and environmental pollution too often float in their wake.

If a substantial area of land surrounded by water equals an island, this gives a magical figure of around four thousand British islands. (One can count another thousand around the coast of the Republic of Ireland which are not part of this book.) But as many of them are tiny and barren and of interest to seabirds alone, this book creams off for description only the most important and most attractive of them. Even so, where does one begin to list them and where end?

The old Scottish definition that 'if it will support a sheep, it is an island; if not, it is a rock', does not, as it were, hold water. For a start, some islands which would not even support a rabbit must be included, because they carry manned lighthouses or are otherwise 'inhabited'; others, though barren, are included for their geographical, geological or other splendour. Again, what will easily be neglected as an anonymous and unnamed lump of granite among the remoter Outer Hebrides would have to be given the status of a Skye or Staffa if it became anchored in the mouth of the Thames or a few hundred yards from Bournemouth Promenade. Resited further south, there are many of these northern islands round which there would be boat trips, post-cards would exist of them and they would even have names, doubtless embossed in pink, in countless souvenirs of rock.

Which fact leads to another of the selection processes of this book. Of all these thousands of islands, by far the largest number have been blessed on the upper west coast of Scotland. Large stretches of the east coast of England, by contrast, have almost no islands alongside them. In the interests of balance, therefore, the author's decision has been to share the entries out on a geo-graphical basis which does not always reflect the truth in numeri-cal terms. Nonetheless, in the end, Scotland need not fear not getting its fair share.

What is included and what excluded in terms of the size and scope of individual entries has not been dictated solely by the size, geographical availability or popularity of the island con-cerned. Indeed, if there is further bias, it has been against the larger or better known islands (the Isle of Man, the Channel Islands, the Scillies, Bute), where there already exists a wealth of readily available literature. But that is not the only reason why these 'popular' islands get less than their fair share of attention. More importantly it is because, given the space available in this one book and bearing in mind that such islands could justifiably be due a book each, it offers a better approach to discuss them relatively briefly, in the overall context of the pattern of all the British Isles. Thus the entries on Jersey or the Isle of Wight are only brief sketches of a massive canvas, while those on much less known islands easily hold their own with anything that has appeared in print heretofore.

There is one further qualification. Very few precise statistics are included in this book relating, for example, to population. To give such figures, particularly for the remoter islands where the number of inhabitants all too often continues to decrease, would be misleading, and the information would rapidly become dated and inaccurate. In any case, most island populations have seasonal fluctuations and grow vastly in holiday periods not just with tourism but by the arrival of those with second homes there. So statistics, including those of size where there are frequent discrepancies in published figures, are given for general illustrative purpose only. (A comparison of major maps has, for example, the isolated far-northern Rona – where it is marked at all – moving around alarmingly.) For such numerical detail, readers should turn to a gazetteer.

The list of the names of the islands tells its own story, from the romantic – the Isle of May and Maiden Bower – to the explicit – Round, Sheep, Mouse, Calf or Asparagus Islands – and on to the less evocative Gugh, Yell and Worms Head, not to mention Dungball and Muck. The approach of the book, is starting with the Channel Islands, to travel round the coast in a clockwise direction. Some geographical groupings are described together for ease of reference, and some other small and less distinguishable groups of islands, or satellites of a larger one, are treated as one entry. What are not included are islands, many of which have a peculiar fascination of their own, which are sited on inland waters, lakes and lochs, or in the upper reaches of rivers. Nor have these neo- or former islands, the Isles of Dogs, Sheppey, Canvey, etc., been given a place in the book; others, in permanent contact with the mainland by road and rail bridge (for example Anglesey and Holy Island in north Wales), are generally disqualified, though how that will re-categorise all Britain when a Channel Bridge or Tunnel is constructed is another matter. High-water islands (Lindisfarne and St Michael's Mount) do however get through the hoop. Right up to the final submission of the manuscript, there were decisions to be made on what to include and what to disqualify, judgements enlivened from time to time by the appearance of evidence of 'new' islands to be vetted, ones which, if marked at all, were known by name and reputation only to some local connoisseur.

What is on offer in this book is a stimulant to wider choice rather than, as with many expert treatises, the provision of more and more information about less and less. It is designed, along with its illustrations, to whet the appetite with glimpses of history, geography, literature, fable and sociology. Also there is the potential for tourism (though detailed descriptions of availability of accommodation and transport are omitted, since they would so soon run out of date), for those who wish to experience the admixture of excitement and peace which even a brief spell of island living brings to everyman.

16

1 The Channel Islands

In the long and intense struggle across the centuries, historical legitimacy has always won out over geography with regard to the allegiances of the Channel Islands. In strict legal terms they have never been part of the United Kingdom, but ever since 1066, when the then Duke of Normandy came to the English throne as William I, they have been and remain dependencies of the British Crown. France, which is roughly ten times closer to them than Britain, has nonetheless left its enduring mark on them, and continues to exert authority over one or two islets in the group. Lest one might be tempted to think that dispute over questions of sovereignty over 'Les Iles Normandes' is something embedded in the past, it was as recently as 1953 that the International Court of Justice finally settled a long-standing feud with France by finding in favour of Britain over the ownership of two groups of rocks, Les Minquiers and Les Ecréhous. Victor Hugo graphically and succinctly described the islands as 'pieces of France fallen into the sea and gathered up by England', though the reasons for this most recent dispute admittedly owed more to adjacent fishing rights than to issues of territorial aggrandisement.

Offshore tax haven, honeymoon resort and retirement refuge; out-of-season tomatoes, flowers and potatoes; occupation by the Germans in the Second World War, and a strange person called the Dame of Sark – these are some commonplace items of school-boy knowledge about the islands. They are all fact; but there is a great deal more to be mentioned, including, at the outset, the surprising number of islands in the group. Jersey, Guernsey, Alderney, Sark and Herm are well known. But there are other islands with less familiar names: Jethou, Lihou, Brecqhou and Crevichon around Sark, Herm and Guernsey; Raz, Burhou, Les Casquets and Ortac near Alderney, and an equal number of islets and reefs along Jersey's southern shore. Together, they offer a

The
Channel Islands

1   Jersey
2   Les Écréhous
3   Les Minquiers (9
    miles south of
    Jersey)
4   L'Islet
5   St Aubin's
6   La Motte
7   Ile au Guerdain
8   Sark
9   Brecqhou
10 Alderney
11 Burhou
12 Raz
13 Les Casquets
14 Herm
15 Crevichon
16 Jethou
17 Guernsey
18 Lihou

varied and picturesque range of experience, with their almost Mediterranean vegetation, mild climate, and gentle mixture of French and English cultures. The names are so often French, the accents distinctive but unmistakably English.

The economy of the islands depends heavily on tourism and on the export of the cattle, fruit, vegetables and flowers for which they are so well known. Financial and tax incentives and the munificent protection of the British system of tariffs produce a high, comfortable and jealously protected standard (though high cost) of living. Despite their apparent vulnerability, they thrive, benefiting equally from their independence and from British protection, which is administered, peculiarly, through the Home Office in London. Such protection was found lacking only from 1940 to 1945 during the German occupation of the islands, when, despite the hardships that the islanders faced, loyalty to Britain remained unshaken. The independence of the islands which was so well demonstrated at that time stretches to forms of self-government which, along with minimal manifestations of the welfare state, often appear to the outsider to owe more to the feudal system than to any modern democratic form. Only the conduct of their international relations remains firmly in the hands of the Foreign and Commonwealth Office in London.

Jersey

As they move through life, most people develop a habit of either gilding or slandering their memories. Events, people and places are much better or much worse than was the reality. Either that, or they are simply forgotten. Retained for Jersey is a memory of flying to land over dense acres of greenhouses, laid out against a rich but well-packed landscape. With a tight area of only forty-five square miles, it is indeed generously populated, but much less so than its neighbour Guernsey, and there are still open spaces and quiet beaches to attract those who wish to shun the crowds. Those forty-five square miles comprise, in more normally understandable terms, a patch of land five miles by nine which floats in a sea of azure blue, and which its tourist authorities claim has, with its mild winters and long-lasting summers, the best sunshine record in the entire British Isles. We will come across other, similar claims on the long journey round the coast but Jersey must, nonetheless, rate high on the blue-sky list. Michael Drayton (1563–1631) put the island in its context:

> O! every happy isles, your heads so high that bear,
> By nature strongly fenced, which never need to fear,
> On Neptune's wat'ry realms, when Æolus raiseth wars,

18

13 11

10 12

14

15 16

18 St Peter Port

17

9 8

2

1

St Helier

5 4

7 6

0   10 miles

0   15 kms

3

And every billow bounds, as though to quench the stars:
Fair Jersey, first of these, here scattered in the deep . . .

An undemanding drive, following the varied coastline, lasts a
bare hour; in that time the old and the new move easily together.
Cloistered green-walled lanes blossom out at one moment into
fields of flowers for harvest, at another to overlook a pink, rock-
framed harbour or crumbling granite-built manor (some constructed by or for the favourites of King William I). Surrounded
by such rural but ordered bliss, prosperous, high-priced cows
ruminate alongside neat rows of seaweed-fertilised potato fields.

Les Ecréhous
Les Minquiers

Like the other islands, the 'States of Jersey' with, in the
Bailiwick, the disputed and sparsely inhabited Ecréhous rocks
and the reef known as Les Minquiers ('The Minkies' is their
anglicised nickname) are self-governing under 'the Monarch in
Council'. The 'State Assembly' or parliament, where French is
the official language, is regulated by an appointed bailiff who,
under the eye of the Queen's lieutenant-governor, doubles as
Speaker of the House and prime minister of a variegated body of
twelve senators, twenty-eight deputies and a dozen constables,
all of them popularly elected. The rich tradition is long and
honoured: Sir Walter Raleigh was Governor for three years from
1600, and later, during the Civil War, it became a staunchly
Royalist retreat. More recent famous children of Jersey include
the controversial 'Jersey Lily', Lillie Langtry, Sir John Everett

*Aerial view of the rich
fishing grounds round
Les Minquiers,
Channel Islands.*

20

Millais, the painter, and the founders of the de la Rue stationery and printing business and the Martell brandy concern.

Seaweed gatherers at L'Etacq, Jersey.

Amid all the charm and careful hospitality (heightened by a walk through the narrow streets of the capital, St Helier), the all-embracing feeling of wellbeing and prosperity is disturbed by one haunting and unromanticised memory. The huge four acres (1.6ha) of underground hospital at St Lawrence, tunnelled out of the rock during the German occupation, is a memorial to an unhappy, perhaps the most unhappy, part of Jersey's history. Cavern after cavern, ward after ward, complete with melancholy operating theatre, none of it ever used, has been worked deep into the hillside. That bitter task, carried out with the lives of grey Russian and Polish labour battalions, has provided its own cenotaph. The tragedy ended only when the British liberation forces landed, with, as some strange whimsy, the arms of the Duke of Normandy gallantly emblazoned on their shoulders.

With this great lesson behind it, the Jersey environment is stringently protected. Would-be immigrants must come exceptionally well heeled. Prosperity is an art. Jersey protects its inheritance.

Half a mile from the St Helier foreshore is the spectacular L'Islet. On it Elizabeth Castle sits tightly on the site of a seventh-century monastery. The castle, refuge for a while to the exiled Charles II,

L'Islet

21

Elizabeth Castle, Jersey. From a print dated 1783.

has long defended the approaches to the harbour. Built, destroyed and rebuilt many times over the years, most recently during the German occupation, it is now accessible to all who, at low tide, walk to it along the causeway. No guns or hostile arrows now; only a bell to signal a warning of the advancing tide. At the

St Aubin's opposite side of the bay is St Aubin's Fort, standing on its islet a short distance from the shore. The fort itself dates from 1542. At the west end of St Clement's Bay, and an island only at high tide,

La Motte is La Motte or Green Island (also a substitute name for Guernsey), where prehistoric remains and an ancient burial ground have

Ile au Guerdain been unearthed. The Ile au Guerdain lies further to the west in Portelet Bay. A structure known as Janvrin's Tower, which dates from the Napoleonic Wars, stands at its centre. It once served as last resting place to a certain plague-stricken sea captain called Janvrin, whose body was taken and left there, unburied for fear of cross-infection.

Sark

In his 'Ballad of Sark' the poet Swinburne wrote:

> Sark, fairer than aught in the world that the lit skies cover,
> Laughs inly behind her cliffs, and the sea-farers mark

22

As a shrine where the sunlight serves, though the blown
clouds hover . . . Sark.

Sark is different from all else. It is called feudal; the laws are
strange and, by the most famous of them, the motorcar is outlawed. It is small but superb. There are no eyesores and few gross
reminders of twentieth-century life. To be precise, it is 'they'
rather than 'it', for there are really two Sarks, joined precariously
by a high ridge of rock, La Coupée, which carries a reluctant cart
road, at times only six feet (1.8m) wide, some three hundred
vertigo-impelling feet (90m) above the sea. Transport, if one
must, is by horse and cart. But because it is only three miles by
one and a half, feet are a good substitute.

With its tiny island neighbour, the privately owned Brecqhou,
Sark is a young explorer's dream of caves and a myriad of rock
pools. Lording the centre of this strange demesne is the person of
'Le Seigneur' (for long the renowned Sybil Hathaway and now
her grandson, Michael Beaumont), Sark's feudal overlord, who
rules this tiny world with the help of a legislature known as the
'Court of Chief Pleas', comprising some forty landowners and a
dozen deputies. One can accuse Sark of feudality, but, in practice, each of these members has the tiny and highly democratic
burden of only ten other inhabitants to represent. This mini-state
has its own court of justice, which, meeting amid the textbooks

Brecqhou

*Non-motorised bliss on
Sark.*

and chalk of the local school, is presided over by the Seneschal, aided by Prévôt (sheriff) and Greffier (clerk). These ancient and ornate titles (and there are many more) allow the holders to sentence any miscreant to up to three days in Sark's tiny prison, for, while Sark comes under the Bailiwick of Guernsey, that larger island's police have to ask permission before landing.

From the harbour at Creux, which is alleged to be the world's smallest, the hinterland is accessible only by means of tunnels through the rock. Dating back to the sixteenth century, these tunnels are their own peculiar introduction to this unique island. Beautiful and strange things there are about Sark, though modern agriculture and hard-nosed tourism supply the economy. But tradition thrives and visitors must beware: only the Seigneur may keep a female dog on the island.

The island of Brecqhou seen from Sark.

Alderney

Nine brief miles off the coast of France lies, as part of the Bailiwick of Guernsey, the island of Alderney, whose uniquely placid and undramatic symbol is the cow. As with its sister island, its present prosperity lies in the twin blessings of agriculture and tourism, both successfully revitalised after the ruin left behind by German occupation. Somehow Alderney is more robust, more remote and more windswept than the other islands of the group and, on an occasional wintry day, has much in common with the Scottish islands to the north. Such unlikely comparison is reinforced by the high cliffs of the island, by the almost total lack of trees and by the dogged nature of its inhabitants who, ruled by a president and an elected body of nine, traditionally have more of the Briton's bluntness than the Gallic *goût* of some of the other Channel Islanders.

The tiny capital of St Anne, with its cobbled streets and clustering shops, is also, to borrow a phrase, 'more Anglo-Saxophone than Francophone'. Whether it was because of this extreme 'Britishness' or not, in the Second World War the entire population of the island was evacuated. German soldiers and the tragic

The tiny harbour of Creux, Sark, reached by tunnels through the rock.

25

slave-labour battalions took their place, frenetically fortifying Alderney well beyond its capacity or strategic importance. It became a concentration camp with a hideous reputation. Equally unhappily, it was turned into a fortress of concrete gun emplacements and military installations, many of which are, sadly, embedded for ever in Alderney's granite.

Burhou   To the west, the Swinge separates Alderney from the uninhabited island of Burhou, a low-lying wildlife and bird sanctuary with much to make it of particular esteem to the naturalist. Round the coast are a number of islets, several of which have ruined **Raz**   defences on them, including the island of Raz, off Longy Bay, which has a fort now converted to a summer chalet. Due west, as **Les Casquets**   another bird-watcher's paradise, are the nefarious Casquets, a group of spiky rocks which have, through the centuries, chewed many ships to their doom. One of these was the famous 'White Ship', which, in the year 1120, ran on to these teeth and sank, drowning its precious cargo, Prince William, heir to the throne of England. Lighthouses have, in consequence, been their most notable and redeeming feature.

Herm

By some freak of nature Herm, a brief one and a half miles by half a mile, is an island built of shells, bank after bank of them, piled up over the centuries. As far back as the seventeenth century, Dorothy Osborne, in one of her stream of letters to the diplomat Sir William Temple, wrote of this crustaceous phenomenon that it was 'next to being out of the world. There we might live like Baucis and Philemon, grow old together in our little cottage ...' Modern writers too have been attracted by its charm: Compton Mackenzie, with his vaunted love of islands, when he moved from the rigours of the Western Isles, bought it for his own before moving on again to neighbouring Jethou.

Crevichon   Unlike Alderney, Herm, with its tiny satellite isles which include Crevichon, is luxuriant, offering what has been called a natural laboratory of study to naturalist, botanist and ornithologist. It is rich too in its past, and the remains of a medieval prison are now part of the great house of the island. Its post-war development has owed most to its leaseholder, Major Peter Wood, who brought it back to life after years of neglect. Day-visitors beware: on Sark no bitches; here you must quit the island before dark.

Jethou   Neighbouring Jethou, a hump of land with a flat top and with its sinister tradition of being the hangman's isle for Guernsey (with witches and smugglers as the gibbet's speciality), has a more modern claim to fame: during his tenancy in the twenties and thirties Compton Mackenzie, who lived in the manor house, built up a large library and wrote over a dozen books, including his novel *Our Street* and the autobiographical *Gallipoli Memories*.

Guernsey

The green isle, 'Greneze', with its many magnificent beaches, demonstrably holds to the reasons for its name. Six miles by four, it should perhaps be listed after Jersey, since it is the other parent isle and has, within its Bailiwick, Alderney, Sark, Herm and Jethou. A self-governing community, it has as its capital St Peter Port. Its mild maritime climate, where frost and snow are rare, has permitted its long traditions of smuggling and privateering to be replaced by a more respectable and prosperous economic base: agriculture with the famous Guernsey cattle, market gardening and, like Jersey, thousands of acres of greenhouses full of tomatoes and flowers. The equally gentle skill of knitting has made the Guernsey pullover known to the world.

Jethou — the hangman's isle, as viewed from Herm.

A dense pattern of Guernsey tomato glasshouses, seen from the air.

Known as 'Sarnia' to the Romans, it has, unlike many of the other islands, never been dominated by one family group. From the fifteenth century it came under the rule of a captain, and later a lieutenant-governor, as the representative of the Sovereign. Nowadays, the governing assembly is presided over by a bailiff, counsellors, elected deputies and ten 'Douzaines' or parish representatives. Alderney contributes a further two deputies to Guernsey's so-called 'States of Deliberation'.

Victor Hugo, as an opponent of the regime of Louis Napoleon, moved to St Peter Port in 1855, and there on the cliff tops he wrote perhaps his most famous novel, *Les Misérables* (1862), and a number of other works, including *Les Travailleurs de la Mer* (1866), an epic which he set in Guernsey. His house, owned by the city of Paris, is now a museum for his life and works.

Guernsey's greatest problem is over-population, a contradiction to what is the usual experience of non-metropolitan islands the world over. Space is at a premium and every inch of land is built on or intensively cultivated. As with Jersey, one has to be rich to buy oneself into this cramped, low-taxed but beautiful world with its wealth of Anglo-Norman traditions. It is an island for all seasons.

28

To the west of Guernsey and accessible by foot only at spring tides, tiny Lihou, only a third of a mile long, is an unspoiled haven for birds, including heron, storm petrel, short-eared owl, brent goose and peregrine. Here are the still visible remnants of the twelfth-century Priory of Mary or Our Lady of the Rock, the chapel of which was destroyed in the mid-eighteenth century to avoid the danger of its occupation and fortification by the French. A remarkable event: the year before the Second World War began Lihou was advertised in *The Times* for the knockdown price of five pounds, a bargain even in those last ominous days before its peace was shattered by its becoming an artillery target for the German forces. In recent years new hope has come to Lihou through the development of a community youth project on the island.

Lihou

All these Channel Islands are variations on a theme, each one an island to itself, individual, even 'insular' in the best sense of the word, yet rich in history and tradition. And the people of these British islands are also particular. As Edith Carey has written of the 'thoroughbred' Channel Islander: 'To the world in general he asserts himself an Englishman, but in the presence of the English he boasts of being a Jersey-man or a Guernsey-man.' Of all the island groupings belonging to Britain, these are the most prosperous, the most 'modern' and the ones for which the future seems most securely assured.

2 The Islands of the South Coast of England

An insubstantial glance at a map of the south coast of England will reveal the mass of the Isle of Wight and, if the scale of the map is sufficiently large, perhaps also show St Michael's Mount. A much more detailed projection is required, however, before one can identify the interesting and varied range of other smaller islands along this seemingly uncomplicated coastline.

The Isle of Wight

The publicity and glossy tourist material about the Isle of Wight is larded with words full of respectable tradition. 'Edward I became Lord of the Isle in the year 1293 . . . Queen Victoria chose the Isle . . . the Prince Consort designed Whippingham Church . . . The Royal Yacht Squadron at Cowes, founded in 1815, is, uniquely, allowed to fly the White Ensign (blackballing Tommy Lipton because, even aged eighty and with every racing success behind him, he was still just a grocer . . .).' The average age of the population rises relentlessly year by year into dignified old age, yet the Isle of Wight has youth, it has vigour and it has modern industry, especially in the aviation field. A tight little corner with tight little attitudes which is very much part of southern England, yet is different.

In any library a dozen books are generally available on the Isle of Wight. It has, throughout the ages, been considered as a sort of England in microcosm, so much like part of the mainland that it hardly deserves the appellation 'island' which, by definition, suggests something remoter, with a distinct character of its own. An island it is, nonetheless, though geologists argue that two hundred and fifty thousand years ago, when Palaeolithic man still roamed the land, it was part of the mainland, giving it an island status which is much more recent than that of the majority of other places mentioned in this book. There are many interest-

Side by side: Queen Victoria's and Prince Albert's desks, Osborne House, Isle of Wight.

30

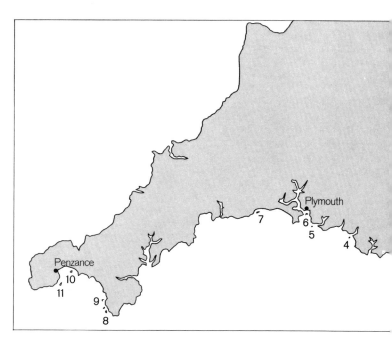

ing archaeological, particularly Bronze-Age, sites scattered across the island, and the Romans, who knew it as 'Vectis', also left their mark; Roman villas have recently been excavated in a number of places, including Carisbrooke.

Throughout its later history, Wight was both refuge and place of exile. Charles I was incarcerated in Carisbrooke Castle, while, at a later age, Queen Victoria and her husband Prince Albert chose the isle for their summer residence when they bought an estate there in the year 1845 and proceeded to erect Osborne House. Despite her long self-imposed exile at Balmoral, the old Queen returned to Osborne to die in the year 1901.

A bare twenty-two miles by thirteen in size, and separated from the mainland by the prosperously shored Solent, Wight is geographically and geologically of interest in possessing one of the thickest chalk layers in the British Isles. This unique stratum is most obvious on the western side of the island, where there is the traditionally evocative prospect of the Needles, three white teeth of rock, riding out into the sea. The last of them has the defiant red-and-white striped lighthouse perched prominently atop it, a 'resolute symbol of man's battle against nature', to quote the local literature. Against this background, it is the twins of tourism and sailing for which the Isle of Wight is most famous. Cowes, at the mouth of the river Medina, is the principal port and an internationally élite yachting centre, while, around the coast, are a host of more modest but agreeably fashionable holiday resorts.

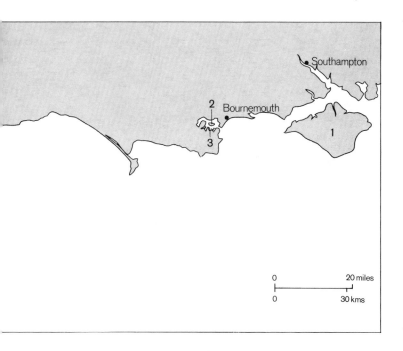

The South Coast of England

1 *The Isle of Wight*
2 *Brownsea*
3 *Other Poole Harbour Islands:*
    Long Island
    Furzey
    Gigger's Island
    Green Island
    Grove Island
    Pergins Island
    Round Island
4 *Burgh Island*
5 *Great Mew Stone*
6 *Drake's Island*
7 *St George's Island*
8 *Asparagus Island and Gull Rock*
9 *Mullion Island*
10 *St Michael's Mount*
11 *St Clement's Isle*

The National Trust has a number of important properties on Wight, including the Culver Downs to the extreme east, and the river, the quays and several miles of Solent coastline round Newtown, providing the setting for an attractive and unspoiled yachting harbour. It also owns seven miles of shoreline in west Wight, an area known for its white chalk cliffs which, alive with seabirds, tower high above the shore.

The Isle of Wight has many literary connections. John Keats stayed there in 1817, suggesting at that time that it should be renamed 'Primrose Island'. Tennyson bought a house at Farringford, near Freshwater, and many notable writers came to visit him, including Kingsley, Lear and Swinburne. There Tennyson was to compose the heroic *Charge of the Light Brigade*; *Maud* was also written there, along with other of his famous works. Longfellow came from the U.S., stayed briefly at an inn at Shanklin, and there wrote one of his less exciting inscriptions:

> Oh traveller, stay thy weary feet;
> Drink of this fountain, pure and sweet;
> It flows for rich and poor the same.
> Then go thy way, remembering still
> The wayside well beneath the hill,
> The cup of water in His name.

With hovercraft, hydrofoil and more traditional ferries, the four-mile stretch of water between the island and mainland is a short trek for holiday-maker and tourist. But it is a long one for

A famous welcome: the Needles from the air.

those involuntary inhabitants of the Isle of Wight. On the island is the famous Parkhurst prison, where those detained at Her Majesty's pleasure find, as Charles I did long before them, that the Isle of Wight is indeed well moated.

Poole Harbour Islands

There is a muddled archipelago of islands in Poole Harbour, that great estuary which, with its two tributaries the Frome and the Piddle, is like a lake almost cut off from the sea. The best known of the eight or nine islands is Brownsea. There were many more once, but over the years erosion and advancing tides have swept

Brownsea

34

them from existence except at the lowest of low water. Brownsea, like all its lesser neighbours, is a blur of sand and heath, but it also has a vigorous area of woodland which frames it and encourages its reputation as a favourite playground for people from Poole. On old maps and sea-charts it is called 'Brank' or 'Brunk Sea' ('Sea' most likely derived from the Viking '*øy*', meaning 'island'). Monks from Cerne Abbey had a chapel there in the twelfth century, dedicated to St Andrew, the patron saint of fishermen, and Henry VIII fortified it in the sixteenth century as a defence against a possible French invasion. The castle was garrisoned by the men of Poole, and during the Civil War was a strong Roundhead post. Thereafter it fell into disrepair.

In the early eighteenth century the owner of Brownsea was the eccentric William Benson who replaced Christopher Wren as Surveyor-General of the King's Works; it was he who converted the castle into a house. He was also a part-time botanist who recorded something of the island's wild flowers and plants. In the mid-nineteenth century a Colonel Waugh bought the 500-acre (202ha) island and tried to develop it, building a village, a church and a school. It was a happy idea and he had schemes to quarry

Brownsea Castle, Poole Harbour.

china clay there, but he brought little advance to the island and to himself only bankruptcy and eventual flight to an exile in Spain. More successfully in terms of long-lasting renown, Baden-Powell, the founder of the Scouting movement, went there in the year 1907 as guest of the then prosperous owner, taking some twenty boys with him to teach them to camp and learn something of woodcraft and survival in the wild. Thus Brownsea has become hallowed to millions, as the virtual birthplace of the Scouting movement. Twenty years later, under a strange woman owner who employed her own personal 'Amazon' to keep out intruders, the island began to fall into decline again.

More recently, the ground has been cleared and, with the help of the National Trust, made into a nature reserve, thereby having brought back to it a spirit of which Baden-Powell himself would have approved. When the Trust took it over it was almost totally neglected and only three people were living on it. Now, an average of sixty thousand people a year visit it and, as well as the nature reserve, there is a holiday centre for the John Lewis Partnership, a Scouts and Guides camping area, an Adventure Centre, a church, a shop and a restaurant. Despite all this activity, it retains its dignity and peace. By contrast with nearby Poole, from the moment one lands on Brownsea, one is in a world of woodland and heath, of quiet beaches and reed-banked marshes. It is teeming with wildlife and is one of the last places where the red squirrel survives in England. But, if you come, bring mosquito repellent: the marshes are their happy breeding ground.

Long Island

Apart from Brownsea, one of the more sizeable islands in the harbour area is Long Island. This, it is said, was once a hide-out for the famous 'Arripey', who, under his English name Harry Paye, was known as one of the great privateers of the fourteenth century. Paye brought many a captured ship from Spain and France to loot it in the safety of Poole Harbour. Long Island is now almost entirely a windblown patch of heath and sand. The other

Furzey

low-lying islands such as Furzey, which in season is ablaze with rhododendron blooms, are all privately owned. Among these

Gigger's Island
Green Island
Grove Island
Pergins Island
Round Island

others are Gigger's Island (difficult to reach because of the mud flats), Green Island (on which Roman remains have been found), Grove, Pergins and Round Island. Green Island was owned by the monks of Milton Abbey in the Middle Ages and here they built a chapel dedicated to St Helen. At one time, too, a causeway, still partly visible, connected it with the mainland.

One has to travel many miles from Poole along the placid south coast of England in a westerly direction before coming to the next island of note. About thirteen miles south-east of Plymouth, at the mouth of the Avon and a quarter of a mile off the caravan-blighted south Devon coast, lies the island of Burgh or Borough. It is accessible at low tide by a walk across the sands and it is now part of a lively holiday centre, specialising in self-catering holiday chalets. At high tide there is a fascinating rubber-wheeled machine which rides through the water, to ferry passengers dry-shod back and forward to the island. Herring gulls, nesting on the island's cliffs, are something of a menace, and their eggs are culled to try and control the population. There are a few indications of an earlier and less commercialised civilisation, including the faint ruins of a chapel, and on the north side of the island there is a pub, dating from the fourteenth century, called 'Pilchard's Inn', that probably takes its name from the specialised fishing for which the island was known until the end of the last century.

Burgh Island

Close inshore off Wembury Point in south Devon lies the Great Mew Stone, a conical rock rising some sixty feet (18m) above the sea. (There is a further Mew Stone east of the entrance to Dart-mouth Harbour.) A family is said once to have lived in a cottage on the three-acre (1ha) island to look after rabbits which were to be bred there as a commercial venture. In an age before that, monks kept an oil lamp burning on a tower on the island, a primitive lighthouse to act as a warning to sailors. The perfor-mance of this traditional function was a common activity of reli-gious settlements on the more dangerous of Britain's offshore islands. Of the several reasons given for the island's name, there is none that stirs the imagination sufficiently for it to be given currency here.

Great Mew Stone

Drake's Island

Of considerable strategic and psychological importance in the history of the south coast of England is Drake's Island, which lies in Plymouth Sound. It has been, in turn, a fort in Henry VIII's reign and then both stronghold and prison to the Roundheads. In the days of Elizabeth I Sir Francis Drake refortified it and is quoted as having said that 'he who holds the island, holds the town'; and with reason, since the fort at its centre does look out impressively over the one navigable approach up the Sound. And, as Sir Henry Newbolt in his own heroic style managed to convey, Drake's views mattered:

'Take my drum to England, hang et by the shore,
Strike et when your powder's runnin' low;
If the Dons sight Devon, I'll quit the port o' Heaven,
An' drum them up the Channel as we drummed them long
ago.'

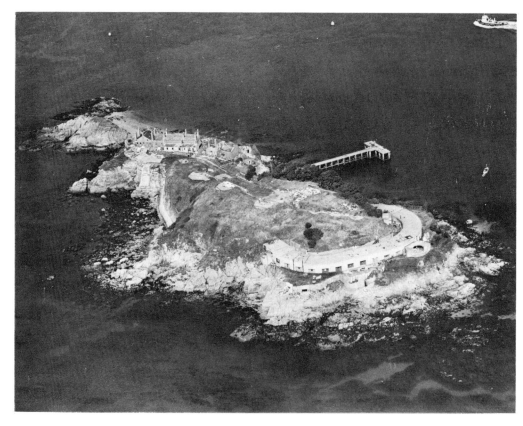

Guardian to Plymouth Sound: Drake's Island.

Landing at a pier that was built just before the Second World War, one reaches the plateau of the tiny island by way of a narrow tunnel-staircase which immediately demonstrates how impregnable the island has been. Nowadays young people, living in what were the nineteenth-century barracks for the garrison, use Drake's Island to constructive purpose, learning to canoe, to sail and to rock-climb. Taking advantage of its varied situation, residential courses in marine biology are also held on the island from time to time.

St George's Island

A mile off Looe in south Cornwall lies the little wooded island of St George, sometimes known as Looe Island. It is privately owned, is a bird sanctuary and now has a daffodil farm, a pottery and a folk-craft centre operating on it. A legend connected with St George's Island is that Joseph of Arimathea landed there on his way to bring the Holy Grail to Glastonbury, and at the highest point there are remains of a chapel which, it is said, was built to commemorate the event. Traditionally a haunt of smugglers, it is easy, and not only for a schoolboy's imagination, to bring the past alive in such a place. It even has treasure caves, reputedly con-

nected by real secret tunnels, there to thwart the most cunning of
excisemen.

In Kynance Cove, west of the Lizard in south Cornwall, is
Asparagus Island. There are in fact several rocky islands along
this coast, and sometimes three of them are grouped together and
called the 'Asparagus Islands'. One of these is Gull Rock, though
as there are four such-named rocks along this section of the south
Cornwall coast alone, this becomes somewhat confusing. The
Asparagus Islands are perhaps best or only known for their
name. While one will have to look hard to find it, asparagus in
England is basically a maritime plant, normally found wild only
near the coast, and tolerant both of sand and salt. Also in this area
is Mullion Island, off Porth Mellin to the east end of Mount's Bay.

Asparagus Island

Gull Rock

Mullion Island

St Michael's Mount

Among the most romantic and best-known islands around the
entire British coastline is the dramatic pyramid island of St
Michael's Mount, which rises to a peak, hundreds of feet high, off
the shore of Mount's Bay in western Cornwall. Milton, much
moved by his first sight of it, called it 'the great Vision of the
guarded mount', and spectacular it is by any standards. At low
tide a causeway links the island to the mainland at Marazion.
Edward the Confessor, by tradition, established a cell on the
island in 1044, granting its administration to the Abbot of Mont-
Saint-Michel in Normandy. From 1425, however, when the alien
priory was suppressed, the Mount became a military stronghold,
which it was to remain for the next two hundred years. Here came
Perkin Warbeck, claiming to be one of the Princes supposedly
murdered in the Tower, and established it as his base. Later, at
the time of the Reformation, it came into the possession of the
Crown, and governors were appointed to it. The castle at the
peak of the island passed to the St Aubyn family in the year 1660,
and they have owned it for over three hundred years, though the
National Trust, who accepted the island itself in 1954, now takes a
major responsibility for the upkeep of the entire property.

Traditionally the entrepôt centre of the medieval tin trade, the
island has many romantic legends connected with it, fed by the
fact that it is every child's fantasy of what a magic island should
be. In form it is very similar to Mont-Saint-Michel in France, and
though the latter is larger and even more dramatic, St Michael's
Mount, with its unique blend of natural and man-made excel-
lence, was well chosen by St Michael himself when he appeared
there in a vision in the year 495. One version of the story of Jack
the Giant-killer also has this as its setting. According to ancient

The most perfect island: St Michael's Mount, Mount's Bay, Cornwall.

Cornish legend, Jack slew a giant called Cormoran there. In terror, the giant's wife dropped the rock she was carrying in her apron pocket on to the shore at Marazion, where it rolled over and over, coming to rest as St Michael's Mount.

The church, dating from the fourteenth century, and the fortified castle, which has been subject to many alterations and additions across the centuries, together crown the island and are reached by a charming cobbled path which winds gracefully up from a harbour lined with fishermen's cottages.

As with so many of the islands around the British mainland, St Michael's Mount has a bitterly conflicting mongrel tradition – Vikings, monks, smugglers and pirates. Here, amid the clutter of plastic tourist trinkets, the best has remained.

St Clement's Isle

No oranges, lemons or much else on the tiny three-acre (1ha) island of St Clement just off Mousehole harbour in Cornwall. It has the sole distinction of being the last island before one turns the corner at Land's End to move towards the Isles of Scilly to the west or round to Lundy and the islands in the Bristol Channel.

A Herm landscape in the Channel Islands.

Asparagus would need to be hardy to cling to its island namesakes.

The tropical luxuriance of Tresco's sheltered gardens.

Bardsey: 'Isle of the Twenty Thousand Saints' off the North Wales coast.

3 The Isles of Scilly

One well-researched book on the Scillies carries the over-bold statement that they are the most remote part of the entire British Isles. Twenty-eight miles south-west of Land's End around two thousand people live permanently on five among scores of disparate islands. (Nowadays the population increases considerably during the summer months.) But to classify them as remotest Britain would be a claim that deserved to be challenged again and again throughout this book. Admittedly, in terms of the rigours of existence, life can be hard on the Scillies, but it can be proven to be harder, by any standards, on the bleaker and more storm-battered islands to the far north. Nonetheless, the Isles of Scilly form an archipelago of contrasts, blasted by winds of typhoon strength, yet a place where the winter daffodils not only bloom but thrive.

In the late twentieth century the Scilly Islands may, to many people, bring cynical memories of a pipe-smoking ex-Prime Minister Wilson seen holding a press conference on some deserted island. More common is the sight, on a cold and wintry metropolitan railway station, of box after box full of inviting Scillies daffodils, shipped across during the months from December to March from these mild western isles. To those more romantically inclined, they are peaks of a submerged Arthurian Avalon or Lyonnesse, or a drowned Atlantis. For the casual reader or armchair travellers, they hit the headlines when ships or yachts are wrecked or take refuge there from the storm. Time and time again they appear in biography and novel as source of the first lights through the night, winking, gleaming or shining to welcome the transatlantic passenger out of Manhattan or some less glamorous part of the New World. The Scilly Isles were, after all, part of the pre-Columbian edge of the world, the mythical Scylla of some unmatched Charybdis, poised on the brink of the known. Men were long certain that the ocean poured, in a

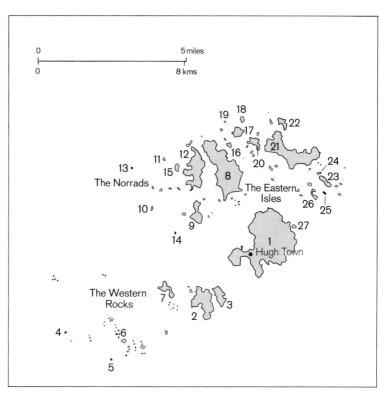

The Isles of Scilly

1 St Mary's
2 St Agnes
3 Gugh
4 Bishop Rock
5 Gilstone
6 Rosevear Island
7 Annet
8 Tresco
9 Samson
10 Mincarlo
11 Scilly Rock
12 Bryher
13 Maiden Bower
14 The Minaltos
15 Gweal
16 Northwethel
17 St Helen's
18 Round Island
19 Men-a-vaur
20 Tean
21 St Martin's
22 White Island
23 Great Ganilly
24 Nornour
25 Ragged Island
26 Great Arthur
27 Toll's Island

gigantic Niagara, off the edge of a flat world only a handful of miles beyond the utmost bounds of the Scillies.

The past constantly beckons to the future in the Scilly Isles, and they have recently been a glamorously successful target for treasure-seekers. Skin-divers, and those with more expensive gear, swim down through the fathoms and back through the centuries, to bring to the surface hoards of pieces of eight and barnacle-encrusted guns from the skeletons of sunken English men-of-war. The Scillies have also been a traditional lair for pirates and smugglers; even nowadays there are not-infrequent attempts to smuggle in a more profitable contraband than silks and brandy.

From the rugged viciousness of the Western Rocks to the palms and banana trees of the botanical gardens on Tresco, from the strange megaliths of Gugh to the British Airways helicopter service which offers its efficient service to and from the mainland, the Isles of Scilly offer a range of attractions to the convivial or to the visitor inclined to solitary pursuits.

Two well-known books on the Isles of Scilly, of roughly the same vintage, give the reader totally different data about the islands, thus reinforcing what this author has said about the

46

dangers of statistics. One of these books states that there are five inhabitated islands, with fifty other satellite isles; the other lists seven inhabited islands and another hundred and thirty-nine islands, some of which latter, the second author admits, are little more than isolated rocks. As was argued above, it entirely depends on how one defines 'inhabited' and 'an island' – so let us say that the truth lies somewhere in between. However defined, this is a particularly wealthy and fascinating pattern of islands. Ignored for centuries, their inhabitants long lived in considerable poverty, largely unrecognised by a British Government and people that were, at the same time, knowledgeable about and outraged by conditions in the furthest parts of the globe. In general, the islands remained relatively unknown till the beginning of this century, and their 'opening-up' to the rest of Britain really postdated the Second World War.

It is argued that one of the most significant social developments in the history of the Scilly Isles arose from the decision of the Duchy of Cornwall, as landlord of all the Scillies, to sell Hugh Town, the capital of the islands, to its sitting tenants at the end of the Second World War. This meant that, at a stroke, there was an immediate creation of civic purpose and organisation to replace purely tenants' organisations, and from then on the isles developed in a multitude of different ways, particularly in terms of the expansion of tourism and of agriculture.

The Scillies, unlike the Channel Islands which, though equally remote from their parent land, are pulled or trapped between the two major landmasses of Britain and France, have nothing between them and the United States of America, thousands of miles away. As a group of islands so remote from the rest of Britain, they inevitably became connected with varied superstitions and myths. To the people of the West Country they were, for example, the graveyards of the fabled knights from the days of King Arthur's Table. There is certain historical evidence that they were the eventual destination of the barges of death, sailing at the verge of dawn, for (like many other western isles with Celtic traditions) the islands are rich in early graveyards and burial mounds.

As Arthur said:

'But now farewell. I am going a long way
With these thou seëst – if indeed I go –
(For all my mind is clouded with a doubt)
To the island-valley of Avilion;
Where falls not hail, or rain, or any snow,
Nor ever wind blows loudly; but it lies
Deep-meadow'd, happy, fair with orchard-lawns
And bowery hollows crown'd with summer sea ...'

47

Meteorological conflicts and Tennyson's hyperbole apart, why not the Isles of Scilly?

St Mary's

Since the end of the Second World War the main and largest of the islands, St Mary's, has taken on a completely new lease of life and has rapidly become a major tourist centre and base from which visitors go on day trips to the other surrounding islands. Boatmen will, on request, take you and maroon you on some deserted island, to have it as your own for the day, leaving you hopeful or sad that weather and tide will probably allow your release before nightfall. St Mary's is best in the spring and autumn when it is less crowded; though the island is only two

Hugh Town Harbour, St Mary's.

and a half miles long at its widest, it is easy to move inland to where one is out of sight of the sea. Standing buried among the flower fields that blanket the centre of the island, one sees the secret of its new prosperity: where Atlantic breakers and the wind reach, only gorse will grow, and all else is bent and misshaped by the blast – but provide some shelter, and everything changes radically and even the rocks seem to bloom.

By day, there is much for an undemanding visitor to see and do, particularly if he is interested in ornithology or natural history, and especially if he comes in the autumn when countless birds use the isles as a staging post on their migration to the south. Expect no riotous, tourist-beckoning nightlife however; the inhabitants of St Mary's are due the peace with prosperity which is now theirs, after centuries during which they were

49

Prehistoric burial chambers, St Mary's.

pillaged, used and abused by every privateer and pirate in the western seas.

St Agnes and Gugh

South-west of St Mary's lies the wilder yet no less charming prospect of St Agnes, with, between them and connected to St Agnes at low water by a sandbar, the island of Gugh (pronounced 'Hugh'). St Agnes is the remotest from the mainland of all the inhabited islands in the group, and due doubtless to the amorous attention of some marauding band of pirates in the past, the inhabitants tend to be of a distinctly darker and more Celtic (some say Mediterranean) origin than those of the other islands.

St Agnes

As befits its turbulent ocean setting, the island's church was built with money raised from salvaging the wreck of a French ship which had run aground (the accusation was that it was deliber-

50

ately wrecked there), in the year 1685. As a gesture or penance to the ship's memory, its bell is still used as the bell of the church itself. The present small population thrive on fishing, flower-growing and subsistence agriculture. But here too some incipient tourism, with the possibility of letting out cottages and encouraging camping, has injected new life into the little community.

The main point of interest on the adjoining island of Gugh is the remarkable series of megaliths which have been found there. Theories as to their origin are as common as the megaliths themselves, but they were undoubtedly of religious or mystical significance and are matched by similar standing stones on other sites around the British coastline. The most prominent of them is one that, standing over nine feet (2.7m) high, is known as 'The Old Man of Gugh'. The island, claiming to have the smallest post office in the world, has, in common with a number of other unusual islands (Lundy and Staffa to name but two), raised a fair revenue from the selling of special postage stamps depicting scenes from the island and its life, a peculiarly modern economic device now adopted by more substantial islands and mini-states

Gugh

The Earl of Lonsdale, *wrecked off St Agnes, 1885.*

The bar leading to Gugh, Isles of Scilly.

around the world. At least a few of Gugh's stamps are used for their intended purpose – as a surcharge to cover the cost of delivery to the GPO in St Agnes; the rest are swallowed up by the apparently insatiable appetite of philatelic markets everywhere.

The Western Rocks

South-west of St Agnes again lie the Western (or Westward) Rocks, the most extreme part of all the Isles of Scilly. These grim and barren teeth have been the ruin of, and stand as gravestones to, many ships throughout the centuries. In the mid-nineteenth century a lighthouse, at 175 feet (53m) one of the highest in Britain, was built on Bishop Rock, which somewhat reduced but by no means eliminated the dangers. The names of this scattered group of rocks themselves have strange undertones of warning as the sea boils round them: the Crim Rocks, the Gunners, the

Bishop Rock

The Crim Rocks
The Gunners

A helicopter landing atop the remote Bishop Rock lighthouse.

The Crebinicks
Melledgan
The Crebawethans
Isinvrank
The Dogs of Scilly
The Hellweathers
Gilstone

Rosevear Island

Crebinicks, Melledgan, the Crebawethans, Isinvrank, the Dogs of Scilly and the Hellweathers are but some of them. Perhaps the most notorious of all is Gilstone, around which, in the year 1707, five ships of the British Fleet which were making for Portsmouth, under the command of Admiral Sir Cloudesley Shovell, were wrecked. A dozen years ago the remains of Shovell's flagship, the *Association*, were discovered, and subsequently large numbers of gold and silver coins and other valuable relics have been found by treasure-seekers. Another bleak neighbour is Rosevear Island (sometimes spelled with a final 'e'). Its claim to fame is that, despite its inhospitable aspect, it was chosen as a just-bearable site for the huts of the workmen who built the lighthouse on Bishop Rock. The men grew vegetables on Rosevear, and even held a ball on the rock during the harsh months of their life there. In a small boat it would have been no easy journey for the guests from the nearby islands, and the lure of the dance floor must have been strong.

Annet

Annet, to the north-west of St Agnes, is renowned for its seabird population, which is so vast that it is almost impossible to walk across the island without stepping on the birds and their nests. From the moment one lands on the island the stench is most pervasive, and at certain seasons becomes unbearable even to the most ardent ornithologist, and in no way is the situation helped by their sound: a never-ending cacophony of noise. Nearly all varieties of seabirds commonly found in the British Isles can be found on Annet, and after the nesting season, during which permission to land on the island is refused, the ground is strewn with the carcasses of the dead, this adding its own peculiarly revolting olfactory experience. Puffin, gannet and shearwater, seen swooping low over the reefs of knife-edged rocks that ring the island, are in consequence best studied from a boat with a *cordon sanitaire* of sea and fresh air between.

Tresco

Tresco, the second largest of the Isles of Scilly and a bare two miles from St Mary's, is popularly considered to be the most attractive of all the Scilly Isles, in the main because of the startling variety of its scenery. Reaction to such accepted opinion may vary slightly according to one's tastes, but from the rocky grandeur of the north-west which is constantly swept by the Atlantic winds, across the Great Pool which appears almost to cut the island in half, to the tropical luxury of the sheltered gardens in the south of the island, round each corner is something new and rewarding. It is, over all, one of the most sheltered of the group, blanketed as it partly is from the full force of the western gales by the island of Bryher. Because of its agreeable climate, it has long been well populated, particularly by religious communities, and there are records of monastic settlements on Tresco since the early tenth century. But, in common with other islands in the group, it has suffered from or been a refuge for the pirates, privateers and other raiders that flourished in the area. From time to time, notably in the year 1209, it was also a place for their execution, and according to the records 112 pirates were beheaded there on one single day.

There are ruins of at least three castles on Tresco: the Old Black House situated at the southern corner of Old Grimsby Harbour, the so-called King Charles's Castle, of which only a few stones now remain, and Cromwell's Castle, which sits on a rocky strip of land on the north-west of the island. This last was built in the middle of the seventeenth century to guard against the remote

Cromwell's Castle, on the north-west of Tresco.

danger of the Dutch landing on the island and using it as a base for further attacks on the British mainland.

Tresco's development over the last hundred and fifty years owes much to an eccentric man by the name of Augustus John Smith, the relevantly named 'Lord Protector' of the island, who moved to Tresco in the year 1834. He in fact took a lease of all the islands, setting up initially on St Mary's before moving to Tresco. Right from the start he worked to change the overgrown jungle he found into an agreeable and agriculturally profitable place to live. In the course of achieving these ends, Smith gained a reputation for extremely ruthless and autocratic behaviour, in that all who dared oppose him were expelled from the islands. Nonetheless, he left behind him for his family, who live there to this day, a handsome legacy of gardens and buildings. His Abbey Gardens, stretching in subtropical splendour for about twelve acres (5ha), are filled with a vast variety of exotic trees and plants, including palms, mimosa, banana, eucalyptus and many other rarities brought there by him from all over the world. Close by is a museum of ship figureheads, aptly named 'Valhalla', a last Viking resting place for all that struggled with the seas.

Ships' figureheads, 'Valhalla' Museum, Tresco.

In more recent years Tresco has developed its little village of Grimsby into an attractive tourist resort. Traditional playground for mermaids, Tresco has become the haunt of lesser but no less demanding mortals in pursuit of their own goals of peace and charm, with or without the prospect of some brief glimpse of flaxen hair suggesting a topless sylph with a fish's tail.

South-west of Tresco, and leased by the same family of Smiths, lies Samson, the largest uninhabited island in the group. Though in the distant past a few people used to live here, there are now no buildings on the island, and it is mainly an undisturbed haunt of seabirds. One of the most unspoilt yet still accessible islands in the entire archipelago, it was, in the eighteenth century, briefly used as a prison colony. Its more recent and even briefer claim to fame was that the former Prime Minister, Harold Wilson, disturbed its peaceful state and held an impromptu press conference while he was picnicking there, to the amusement if not the enlightenment of the ever-venturesome members of the fourth estate.

Samson

To the west of Samson is rocky Mincarlo, one of the most storm-torn islets in the entire pattern, while to the west of Bryher is the so-called Scilly Rock which, Latin tradition suggests, may have given its name to the Scillies themselves – the original deadly Scylla which matched the mythological Charybdis.

Mincarlo

Scilly Rock

Bryher itself now has a population of just under fifty. Before the last war the number was somewhat greater, but there has been a gradual and inevitable drift away towards the larger islands and to the mainland, a tendency repeated with monotonous regularity all round the British Isles. The main occupation is farming, with some fishing, though by and large it is too exposed to the elements for any of the prosperous and intensive agriculture one finds on Tresco and on the warmer, more central islands of the group. A twenty-four-bedroom hotel has recently been completed which will add an impetus to the incipient tourist trade. Also to the west of Bryher are a group of rocks known as the Norrads, including the inaptly named Maiden Bower. The name must have been chosen to emphasise the opposite: the rocks, with another group of two called the Minaltos, which lie to the south-west of Samson, are extremely vicious projections on which it is almost impossible to land, should one, strangely, feel compelled to do so. All this pattern of wild rocky outcrop, plus the additional eight acres (3ha) of barren Gweal, has again and again been the site of wrecks across the years. But even the most intrepid and well-equipped treasure-seekers leave these particular ones safely buried by the wild inhospitality of the surrounding seas.

Bryher

The Norrads
Maiden Bower
The Minaltos

Gweal

North-east of Tresco lies a group of islands, including North-

Northwethel

St Helen's
Round Island
Men-a-vaur

A pattern of islets, Hell Bay, Bryher.

wethel, St Helen's, Round Island and Men-a-vaur. While Northwethel has only faint evidence of prehistoric habitation, St Helen's, known once as St Elid's Isle and now among the larger uninhabited islands of the Scillies, has a Viking inheritance, and traces of a later monastic settlement have recently been uncovered. Further to the north of St Helen's is Round Island, whose prominent lighthouse is often the first welcoming sight of land when approaching by ship from the United States. Its name accurately describes its shape – a dome or regular mound of granite rock. The lighthouse, built in the year 1887, has a precipitous run of steps carved into the rock to allow the lighthouse-keeper to reach it from the uneasy landing stage. To the north again, the peculiarly named Men-a-vaur is an almost entirely barren rock, less than a sixth of a mile long. Despite suggestions that its name is an unexplained confusion of 'men-of-war', the real origin is unproven, though it may come from the old Cornish for 'big rock'. Finally, to the north-east of Tresco and close to St Martin's is the uninhabited island of Tean. Always a popular picnic spot, it has recently provided teams of archaeologists with the finds of fifth-century remains, as well as some earlier megalithic graves. Tean was at one time an important site of the kelp industry. A product of burnt seaweed, kelp was much used, from the seventeenth century onwards, in making soda and iodine, and in the manufacture of soap and glass.

Tean

St Martin's

St Martin's is the third largest of the Isles of Scilly. It is particularly favoured with good bathing beaches and has become a popular tourist centre, with, again, spring flower-growing as a main occupation. The general tendency of authors of a number of books written about the Scillies has been to suggest that St Martin's is the least interesting of all the islands, by this presumably inferring that it is more like the mainland than any of the others. To an extent this is true, but, whatever it lacks, it is still very much an island; boats ply their way to and from it, collecting the flowers, delivering foodstuffs and mail and, in the summer season, off-loading the many tourists. Communications, schooling, and the problems of an isolated community of under a hundred people are just as prevalent on St Martin's as anywhere. Perhaps the most notorious sight on the island is a huge and hideous red-and-white striped tower which stands on the north-eastern point of the island. Built in the year 1683 as a guide to shipping, it is almost universally considered to rank top of the list of Britain's most ancient eyesores.

To the north of St Martin's lies White Island (pronounced 'Whit'), one of two of that name in the Scillies, the other being due west of Samson. At low water, across a bay known as Porth Morran, this White Island is joined by a causeway to St Martin's, and its beaches too were once used as a site for collecting and burning seaweed for kelp.

White Island

Further towards St Mary's, the so-called Eastern Isles are often referred to as an 'archipelago within the archipelago'. There are around a dozen of these tiny islands, the largest of which are Great Ganilly, Nornour, Ragged Island and Great Arthur. The whole area is a maze of rock and sea, and, even with the definitions used in this book, it is often very difficult to distinguish

Eastern Isles

Great Ganilly
Nornour
Ragged Island
Great Arthur

59

Kelp burning on White Island, to the north of St Martin's.

which is an island and which is not. On Nornour, Roman remains, including an important collection of brooches, have been found, and there is some slight evidence that at an early period of this Roman occupation it was used as a penal colony or a place of exile for undesirables. In the centre of the group, Great Ganilly, also a kelp-producing site, is now a popular picnic island for day-visitors from St Mary's.

Toll's Island

Finally on this brief tour of the Scilly Islands there is Toll's Island, which lies to the east of St Mary's. Only an acre (0.4ha) in area, it too is an attractive place for an undisturbed picnic, and one can reach it across the sands at low tide. Here are old fortifications or earthworks, known locally as Pellew's Redoubt, which date from the Royalist occupation of the island during the seventeenth century.

The variety, the peace yet the vigour of the Scilly Islands has only been touched on. They, for all their differences, are a world of their own, cast and scattered across the seas on what was once the furthest edge of the known world, beyond which was void. Here, off the toe of England, one can sit in the February sun amid the spring flowers, remote, silent and free, and, above all, aware of the mystery of the past.

4 The Islands of North Devon and Cornwall and the Bristol Channel

Until one hits the island of Lundy, which is some eleven miles north of Hartland Point in Devon, there are few islands of particular distinction off the northern shores of Devon and Cornwall. Worthy of brief mention however are the Brisons, two uninhabited but attractive rocky islets which are just half a mile to the south-west of Cape Cornwall. A little further along the splendid rocky coast, at the north-east end of St Ives Bay in northern Cornwall, are a further two islands, again uninhabited, known as the Godrevy Islands, on one of which is an unmanned lighthouse which is the supposed setting for Virginia Woolf's book *To the Lighthouse*. There is a submarine reef which runs to the north-west out from the island and which used to be called 'Plenty-to-come-yet', a name relating to the fact that it was an excellent ground for lobster fishing. It is now a popular skin-diving area, and a breeding ground for seals. In the year 1649 a ship, carrying, among other things, the wardrobe of King Charles I, was wrecked there with the loss of sixty lives. Only a ship's boy and a dog were saved and they took refuge on the island along with many of the King's vestments. A later shipwreck, of the steamer *Nile* in 1854, led to the building of the lighthouse in 1859.

    Further north-east again, at the mouth of Padstow Bay, one comes to Newland, a pillar of rock which, reaching to a height of 120 feet (37m), is constantly beflecked by hundreds of seabirds wheeling round it. Close by, round to the north-east of Pentire Point, is the rocky islet, the Mouls, which rises to 165 feet (50m) and is now owned by the National Trust who had it bought, along with Pentire Farm, by public appeal in 1936 to save the area from being turned into building land. Its main, if not sole, claim to fame is that, one day early in the Great War, the poet Laurence Binyon is said to have landed on the island from a small boat and been so moved by the peace and solitude that he found there, in an age of such great tragedy and turmoil, that he wrote the

The Brisons

Godrevy Islands

Newland

The Mouls

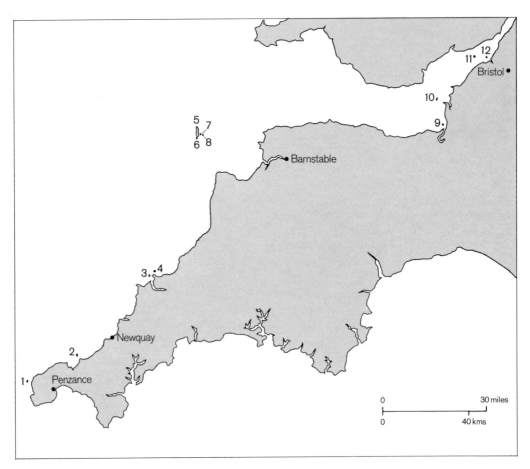

immortal Remembrance-Day verse:

England mourns for her dead across the sea. . . .

They shall grow not old, as we that are left grow old:
Age shall not weary them, nor the years condemn.
At the going down of the sun and in the morning
We will remember them.

Lundy

Standing on the soft moss beside the huge, now de-beamed lighthouse which is the most prominent of the three which Lundy boasts, the imaginative visitor may think that the island resembles nothing less than a huge ship, moored for ever in the southern reaches of the Bristol Channel. Even its shape, a pointed northern prow and blunt stern with the Old Light for a truncated mast, adds to that metaphor. But then, so quickly, the mist and the rain can descend like a dripping blanket, wiping everything out and producing a lonely desolation with, as the only sounds, the wind, the seabird cries and the waves pounding hundreds of feet below. Then it is easy to lose both path and footing, and, as all the edges of Lundy are sheer cliff, a slip means certain death. This danger is real, though on one occasion, for the author, it was prevented by a typically Lundy piece of advice on how to get back to the famous Marisco Tavern. 'It is easy', advised the guide. 'Keep close to the wall for shelter. Then turn left when you get to the cow . . .' Such was, and I suspect still is, the timelessness of Lundy.

Lundy is by far the most impressive and important island in the whole area. Eleven miles off Hartland Point on the coast of north Devon, it is a high bluff of granite three and a quarter miles long by just over half a mile wide, with, all around, these dramatic cliff-falls to the sea which sometimes reach 400 feet (120m). The flat plateau of the island is reached by one rough cart track which zigzags upwards from the sheltered landing beach. A ruined castle lies guarding the cliff top overlooking the bay, while, in the wooded copse to the right of the track, is elegant Millcombe House, built around 1840 and belonging to the owners of the island. A cluster of buildings round the generous and ever-open Marisco Tavern, the Manor Farm Hotel, one or two other houses dotted remotely to the north, the lighthouse on the south of the island, another at the north and the Old Light in the southern third, these are Lundy's main habitations. There is also the Victorian church of St Helena which stands prominent amid the green and crumbling ruins of other lost generations.

Lundy has gone through a strangely entrancing and mixed history, much of it enhanced by myth, and even in this century it has been the subject of controversy and conflict. Perhaps one of the most interesting recent proprietors was Mr Martin Harman, who was affected, like so many, by feeling himself a 'king' in such an isolated place. As successor in line to the Mariscos and the family of believers aptly named Heaven, who owned the island before him, he put an agent on the island and introduced a large number of innovations, including the establishment of a unique postal and telegraphic service to the mainland. Amid much dispute, he had stamps and coins made for the island and this led to him to being taken to court by the Crown. After a long and somewhat light-hearted court case, he was fined the substantial sum of five pounds. In the longer run he benefited: the coins and stamps that he had had produced soon became valuable collectors' pieces. Whatever else, Lundy still has no rates or licensing laws, nor is income tax payable on money earned on the island.

Lundy has been populated for many centuries and there are

North Devon and
Cornwall

1   The Brisons
2   Godrevy Islands
3   Newland
4   The Mouls
5   Lundy
6   Little Shutter
    Rock
7   Rat Island
8   Mouse Island
9   Stert
10 Steep Holm
11 Denny
12 Dungball

archaeological remains such as the Neolithic 'Giants' Graves', discovered in the eighteen-sixties, which, by dubious tradition, were found to contain skeletons over eight feet (2.5m) tall. The island had close historical connections with the Welsh, particularly with Prince Madoc, who is reputed to have sailed the Atlantic, discovering America some three centuries before Columbus (though perhaps a shade after Leif Erikson of Norway). Then came a long Norman connection with the family of Marisco, who were granted a charter to it in 1153 and who built the castle. Sadly they are now remembered only by the gift of their name to the pub. While today Lundy has a population of only a dozen or so permanent residents, at one period in the nineteenth century it reached the two-hundred mark, many of them doubtless the descendants of the pirates and smugglers who once made it their home and earned it the rebellious title of 'Tollgate of the Channel'. Charles Kingsley, who visited the island in 1849, recorded of his stay: 'O that I had been a painter for that day at least', and it obviously made a significant impression on him, because the final scene of his book *Westward Ho!* is set on the Little Shutter Rock, south of Lundy.

Little Shutter Rock

> On their left hand as they broached-to, the wall of granite sloped down from the clouds towards an isolated peak of rock, some two hundred feet in height. Then a hundred yards of roaring breaker upon a sunken shelf, across which the race of the tide poured like a cataract; then, amid a column of salt smoke, the Shutter, like a huge black fang, rose waiting for its prey . . .

Most recently of all, Lundy was put up for auction, and Mr Jack Hayward (who was later to be much involved in the trial of the Liberal leader Jeremy Thorpe) donated £150,000 to the National Trust to enable them to acquire Lundy, though it is in practice administered by the Landmark Trust.

Above all, to the bird-lover, Lundy is a paradise. The puffin breeds there, burrowed into the grassy slopes, and many other species of birds, all rare in other parts of the British Isles, visit it. The Royal Society for the Protection of Birds has, in consequence, kept an observation post on the island for many years. There are animal peculiarities too. Even the rabbits have their oddities as the result of inbreeding, as does a type of New Forest pony, imported to the island in the late thirties. Then there is a unique type of wild cabbage with yellow flowers . . . Lundy is never normal.

The strange tranquillity is disturbed only when the day-trippers come, and they do by the score. While most of them do not get very much further than the ever-available delights of the pub, the more adventurous can make the upper reaches of the

The island of Godrevy's lighthouse, off the north Cornish coast.

A Victorian watercolour of Steep Holm.

island to see, for example, the strange granite death slope known as the Devil's Slide, which runs smoothly for hundreds of feet from the plateau down to the sea itself.

Rat Island
Mouse Island

At the southern tip of Lundy are two rocky islands, one called Rat Island, the other Mouse Island, which, with Little Shutter Rock itself, have been the teeth on which many a ship has been wrecked across the years.

Stert

The half-dozen islands of the upper Bristol Channel are of disappointingly little interest or note. They include the island of Stert, or Steart, which lies off Burnham-on-Sea in Somerset and is really nothing more than an elongated sandbank which came into existence probably during the eighteenth century. Then come the

Steep Holm

two islands Steep Holm and Flat Holm (both of which are sometimes listed with a final 'e'), which lie two and a half miles apart off the South Glamorgan coast. Steep Holm, squat and precipitous and once known as Echri, is now principally a wildlife sanctuary, administered by the Steep Holm Trust.

Prehistoric and early Christian remains have been discovered on the island, and when a military battery was being built there in 1867, the walls of an old priory were still standing, once the reputed refuge of a sixth-century saint, Gildas, who worshipped

66

there until driven away by pirates. Now the ruins have disappeared, but there is still visible evidence that Steep Holm was used as a sacred burial ground by people living on the adjacent mainland, one of many such offshore graveyards round the coasts of Britain. Numerous islands have been imbued with particular mystical or religious significance, perhaps because they were sanctified by some hermit, priest or religious community that lived in seclusion on them. But, equally possibly, they were utilised as a primitive form of protection against infection. If the deceased had died diseased, surely it was better to ferry the corpse to as isolated a place as possible, to avoid spreading sickness to the wider community.

Like Lundy, Steep Holm, which is another major sentinel for the Bristol Channel, was used as a base by the Vikings in their raids on the mainland, and in later centuries it was also a refuge for pirates. Its twin isle, Flat Holm, is part of the Principality of Wales and will be described in that section.

Much higher up the Channel, in the mouth of the Severn and surrounded by an otherwise industrial landscape, is Denny, an uninhabited island some twenty acres (8ha) in area. It is flat and barren and mainly of interest to fishermen, though it serves to mark the boundary in the estuary between England and Wales.

Denny

The final island in the upper reaches of the Bristol Channel is the one with perhaps the most unattractive name in this book; the sad, non-island of Dungball or, more politely, Dunball. Marked at the mouth of the Avon on some early maps and navigation charts, in recent time it has disappeared below the surface of the water. The name probably came from the basic, unromantic, yet necessary fact that it was a dumping ground for refuse from the catchment area of the upper Bristol Channel, though according to one story it was started as a wharf in 1844 by some coal merchants involved with the Bristol to Exeter railway. Alas, poor Dungball: it was nonetheless an island.

Dungball

5 The Islands of Wales

Given their variety, the islands of Wales have a character unique to themselves. Religious isles, isles of saints, then of pirates, and now largely of bird-wardens and tourists. They have been, in turn, refuges for the godly and the ungodly; they have a beauty and remoteness, even when close, or perhaps for the very reason of their proximity, to large concentrations of people. By and large none of these islands have inherited indigenous populations. If they are inhabited at all, it is by new generations who have arrived to escape and to settle in small numbers. Here are Caldey, Ramsey and Bardsey, but also many more, rich both in tradition and in present-day attractions. And they have taken to themselves those characteristics peculiar to the Principality, of charm, of mystery, of fable, of temperament. Wales would be much poorer without them; national pride would be diminished by loss of some of that sense of identity and independence and fortitude which these islands underline.

Flat Holm

As one skirts the southern shores of Wales the first island of significance that appears is Flat Holm, twin isle of Steep Holm and a low-lying fifty acres (20ha) of land. Now owned by Trinity House, which maintains a lighthouse there, it has a well on it that is said to ebb and flow with the tides. Its most recent history is interesting in that it was from here that Marconi conducted his early radio experiments in the year 1897, transmitting the first-ever wireless message across water in May of that year. The first words were the not over-inspiring: 'Are you ready?' Flat Holm was used as a base for the Viking fleet in the tenth century, and in the nineteenth century, as well as housing three gun batteries erected as defence against possible French invasion, it was, for a brief time, the site of a cholera hospital for the town of Cardiff. In very recent times it was proposed that it (like Osea Island) should be used as a home for alcoholics, but this particular proposition

St Catherine's Island, with bathing machines in the mid-1890s.

68

was never followed through, and the island is now distinguished primarily for its correction with Marconi.

Along the coast is Worms Head, which, with its adjacent shoreline of cliffs that fringe the west of the Gower Peninsula in West Glamorgan, is now owned by the National Trust. Worms Head is really two tidal islets, connected by the so-called 'Devil's Bridge', a narrow track running over a neck of rock. Despite its closeness to Swansea, the whole area is beautifully unspoiled, and the view over the Rhossili beach is striking and impressive. The word 'worm' is from *'wyrm'*, an Old English name for a dragon, and people say that in certain lights they can see this twin island shaped in such a form. Here too, at the north end of Rhossili Bay, is the tidal islet of Burry Holms, which is accessible for two and a half hours each side of low water. On the islet are traces of Iron-Age earthworks and an early religious settlement, and round the shoreline, treasure from a wrecked seventeenth-century Spanish galleon has been found.

Further along the coast and close to Tenby is the tiny but picturesque high-water island of St Catherine. This bare half-dozen acres (2.5ha) of precipitous rock is topped by a fort which was built in solid Victorian times as a defence against nothing except, perhaps, a surfeit of money. It has recently served as a zoo. Access to it is by steps up the cliff face.

Worms Head

Burry Holms

St Catherine's Island

Caldey Island

Wales

1   Flat Holm
2   Worms Head
3   Burry Holms
4   St Catherine's
     Island
5   Caldey Island
6   St Margaret's
     Island
7   Thorn Island
8   Sheep Island
9   Skomer Island
10 Midland Isle
11 Mew Stone
12 Gateholm
13 Skokholm
14 Grassholme
15 The Smalls
16 Ramsey Island
17 Ynys Bery
18 Ynyscantwr
19 Ynys Eilun
20 The Bishops and
     Clerks
21 Carreg Rhoson
22 Cardigan Island
23 Ynys-Lochtyn
24 Shell Island
25 St Tudwal's
     Islands
26 Ynys Gwylan
27 Bardsey
28 Llanddwyn
29 North Stack
30 South Stack
31 The Skerries
32 Mouse Islands
33 Ynys Dulas
34 Puffin Island

The next island on the journey is one of a number of so-called 'Islands of the Saints', haunting, history-laden Caldey Island, also known as Ynys Pyr. It has been the home of a monastery or religious foundation of one form or another from the sixth century onwards, if not before. During the Middle Ages it belonged to a Benedictine Order but, from the time of the Dissolution of the Monasteries in the reign of Henry VIII, it remained in secular hands until 1906, when it fell into the hands of a High Anglican community. When in 1913 that community was welcomed into the Church of Rome, there was a hiatus until, in 1928, the buildings were sold to an order of Cistercian Trappist monks from Belgium.

Caldey Island, one mile off the Dyfed coast, along from Tenby, is one and a half miles long and two-thirds of a mile wide. The Monastery was raised to the status of the Abbey of St Samson in 1958. Its quaint church, dating in part from the twelfth century, with its strangely out-of-true stone steeple, and its other buildings, all with attractive whitewashed walls and high red-tiled roofs, are the centre of life on the island. The monks, with some secular help, farm the surrounding fields on successful commercial lines, as well as pursuing their strange traditional craft of distilling perfumes. One trace of the earliest Celtic monastery is a famous stone called the Caldey Ogham Stone, which is a slab of sandstone with a cross and a double inscription carved on it, one in the ancient and charmingly simple ogham script and the other in Latin. One theory is that this stone was, with earlier, now defaced inscriptions, a religious symbol of the sun-worshippers of pre-Christian times.

Until recently the monks on Caldey observed strict rules of silence, but these conventions have been relaxed and contact with the mainland is thriving, with tourism, flowing in from nearby Tenby by the regular motorboat service, now a major factor of Caldey life. But the monastery itself is still prohibited to women visitors.

The cliffs of the island are said to be haunted by the ghost of the notorious pirate Paul Jones, who can be seen walking them. There are a number of curious caves on the island, the most magnificent of which is the 'Cathedral Cave', which is lit by daylight from natural hidden crevices and has a huge nave, the main part of which is sixty feet (18m) high, forty feet (12m) wide and nearly three hundred feet (92m) long. In another cave, bones of mammoth and rhinoceros have been found, demonstrating that, in an earlier age, Caldey was firmly part of the mainland. At the south-east corner, the highest point of the island, there is a

prominent lighthouse. The shoreline to the west of it provides good places for watching seabirds and the occasional seal.

St Margaret's Island

Close by the north-west tip of Caldey is St Margaret's Island, also famed for its cliffs and its bird life. It is now a nature reserve and bird sanctuary managed by the West Wales Naturalists' Trust. There is an old eleventh-century watchtower, which overlooks the landing bay. While at low tide one can wade out to the island across the rocks, permission is needed for a visit.

Thorn Island

About a quarter of a mile from the Angle Peninsula in southern Dyfed is a small rocky island known as Thorn Island on which is a fort, built as a defence for Milford Haven during the Napoleonic Wars. It has now been converted into a private hotel and restaurant. At the southern sea end of the peninsula is Thorn Island's

Sheep Island

twin, Sheep Island, which lies close in to the shore.

Skomer Island

The most prominent of a group of islands to the south of St Brides Bay is Skomer Island, three-quarters of a mile west of Wooltack Point; it is now a national nature reserve, owned by the Nature Conservancy and administered by the West Wales Naturalists' Trust. It is renowned for its seabirds, its abundance of wild flowers, and a unique subspecies of vole, as well as being a breeding ground for seals. Because of this, it is necessary to ask for permission from the resident warden before landing on the island. Rising over 200 sharp and dramatic feet (60m) above sea level to a flat plateau, Skomer is in two distinct parts, joined by a narrow isthmus of land. As with many of the other islands along the Welsh coast, there is much evidence of early Iron-Age inhabitation, and substantial traces of fortifications, huts and burial barrows date from that period. Between Skomer and the main-

Midland Isle

land is Midland Isle (sometimes called Middle Island or Middleholm), which was once used for rabbit farming and is now privately owned. Off the south tip of Skomer is yet another rock

Mew Stone

with the name Mew Stone.

Gateholm

Close by, hugging the coast a little to the south-east, is the tiny island of Gateholm on which no less than 130 hut-circles, dating from Roman times, have been identified. Despite this strangely thriving past, it is now totally uninhabited.

Skokholm

Two other islands in the area are Skokholm and Grassholme. The former, to the south of Skomer, is some three miles off the Dyfed coast and is the reputed site of the first bird observatory in the British Isles. It, with its flat top and dark red cliffs, is also manned by wardens from the West Wales Naturalists' Trust. Teams of ornithologists have recorded over a hundred and fifty different species of birds on the island. Like its northern neighbour, Skokholm was at one time occupied by Vikings and

A monk prepares perfume from an old recipe at Caldey Island's monastery.

Grassholme

(Above) *The nature reserve of Skomer Island.*

(Opposite) *Gateholm Island and Skokholm, both rich in wild life and prehistoric remains.*

numerous traces of early and medieval settlement exist on the island. Mr R. M. Lockley, who made his home on the island in 1933 and who founded the bird observatory, has written a fascinating account of life on Skokholm in his book *I Know an Island*.

The twenty-acre (8ha) island of Grassholme, which lies eight miles out from Skomer to the west, has one of the largest gannetries in the British Isles and was bought, in 1948, by the Royal Society for the Protection of Birds. Surrounded by fierce tidal races and well exposed to the Atlantic, it is always difficult to effect a landing on it. Grassholme has been identified as the 'Gwales in Penfro' of medieval Welsh mythology, where the followers of Bran the Blessed 'rested for eighty years, oblivious to time, in a place overlooking the sea, with three doors, two of which were open and the third, which looked towards Cornwall, closed to them'. When one of their number eventually opened the forbidden door, the scales of time fell away and they all realised their destiny – to defend their country against foreign invasion.

Fifteen miles to the west of Skomer are some rocks known as the Smalls. Here, too, the major interest is its bird life, though, for students of lighthouses, the first one on these rocks was made

The Smalls largely of wood and erected in the year 1776. The builder was a Liverpool musical-instrument maker, who, as often in those years, doubtless hoped to profit, if he could, by collecting dues from passing vessels.

Ramsey Island

There are few Celtic saints whose names are not in one way or another connected with Ramsey Island which, reached from St David's, lies a mile off the west Dyfed coast. Covering an area of some 650 acres (263ha), it has twin hills which rise to over 400 feet (120m), and the whole island is surrounded by tidal races of differing intensities and dangers. Known also by its Welsh name, Ynys Dewi, it has a tiny resident population and at the time of going to press is up for sale at an undisclosed price. As with a number of islands here, the bird colony needs protection from natural rather than human enemies: rats have decimated the colonies of puffin and shearwater. Ramsey's beaches and the caves at the foot of its high cliffs are a breeding place for seals.

Tradition and history are, as often, blurred, but the island is said to have had a monastery which was founded by St Devynog in the second century. It was visited in turn by St David, St Patrick and St Justinian; the last of the triumvirate is reputed to have been murdered on Ramsey. There are many ancient graves, presumably of the monks who lived in the monastery.

To the south of Ramsey are three uninhabited little islands which have, at various times, been used for summer grazing. The
Ynys Bery largest is Ynys Bery and the others are called Ynyscantwr and
Ynyscantwr Ynys Eilun.
Ynys Eilun

Out to sea beyond Ramsey can be seen the spectacular little
The Bishops and Clerks group known as the Bishops and Clerks, or alternatively, 'The Bishop and his Clerks'. They are more rocks than islands, but are rich in bird life and on the most southerly of the rocks stands the South Bishop lighthouse. Almost in the middle of the group is an
Carreg Rhoson island, Carreg Rhoson, which again is of interest mainly to ornithologists. It too was, in the past, used for sheep-grazing, until the labour of landing and taking off the animals (still practised in some parts of the Western Isles of Scotland) became too unprofitable.

Much further round the north Dyfed coast is the cliff-bound
Cardigan Island Cardigan Island, now a protected nature reserve and bird sanctuary, though its once famous puffin colony has deserted it. The island is also a breeding ground for seals and there are a few half-wild Soay sheep on it. Further east along the shore, over a mile north-east of Llangranog, lies the uninhabited island of

Ynys-Lochtyn, a tiny ten acres (4ha) which, with the surrounding coastline, has since 1965 been the property of the National Trust. The whole seaboard along this stretch is magnificent and rich with an abundance of bird- and wild-life.

Ynys-Lochtyn

Further to the north up the coast of Wales and inside the hook of the Lleyn Peninsula, in Cardigan Bay, is the high-tide island Mochras, more commonly known as Shell Island, which lies two miles west of Llanbedr. It is, as its alternative name suggests, best known for its shells, over two hundred varieties of them, and harvesting these is particularly rewarding after stormy weather. The island is also popular with the local lobster fishermen. From here, exposed at low tide, is a line of rocks known as Sarn Badrig or St Patrick's Causeway, which by tradition was the road to the flooded land known as the 'Lowland Hundreds' whose church bells still ring from below the water.

Shell Island

To the south of St Tudwal's Bay, a mile from the Lleyn Peninsula in Gwynedd, are the twin St Tudwal's Islands. On the eastern of the two are the remains of a small medieval priory dating from the twelfth century. On the western island is a lighthouse which has now been redesigned as a private home. Then, further to the west, by Aberdaron Bay is the group of rocky islets, inhabited by birds, known collectively as Ynys Gwylan.

St Tudwal's Islands

Ynys Gwylan

Bardsey

At the western end of the Lleyn Peninsula, with a dangerous tidal race running between it and the mainland, is the island of Bardsey, or, in Welsh, Ynys Enlli, also traditionally named the 'Isle of the Twenty Thousand Saints'. It is reached by boat from Aberdaron.

Nearly every island along this stretch of the Welsh coast appears to have a long religious and monastic history. On some, early Christian relics date back to the sixth century. Bardsey is exceptional in that everything is there in much fuller measure. Meilyr, a twelfth-century poet, saw it thus:

The isle of wondrous Mary,
Holy isle of the Saints,
With its graveyard in the bosom of the sea.

It was very much a place of pilgrimage in the Middle Ages, three trips to Bardsey equating, in some strange balance of holy worth, with one to Rome, until that later stage when, like those of so many islands, its priests were replaced by pirates.

The bell tower of the thirteenth-century Augustinian Abbey of St Mary is still there, while in the churchyard there are Celtic crosses in white marble, one of which is a memorial to the reputed

The lighthouse on Bardsey Island. A refuge for numerous types of birds, the island, sadly, spells death for others — migrating flocks attracted to the light.

twenty thousand saints. Saints some may have been, but since it was commonplace Celtic tradition that burial should always be in the west and Bardsey was as far that way as one could easily go, it would also have served as a graveyard for all west Wales.

Four hundred and fifty acres (182ha) in size and rising to a height of 500 feet (152m), Bardsey nowadays is sparsely populated and is known principally as a nature reserve. There is a permanent bird observatory on the island, first manned in 1953.

In 1977 the Bardsey Island Trust acquired the option to buy the island, which they finally managed to do in 1979. It is not only a refuge for many types of birds, fulmars, guillemots, razorbills and Manx shearwaters, but also a deathtrap for migratory flocks. Each morning the ground at the base of the lighthouse is littered with the corpses of a wide variety of birds that have flown into it to their death. With the help of Trinity House, the bird-wardens on the island are now experimenting with false lights at other points on the island, to try and decrease the death rate.

One quaint custom is concerned with the peasant monarchs, the 'kings of Bardsey', and stems from one of the traditional owners of the island, Lord Newborough, who wisely appointed one of the most prominent of the then somewhat turbulent inhabitants as local head man. The 'King' was given a 'crown' of brass, a 'treasure' in the shape of a silver casket, and an 'army' which comprised the painted wooden effigy of a soldier.

Overall, however, Bardsey's reputation has, as with Iona to the north, always been as an oasis of sanctity and isolation for those of religious faith. In later times it also became a refuge for those fleeing the law. Now, thousands visit it annually to study its natural inheritance. Despite that, the peace of the island remains.

If one is looking for information on Anglesey and Holy Island, this book does not offer it since, as was explained in the Introduction, they have umbilical links to the mainland with their permanent road and rail bridges; they therefore relinquish their rights (doubtless something to which the inhabitants would object) to island status. The Britannia Tubular Rail Bridge, the Menai Suspension Bridge and the causeway to Holyhead are permanent and disqualifying bonds.

Llanddwyn

At the south of Anglesey, however, is the island of Llanddwyn, a high-tide island with, as a package of almost statutory requirements along this coast, bird sanctuary, monastic remains and a

North Stack
South Stack

lighthouse. At the north-west points of Holy Island are the North and South Stacks, the latter with its famous lighthouse (built by David Alexander, who also constructed Dartmoor Prison). It can be reached by a suspension bridge, thus banning it from being an

The Skerries

island proper. To the north-west of Anglesey itself are the Sker-

78

ries, with a lighthouse which dates from the eighteenth century.

Mouse Islands Some miles east are the three so-called Mouse Islands, which lie strung out between the Skerries and Amlwch. Along this coast

Ynys Dulas are a number of other islets, including Ynys Dulas in Dulas Bay, a well-known picnic spot, on which there is a nineteenth-century tower, built as a marker for ships.

Lastly, at the north-east corner of Anglesey and half a mile

Puffin Island offshore, is white-cliffed Puffin Island, otherwise known as Priestholm or Ynys Seiriol after a saint who established a settlement there in the sixth century. The Danes arrived and destroyed the monastery in the year 853. Because pickled puffins became too much of a high-society delicacy in the eighteenth and nineteenth centuries, the puffin population, not surprisingly, declined enormously. Perhaps a more devastating reason for the colony's decline was the rats which came ashore from a shipwreck in the early nineteenth century. They are now the enemy, gradually destroying the remaining bird life and, with their burrowing, making casual exploration of the island by mere humans difficult and dangerous underfoot.

6 The Isle of Man and the Islands of North-West England

The Isle of Man

'Gules, three armed legs proper conjoined in fess, at the upper part of the thigh, flexed in triangle, garnished and spurred' – thus the heraldic description of the strange three-legged device of the Isle of Man. The tale of Mannanin, the warlock, traditionally gives the island its name. St Patrick, attempting to rid the island of his evil spell, changed him or had him changed into the three-legged symbol that, with the warlock's last defiant cry – 'Whichever way you throw me, I stand' – is now the emblem.

Taken to the International Court over the much-publicised continuance of judicial birching; envied for its considerable tax benefits; governed, under a system which allows plural voting, by a parliament older than Westminster; famous for motorcycle racing, for a form of tailless cat, and for an adjective 'Manx': these are the items of conventional knowledge about Man. On the one hand Manxmen have a reputation for being puritanical, on the other hand they are in many ways in advance of the rest of the United Kingdom. A haven for tourists, the isle has beautiful beaches, a mountain (Snaefell), rivers and magnificent scenery. From the holiday-resort vulgarity of Douglas to the relative peace of some of the smaller towns, the Isle of Man has range and diversity and, for all its reputation of being crowded, it is big enough for the visitor to find real solitude there.

The ancient capital of Man is Castletown, which has medieval Castle Rushen at its centre and boasts a fascinating museum concerned with witchcraft – a peculiarly Manx phenomenon. About a mile north-west of Douglas the poet T. E. Brown, one of many literary figures with Manx connections, lived out his childhood, and later, in England, wrote in 'Braddan Vicarage':

I wonder if in that far isle
Some child is growing now, like me
When I was child: care pricked, yet healed the while
With balm of rock and sea.

Following in the footsteps of St Patrick, early Irish missionaries used the Isle of Man as a major stepping-off base; the Celtic influence was strong in the language, and the Manx tongue was in common use until the first half of the last century. As with the majority of the islands down the western littoral of Britain, it was a Viking dependency from the ninth century until it was sold to Scotland in the year 1266. The island, known to the Romans as Mona or Monapia, passed from Scottish into English hands and was granted in 1405 to Sir John Stanley. His descendants, the earls of Derby, held the title 'Lord of Man' until this passed with the island itself to the Duke of Atholl in 1765. He soon afterwards sold sovereignty of the island to the British Crown, though the

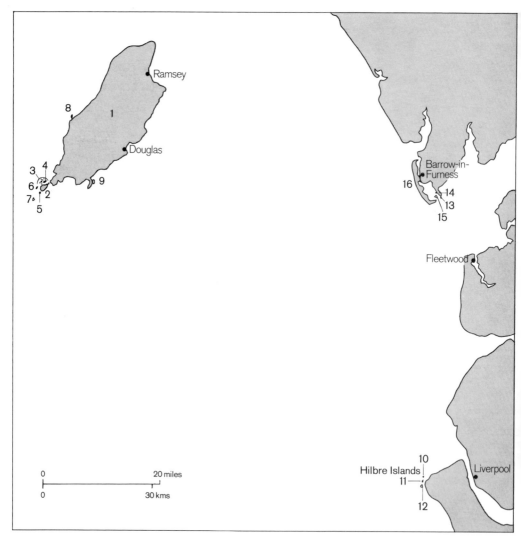

Atholl family did not cede all their claims to the Isle of Man until 1829.

Today Her Majesty the Queen is the Lord of Man, but the title is not used by her except on the island, nor is it one by which the Sovereign is proclaimed. Man is administered by the Home Office, but has, nonetheless, considerable powers of self-government, and is consequently deprived of the right to elect or send Members of Parliament to the House of Commons. A lieutenant-governor is appointed by the Monarch, there is a Council or Upper House, and the lower chamber is the famous twenty-four-member House of Keys. Together they form the thousand-year-old Court of Tynwald and any Act of the West-minster Parliament has to be endorsed by it before it applies equally to Man.

Man, with the Isle of Wight which is almost its equal in size, is among England's largest islands. Yet it has only half Wight's population and, again unlike Wight, is very different from the closest mainland. Its centuries of tradition, carefully husbanded and guarded even today – Tynwald Day in July is the most important date in the Manx calendar – stress its individuality of

Victorian prosperity: Douglas, Isle of Man, in the year 1895.

The North-West of England

1   The Isle of Man
2   Calf of Man
3   Calf Islands
4   Kitterland
5   The Burroo
6   The Stack
7   Chicken Rock
8   St Patrick's Isle
9   St Michael's Island
10 Hilbre
11 Little Hilbre
12 Little Eye
13 Foulney
14 Roa Island
15 Piel Island
16 Isle of Walney

(Above) *The Queen, as Lord of Man, attends the thousandth parliament, the Tynwald, in July 1979.*

(Opposite) *Peel Castle on St Patrick's Isle.*

character, its curious blend of timelessness and modernity that makes it an island to itself.

A bare half-mile off the south-west coast of the Isle of Man is the National Trust-owned island, the 616-acre (249ha) Calf of Man, now principally a nature reserve. The study of the bird life there is carried out in a highly organised manner. The fact that it is on a main migration route down the west coast of Britain makes it possible to ring thousands of birds there every year. A ruined church, two ruined lighthouses and other relics indicate a more populous past. Here, as on Priestholm, puffins were exported in large quantities to be pickled as a table delicacy for past genera-

Calf of Man

tions. The Calf of Man, with Lundy and Herm in the Channel Islands, has, as a result of the whim of previous proprietors, its own stamps which must be affixed to a letter as surcharge before it will be passed into the safe hands of the GPO on the Isle of Man itself.

Calf Islands
Kitterland
The Burroo
The Stack

Between the Calf and Man are a group of half a dozen islets known as the Calf Islands, the largest of which is called Kitterland. South and west of this island are two remarkable rocks, the Burroo and the Stack, both of which rise a hundred feet (30m) above sea level, while three-quarters of a mile south-west is the Chicken's Lighthouse on its dangerous Chicken Rock. On the west side of the Isle of Man, near Peel, is St Patrick's Isle or Innis Patrick (now strictly not an island as it has a permanent causeway, but thus part of Man), most of which is occupied by the ruins of St Germain's Cathedral and by Peel Castle's majestic walls. Inside these lurks the ghost of a wolfhound which appears to haunt the ramparts by moonlight, a myth referred to by Sir Walter Scott in *Peveril of the Peak* and *The Lay of the Last Minstrel*. The castle has, variously, been a defence against the Vikings and, in the fifteen-hundreds, against the Scots. Later it became a prison. The cathedral is said to be modelled on that on Iona, as a result of the abbot of the day having served his time on both islands. It also has its own convenient ecclesiastical prison beside its crypt, which was, in the past, used to incarcerate blasphemers and other anti-clerical elements. At another age, the castle was the principal residence of the kings of Man.

The east coast of Man has but one small island, which is connected to it by a low-water causeway. St Michael's (or Fort) Island, just off the north-east corner of the Langness Peninsula, bears the remains of a circular fort and a thirteenth-century church. A slim tradition has it that a horse race – the forefather of

Chicken Rock
St Patrick's Isle

St Michael's Island

today's Derby – was held on a neck of land close by. The fort was built about 1540 as part of a chain of coastal defences thrown up in the reign of Henry VIII.

Hilbre Islands

Leaving the Isle of Man and turning eastwards towards the mainland, one finds only a tiny handful of islands along the northwestern coast of England. Moving in a northerly direction, the first one reaches are the almost uninhabited Hilbre Islands, a mile off Hilbre Point on the Wirral Peninsula, three of them in all, and of interest mainly to ornithologists. At low tide they can be reached across the Dee Estuary mud flats, though before setting out one should be sure of the route since the risk of being trapped is high. Remember the Charles Kingsley poem which begins 'O Mary, go and call the cattle home':

> The western tide crept up along the sand . . .
> The rolling mist came down and hid the land;
> And never home came she.

A small order of Benedictine monks once had a settlement on the main island of the group. It was maintained until the suppression of its parent abbey at Chester in the year 1541.

Hilbre
Little Hilbre
Little Eye

Hilbre itself is only eleven acres (4ha) in size, Little Hilbre three acres (1ha), and Little Eye half an acre (0.2ha), each of them separate though earlier maps show them as one island. Today, all three are joined at low tide by sandstone reefs. In Queen Elizabeth I's reign, the English army encamped on them on their way to fight in Ireland. Since 1945 these islands have been owned by the local district council, which has a permanent keeper on them. They have a number of well-known caves: the Devil's Hole on Little Hilbre is said to have been used by smugglers, and on Hilbre itself is Lady's Cave, where a shipwrecked woman, fleeing her father's wrath, took refuge till she died.

Foulney

South of Barrow-in-Furness and joined by a causeway to Roa Island is Foulney, an uninhabited and somewhat desolate stretch of land, little more than a bleak breeding ground for terns. Neither of these is now really an island, permanently linked as each is to the mainland. Roa, with its little village which occupies almost all the land area, is a well-known sailing centre. Here the Trinity House pilots had their houses.

Roa Island

Piel Island

Piel Island, three and a half miles south-east of Barrow-in-Furness and close to the Isle of Walney, is a grassy twenty-six acres (11ha) of play and picnic area for day-visitors and has long been a destination for tourist steamers from Morecambe and elsewhere. Here too are the ruins of a twelfth-century castle, known as the Pile of Fouldray, and for a brief period before the Dissolution of the Monasteries it was used as a religious retreat by the Abbey of Furness. Its thick concentric walls and internal keep were defended by towers and deep ditches. In June 1487, Lambert Simnel landed from Ireland and, proclaimed 'King Edward IV', held brief court there.

A hotel flourished on Piel in the nineteenth century. Its landlord was 'king' of the island, and he instituted the presumably commercial device of initiating 'knights of Piel' – a ceremony mainly of drink and horseplay. For reward, those knighted who were 'wrecked or drowned' in alcohol were granted free bed and board until they recovered.

The Isle of Walney is not, by all the definitions of this book, an island any more, since it has, from the end of the nineteenth century, been permanently linked by a road bridge to Barrow-in-Furness. It has, nonetheless, certain island characteristics, among them its well-protected nature reserve. But residential development on the island is increasing rapidly and it will, in all likelihood, rapidly become totally indistinguishable from the mainland.

Isle of Walney

The Island of Hilbre from the air. The slipway of the old lifeboat station is still highly visible.

7 The Islands of Northern Ireland

While there are hundreds of islands along the south and west coasts of Ireland, the islands of Northern Ireland are relatively few. Moving from the border up the east coast of the Six Counties, one finds some tiny islands, including **Blockhouse Island** and **Green Island**, at the entrance to Carlingford Lough, both owned by the National Trust and both important breeding grounds for terns.

Blockhouse Island
Green Island

Just off the coastal hamlet of Ballyhornan, seven miles to the east of Downpatrick, lies the uninhabited **Guns Island**. It gets its name from cannon which were washed up from a wrecked man-of-war many years ago. One of the cannon is still close by – marking a gateway in Ballyhornan village.

Guns Island

There are a number of substantial islands in Strangford Lough. The lough, which was given the Viking name *'Strang Fjord'* because of the swiftness of the current at its mouth, is a twenty-mile-long arm of the sea, matching in size the gentle rolling hills of the Ards Peninsula that shelters it; something like thirty-five separate islands are embraced by it. Due to the narrowness of the channel at the entrance of the lough, these islands have been deprived of any ruggedness and have an appearance that is almost entirely inland in character. Most of them are the summits of what are called drowned 'drumlins', a geological term used to describe ridges formed under the ice sheet in the glacial period of the earth's evolution. The entire foreshore of the lough itself, along with its islands, has been designated as a wildlife and ornithological reserve, for, besides being an area of outstanding natural beauty, it has much to interest botanists, biologists and geologists. There is also much of archaeological interest, since this has been a land much inhabited by man ever since very primitive times. There are numerous burial sites, monoliths and stone circles which long predate St Patrick, who arrived to begin his great Christian mission in this part of Ireland.

Strangford Lough Islands

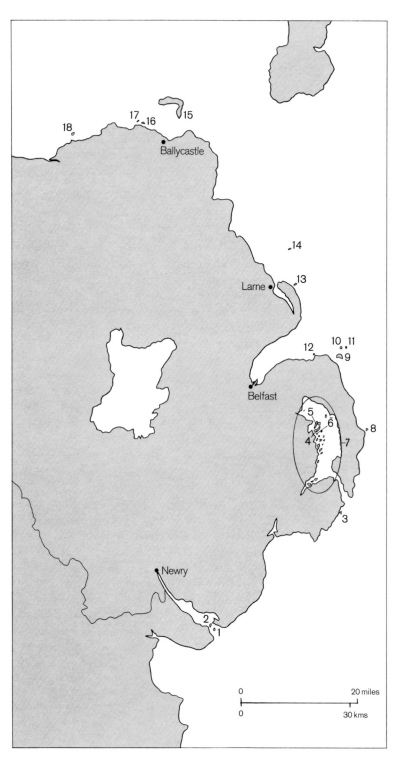

Northern Ireland

1 *Blockhouse Island*
2 *Green Island*
3 *Guns Island*
4 *Mahee*
5 *Reagh Island*
6 *Sketrick Island*
7 *Other Strangford*
  Loch Islands:
   Trainor Island
   Shoan Island
   Chapel Island
   Islandmore
   Island Taggart
   Dunsey Rock
   Parton
    Inishanier
   Pig Island
   Hen Island
   Round Island
   Long Island
   Sheelah's Island
   Peggy's Island
   Jane's Rock
8 *Burial Island*
9 *Copeland*
10 *Lighthouse Island*
11 *Mew Island*
12 *Cockle Island*
13 *Isle of Muck*
14 *The Maidens*
15 *Rathlin*
16 *Carrick-a-Rede*
17 *Sheep Island*
18 *Skerry Islands:*
  Castle Island

The largest of the lough's islands, lying to the north-west, is the crescent-shaped Mahee. With its delightful woodlands, it is also sometimes called Bird Island, and it is connected to the mainland by a causeway that passes the ruins of the sixteenth-century 'Captain Brown's Castle'. On the island itself are the ruins of a monastery reputedly founded by the fifth-century saint Mochaoi. Called Nendrum (literally 'nine ridges'), it flourished from 450 till its destruction by the Norsemen in the late tenth century. It was partly restored in 1922, and includes the remains of a tenth-century round tower and a church with an unusual sundial built into it.

This pattern of near landlocked islands with their myriad variety is arguably one of the most beautiful parts of all Northern Ireland. To make it more accessible, an enterprising Wildlife Scheme has recently been established, a programme through which the public may see something of the natural history of the area at close hand. There are special areas, as on Reagh Island, where birds can be studied under conditions that have been described as those of an 'outdoor nature classroom'. Other bird sanctuaries are on Trainor and Shoan islands, where hundreds of varieties of wildfowl have their breeding grounds.

Surprising for such an inland lough, the smaller islands are also a safe breeding ground for seals, and the whole area, 'standing at the confluence of two tidal streams', is of such varied interest to marine biologists that much research is now undertaken by a research centre at Portaferry, operated under the auspices of Queen's University, Belfast.

Many of the islands are privately owned and a number of them have standing on them the ruins of tower houses which were first built by the Normans during the thirteenth century, to be taken over later by the new wave of seventeenth-century Ulster land-owners. Some of these islands are connected to the mainland by causeways, sometimes dating back to the days when the islands were settled by monks and Vikings. One island, close to Mahee, is Sketrick Island on which stands a well-preserved castle of the same name. And the names of many of the other islands have their own attraction: Chapel Island, Islandmore, Island Taggart, Dunsey Rock, Parton Inishanier, Pig, Hen, Round, Long islands, along with those named after women of the past, Sheelah's and Peggy's islands and Jane's Rock.

On the seaward side of the Ards Peninsula, near Ballyhalbert, is Burial Island, which probably was just that, but is mentioned in the literature solely as the most easterly part of all Ireland.

On the southern shore as one turns into Belfast Lough are the three Copeland islands, Copeland itself, the largest and nearest

Mahee

Reagh Island

Trainor Island
Shoan Island

Sketrick Island
Chapel Island
Islandmore
Island Taggart
Dunsey Rock
Parton
Inishanier
Pig Island
Hen Island
Round Island
Long Island
Sheelah's Island
Peggy's Island
Jane's Rock

Burial Island

An aerial view of the ruins of Neudrum Monastery, on Mahee Island.

Copeland
Lighthouse Island
Mew Island

to the shore, to the north of which is Lighthouse Island (without a lighthouse any longer but with a bird observatory owned by the National Trust) and the twenty-six acres (11ha) of Mew Island whose powerful light, by contrast, is a major shipping marker for the entrance to Belfast harbour. Copeland, which takes its name from an English family that settled there, is a mile long by half a mile wide. It is uninhabited, but it had a community in the past and there are traces of a chapel surrounded by a long-abandoned

Cockle Island

graveyard. Further up the lough is Cockle Island, close inshore by Groomsport harbour, privately owned but now managed by the National Trust. Further north, just off Island Magee (County

Isle of Muck

Antrim), lies the tiny rocky Isle of Muck, now a bird sanctuary ('*muc*' in Irish means 'pig' and is a common component of Irish placenames). The island is sited close to Portmuck, which has a small harbour and the site of a ruined castle said to have been that of an Island Magee chief.

About eight miles north-east of Larne, a group of dangerous

The Maidens

rocks, known as the Maidens, are marked by two lighthouses. From the shore at Larne, the effect is that of two warships lying out to sea.

Rathlin

Eight miles north of Ballycastle, a fifty-minute boat trip across the dangerous race of Sloch-na-Marra, or the 'Valley of the Sea', is Rathlin, also known as Raghery or Rechra. Some six miles long and a mile across, it is shaped like a foot, with the toe pointing at Ballycastle Bay. It is almost totally circumscribed by white cliffs that, to the north-west side of the island, rise to a height of over four hundred feet (120m). The island is now a bird sanctuary, and every inch of it seems to be permanently teeming with seabirds.

The greatest of all the Scots–Irish saints, Columba, is said to have stayed there on his way to the innumerable Scottish isles with which he is associated. One of the main sites of historical interest on Rathlin is Bruce's Cave, where, in the year 1306, Robert the Bruce is said to have watched the spider repeatedly trying to bridge its web across the mouth of the cave, thereby inspiring Bruce himself to try again too, which he did by returning to his native Scotland and defeating the English at the Battle of Bannockburn. (There are a number of other caves, including one on Arran and another on the northern shores of the Firth of

(Opposite) *The Isle of Muck, which lies off the coast of industrial County Antrim.*

(Below) *The dangerous rocks called the Maidens with their two lighthouses.*

Forth, that lay claim to being the site of the same famous incident.) On a neighbouring rock at the heel of the island stand the scant ruins of Bruce's Castle to add their weight to Rathlin's claim to the Scottish hero. Whatever else, the story illustrates the justification for the reputation of the few hundred or so inhabitants of Rathlin, that they are more Scots than Irish in their accents and traditions. Since the island is only fourteen miles from the Mull of Kintyre in Scotland, and is easily visible on a clear day from as far north as Arran in the Firth of Clyde, this is an understandable conclusion to draw.

Rathlin's people, the descendants of survivors of many massacres that were bad and bloody even in terms of Irish history, are farmers or fishermen, most of them living at Church Bay, the main landing place for the island. Rathlin once contained an early Christian monastic settlement, repeatedly plundered by the Vikings and finally extinguished in the eleventh century. There are traces of the settlement at Knockans and there is also a stone 'sweat house' – an early Scots–Irish type of sauna. Geologically interesting, in earliest times Rathlin was an important source of flint implements which, there is much evidence to prove, were exported to all the surrounding areas of mainland Britain and Ireland. Rathlin also has impressive basalt rock formations that

The fragile-looking rope bridge that spans the chasm to Carrick-a-Rede.

94

(in common with those of Staffa, Mull and Islay) are in many ways similar to those of the Giant's Causeway, while its alternately black and white cliffs led Kingsley in his novel *Westward Ho!* to describe it as 'a drowned magpie'.

Close to the shore five miles north-west of Ballycastle is the precipitous basalt stack Carrick-a-Rede, connected to the mainland during the fishing season by a fearsome rope bridge with a wooden walkway across a sixty-foot (18m)-wide and eighty-foot (24m)-deep chasm. The name of the island is Celtic for 'rock on the road', the road in this case meaning the road the salmon take to the northern rivers; the bridge itself, while presenting a considerable challenge to casual visitors, is used by fishermen to get to the valuable fishing on the island. The semi-permanency of this frail link may, in strictest terms, disqualify Carrick-a-Rede from being classified as an island, but, as crossing it is a journey only for those who do not suffer from vertigo, it is a thin distinction.

Carrick-a-Rede

Further along the coast, about a mile off Ballintoy in County Antrim, is Sheep Island, one of a cluster of rocky isles now part of a controlled bird sanctuary; both it and Carrick-a-Rede are owned by the National Trust. Finally, off Portrush, lie the Skerry Islands, the last Irish habitat of the now extinct great auk. They include Castle Island, a straight-line reef of rocks which provides the harbour with a natural breakwater and a convenient play area for holiday-makers from the town itself. Here, by tradition, the notorious Scottish brigand, Tavish Dhu, lies buried. From all these islands along the coast of County Antrim one can, on a clear day, see north to Islay and the Paps of Jura, a visual link with which history has long played.

Sheep Island

Skerry Islands

Castle Island

8 The Islands of South-West Scotland and the Firth of Clyde

According to a much-quoted Scottish census of 1861, an island is 'any piece of solid land surrounded by water, which affords sufficient vegetation to support one or more sheep or which is inhabited by man'. This produced, according to that census, a total of around 590 islands off the west coast of Scotland and another 200-odd elsewhere round Scotland, which latter figure includes the Orkneys and Shetlands. Today, of the five or six hundred islands commonly known as the Hebrides (which include by tradition those islands situated in the western sea lochs) between fifty and sixty can, according to the established conventions, be classified as being inhabited by man. The total number of inhabited islands in Scottish waters comes then to around a hundred and thirty.

For the purpose of this book, I have classified the Scottish islands into a number of separate groups: those in the Solway and the Firth of Clyde; the Inner Hebrides, which lie sprinkled close to the west coast; the Outer Hebrides, which stretch in a chain from Barra Head to the Butt of Lewis; the 'Far Isles', which include the St Kilda group; the islands of the north-west and north; the Orkneys; the Shetlands; and finally those few islands along the east coast of Scotland, which are mainly sheltered in the Firth of Forth. As we progress, these groups will have to be subdivided yet again, since many fall into natural geographical patterns distinct from each other.

Rough Island In Rough Firth, on the Dumfries and Galloway coast of the Solway, is the eighteen-acre (7ha) Rough Island, which is owned by the National Trust for Scotland and is now a bird sanctuary. It can be reached by foot at low tide from the village of Rockcliffe.

Hestan A couple of miles south at the entrance to Auchencairn Bay, and connected at low tide by a strip of gravel to the mainland at Almorness Point, is the haunting and historic island of Hestan.

96

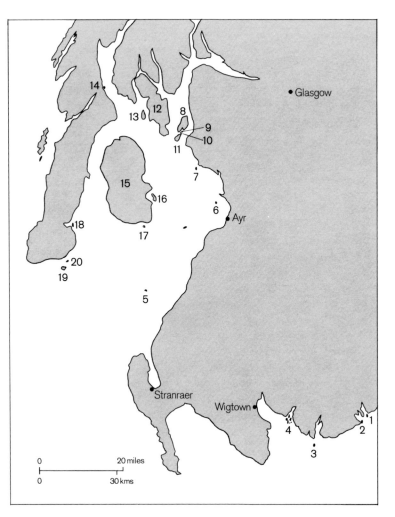

South-West Scotland

1 *Rough Island*
2 *Hestan*
3 *Little Ross*
4 *Islands of Fleet:*
   Ardwall Island
   Barlocco
   Murray's Isles
5 *Ailsa Craig*
6 *Lady Isle*
7 *Horse Isle*
8 *Great Cumbrae*
9 *Inner Eileans*
10 *Outer Eileans*
11 *Little Cumbrae*
12 *Bute*
13 *Inchmarnock*
14 *Cock Island*
15 *Arran*
16 *Holy Island*
17 *Pladda*
18 *Davaar Island*
19 *Sanda*
20 *Sheep Island*

Archaeologists have found a large and interesting 'midden' of oyster shells there which probably dates from the Mesolithic period, while at the north end of the island stand the ruins of the manor from where Edward Balliol, the puppet king of Scotland, ruled during a brief few years from 1332. Crowned at the ancient palace of Scone, he had little or no power over Scotland as a whole, though he did retain some hold over the south-west and issued edicts under the Great Seal of Scotland 'at our place of Estholm', in other words, Hestan itself.

A lighthouse and a nineteenth-century farm now remain on the island, which is also home to a significant colony of arctic terns. It is the reputed model for 'Isle Rathan' in S. R. Crockett's *The Raiders* and there are said to be secret underground caverns on the island which were used by smugglers in the seventeenth and eighteenth centuries. Crockett's description measures up well:

> Rathan Island lay in the roughest tumble of the seas. Its southern point took the full sweep of the Solway tides as they rushed and surged upwards to cover the great deadly sands of Barnhourie. From Sea Point (as we named it), the island stretched northward in many rocky steeps and cliffs riddled with caves. For just at this point, the softer sandstone that you meet with on the Cumberland shore, set its nose out of the brine. So the island was more easily worn into sea caves and strange arches, towers and haystacks, all of stone, sitting by themselves out in the tideway.

Little Ross

Further along the coast, at the entrance to Kirkcudbright Bay, is the island of Little Ross with a lighthouse and two ruined houses on it.

Ardwall Island
Islands of Fleet

Barlocco
Murray's Isles

To the north-west, hugging the eastern coast of Wigtown Bay, is Ardwall Island, also called Larry's Isle, one of the several Islands of Fleet. On Ardwall are the remains of a stone-built church dating from the beginning of the ninth century. Various early stone crosses and an inscription of the Northumbrian period have also been found there. At low tide the island is connected to the mainland, which made it a favourite haunt for smugglers. Barlocco, another of the Islands of Fleet, is a high-water island and privately owned, as are the twin Murray's Isles, the two most northerly of this group of islands, which stand at the entrance to Fleet Bay.

Ailsa Craig

Travelling up the Ayrshire coast and into the calmer waters of the Firth of Clyde, one comes first to an island which is visible from a great distance, the spectacular rock, Ailsa Craig. Nicknamed 'Paddy's Milestone' since it was on the well-worn sea route from Ireland during the potato famines, when poor Irish immigrants made for the bleak but expanding industries of nineteenth-century Glasgow, it rises a magnificent sentinel, 1,113 feet (338m) of granite. Teeming with seabirds, particularly gannet and puffin, it is now a favoured goal for ornithologists. Like many other islands along the coast, Ailsa Craig was, up to the middle of the last century, a source of gannets and their eggs; both were exported and sold on the mainland as a much cheaper source of protein than the lamb and beef which tended to be beyond the pocket of the majority.

There is a quarry on the island which was much valued for its top-quality stone, known as blue granite and used in that peculiarly Scottish game of curling, as well as, more pedestrianly, for kerbstones. In popular reputation, Ailsa Craig is a replica of that

other great rock on the east coast, the Bass Rock which guards the approaches to the Firth of Forth. On this western rock there is a solid lighthouse, the ruins of an old fort and an overwhelming aura of natural magnificence. It was this grandeur which inspired Wordsworth and, in his turn, Keats. The latter composed this sonnet 'To Ailsa Rock':

A Victorian engraving of Ailsa Craig.

> Hearken, thou craggy ocean-pyramid!
> Give answer from thy voice, the sea-fowl's screams!
> When were thy shoulders mantled in huge streams?
> When, from the sun, was thy broad forehead hid?
> How long is't since the mighty power bid
>   Thee heave to airy sleep from fathom dreams?
>   Sleep in the lap of thunder or sunbeams,
> Or when grey clouds are thy cold coverlid.
> Thou answer'st not; for thou art dead asleep.
>   Thy life is but two dead eternities –
> The last in air, the former in the deep;
>   First with the whales, last with the eagle-skies
> Drown'd wast thou till an earthquake made thee steep,
>   Another cannot wake thy giant size.

*   *   *

Lady Isle   A desolate rocky islet, Lady Isle stands, with its lighthouse, two miles west-south-west from Troon, and apart from being a marker to the Clyde's approaches, it is valued as a sanctuary by the seabirds and by yachtsmen sheltering in its lee from an unexpected squall. It has, nonetheless, to be approached with care because of the abundance of rocks hiding just below the surface all around it.

Horse Isle   The five acres (2ha) of Horse Isle, just off the Strathclyde coast by Ardrossan, stand close to the ferry route to Arran. Less than a mile long and about a sixth of a mile in breadth, the island gives the appearance of being little more than a strip of shingle. But it is teeming with wildlife, and in summer many species of butterflies can be found there. In the tower on the island, because of the lack of fresh water, a barrel of drinking water used to be replenished to act as a supply for any shipwrecked sailor.

The Cumbraes

A 19th-century harbour scene at Rothesay, Bute.

To the north-west, lying north–south between the Bute headlands and the Ayrshire coast and in part echoing the pastoral tranquillity of the latter, are the two Cumbraes, the Great and the Little, separated by half a mile of water known as 'The Tan'. The larger island, calm and green, is about four miles by two, with the

S.S. "Columba" approaching Pier, Rothesay   72865 JV

holiday town of Millport at the southern end, at the head of a picturesque bay. Here two groups of islets, the Inner and Outer Eileans, known also by their anglicised name, 'The Allans', add to the lively scenery of the whole area.

Inner Eileans
Outer Eileans

Great Cumbrae has a long ecclesiastical history; there is a charming story that its population's insularity led to one early nineteenth-century minister of the 'Episcopal Cathedral of Argyll and the Isles', the Reverend James Adam, praying for 'the Cumbraes' and 'for the adjacent islands of Great Britain and Ireland'. At Keppel on the east coast there is a museum and an aquarium belonging to the Scottish Marine Biological Station which, among other projects, carries out research into seaweed. The whole island, with its sandy beaches and much-pictured views, has, ever since the late eighteenth century, been a popular play-area for the Greater Glasgow conurbation.

Great Cumbrae

On Little Cumbrae stands a ruined castle, once the seat of King Robert II. It had an important part to play in Scottish history until its eventual destruction by Cromwell's forces in the year 1653. Nearby, on the westernmost point of the island, are the remains of an old lighthouse which dates from the mid-eighteenth century, in which age it burned coal to produce its light.

Little Cumbrae

Bute

The Clyde coast contains some of the most beautiful scenery in the entire British Isles, and one of its highlights is the so-called Kyles of Bute, a narrow, winding, twelve-mile stretch of water that, never more than two miles wide, separates Bute itself from the mainland. It is a yachtsman's paradise; blustery and challenging winds, but plenty of convenient shelter in a storm. Bute fits so closely with the protective arm of the Cowal peninsula that, sailing up the Kyles, one is again and again tricked into believing that the boat is going to run out of sea room. By the time that one emerges, one has encompassed an angle of about three hundred degrees, emerging on an almost reciprocal course.

Bute itself is renowned as a tourist and holiday resort with its main town the much-praised (and mocked) Rothesay. Rothesay has too much character and beauty to deserve its reputation as a sort of northern Blackpool, though at the height of the 'Clyde Fortnight' (a lengthy summer bank holiday), helped on by a long naval tradition maintained at the submarine base there, it takes on an air of alcoholic revelry as the Glasgow crowds descend by the boatload to disturb its genteel tranquillity. Ever since the steamboats were introduced to the Clyde a hundred and fifty years ago, Rothesay has provided even the poorer inhabitants of the industrial west with fresh air, fun and beauty, so well matched by the song styles of Sir Harry Lauder. In more romantic mood, Mrs Craik's old song 'Rothesay Bay' tells how:

> ... the great black hills, like sleepin' kings,
> Sit grand roun' Rothesay Bay.

Rothesay, and Bute itself, has a long and varied history. Rothesay Castle dates from the end of the eleventh century, once a leading Norse stronghold and now a remarkable medieval survival. The castle's history is deserving of a book on its own as it was a major residence for many of the kings of Scotland. The title of 'Duke of Rothesay' is vested on the heir to the Throne of Scotland, the Prince of Wales, by an Act of the Scottish Parliament dating from the year 1469. The Bute family, however, are hereditary keepers of Rothesay Castle.

Apart from tourism, Bute has a thriving agriculture, particularly in dairy farming. Other attractions for the tourist include the fourteenth-century Kames Castle and, to the east of Kilmichael, Glen More, with a splendour outstanding even amid so much other natural competition.

Inchmarnock
To the west of Bute lies its vassal island, Inchmarnock, which is otherwise known (a popular piece of island nomenclature) as the 'Calf' of Bute. It is a peaceful and, in contrast to the drama of its surroundings, featureless island, the home of two farms, which exist without benefit of telephone or postal service. A half mile wide by two and a half long, it seems as remote as any western isle, though it is a bare forty miles from Glasgow. Inchmarnock also has its ancient monastic ruins and its burial grounds; a number of interesting archaeological finds have been made there, including that of the exquisite Inchmarnock necklace, which is dated at around 1500 BC. There are stories of the island having been used at one time as a place of banishment for drunkards. More mundanely, during the Second World War it was evacuated and used as a target range, one of many in that conveniently accessible part of western Scotland.

Cock Island
There are numerous other small islands and islets in the Kyles, and more in Loch Fyne. Worth brief mention is Cock Island, just off Tarbert harbour. Though tiny, it has a miniature plantation of silver birch trees on it, a charming surprise of an islet on a frosty morning.

Arran

Brodick Castle, Arran. The ancient seat of the Dukes of Hamilton.

Arran, inboard of and at the extreme south of that loose pattern of islands which form the Inner Hebrides, is an island with a highland outlook in a lowland setting. It is spectacular to approach across the Firth of Clyde on a clear day – particularly when it is

102

The mountain peaks of the Isle of Arran.

unobscured by the slightest blurring of mist and the winds are in the west or north. Its jagged and lofty heights, beloved of geologist, hill-walker and mountaineer, gradually slope down towards a quieter and more fertile south and provide the visitor with 'instant highlands' or, as more commonly expressed, 'Scotland in miniature'. But despite the grandeur of its scenery – and that is unchallengeable – there is the less flattering opinion that, when viewed from the air or seen on a map, Arran is shaped more like a homely potato. Indeed, much of the island's fame derives from the successful strains of Arran seed potatoes that have been developed there.

While, because of its accessibility, it is generally considered to

be part of southern Scotland, it is, historically, geologically and culturally (with the exception of the three almost suburban east-coast holiday resorts of Brodick, Lamlash and Whiting Bay), more Celtic in nature; for example, it has an agricultural landscape typical of that bleak pattern created by the Clearances. Most of the place names, though often anglicised, also have a Gaelic or Norse inheritance. But, as regards language, spoken Gaelic has almost entirely disappeared. It was once highly populated but now has around three and a half thousand permanent residents. There are many ruins of the past: old black houses (black because they were built simply round a fire which was in the centre of the room, the smoke escaping through a hole in the roof), religious ruins and, predating these, monoliths, stone circles and graves dating back five thousand years. But unlike the majority of the more northerly isles, Arran has, since Victorian times, retained a respectable prosperity built on its summer tourism. (Such prosperity is of course relative, since when further compared, for example with the Isle of Wight which is of much the same geographical size, it has less than a twentieth of the number of both tourists and inhabitants.)

Brodick Castle, once owned by the Hamilton family and now by the National Trust for Scotland, is one of the more formal treasures of the island. It houses an excellent collection of paintings, including some by Gainsborough and Turner, and itself stands in a superb garden setting overlooking Brodick Bay.

Many well-known people have had connections with Arran. Browning visited it and Charles Dodgson, better known as Lewis Carroll, came in 1871 in search of the artist Noël Paton who was staying on the island and whom Carroll hoped to get to illustrate his *Through the Looking Glass.* The village of Corrie was the birthplace of Daniel Macmillan, founder of the famous publishing house and forefather of Harold Macmillan.

And then there was Sir Walter Scott. Even today, Lochranza, in the north-western part of Arran, with its square keep of a castle guarding its approaches, is not too different from Scott's description of it in *The Lord of the Isles.* Much of the action of this dramatic poem is set on the island.

> On fair Loch Ranza streamed the early day;
> Thin wreaths of cottage-smoke are upwards curled
> From the lone hamlet, which her inland bay
> And circling mountains sever from the world;
> And there the fisherman his sail unfurled,
> The Goat-herd drove his kids to steep Ben-Ghoil,
> Before the hut the dame her spindle twirled
> Courting the sunbeam as she plied her toil.

On the south-west of Arran, at Blackwaterfoot, is another of the many caves where, in the year 1306, Robert the Bruce is said to have watched that indefatigable spider spin its web.

It is impossible to do more in this limited space than to give a brief glimpse of a magnificent island, where, at Kildonan, the Author had a home for many years. It can be bleak; it can be cold; it is always beautiful. And over it towers the mountain, Goat Fell, at 2,866 feet (874m) the highest peak on Arran. (According to one source, the name may have nothing to do with goats but be a corruption of its Gaelic calling, Goadh Bhein, 'The Mountain of the Winds'. More likely it is from the Viking '*Geita Fjall*', 'Goat Mountain'.) With its rugged charm and character, with its scenery second to little, Arran offers, at every corner turned, a new range and view. Tinted everywhere in season by rhododendrons of great variety and colour, and by moors of heathers shrinking amid the relentless march of Forestry Commission pines, Arran is an island for every mood and season.

Holy Island

Holy Island, in Gaelic 'Eilean Molaise', stands lowering over a thousand feet (300m) high in the middle of Lamlash Bay, providing in its two-mile lee one of the best natural harbours in the Firth of Clyde. Nowadays the Royal Navy and many yachtsmen share the anchorage between them, but perhaps the most famous occasion on which it was used was when the fleet of King Haakon regrouped there before the Norwegian defeat at the Battle of Largs in 1263.

The name 'Holy Island' is taken from its association with the unfamiliar saint, Molio (or Molaise), who was a disciple of St Columba. His monastic cell, which he occupied during the latter part of the sixth century, is still to be seen, a wind- and sea-worn hollow in the red sandstone rock, with some curious runic inscriptions and Viking names carved on the roof. There is also a farm on the island and houses for the keepers of its two lights.

Pladda

At the southern end of Arran, off Kildonan, is the pear-shaped island of Pladda which has, as well as a lighthouse, a coastguard station from where the arrival of vessels at the Clyde is notified to Glasgow and Greenock. It also has the reputed site of a chapel dedicated to St Blaise.

Davaar Island

Off the east coast of Kintyre, the dark mass of the square-shaped Davaar Island blocks the entrance to Campbeltown from the sea. A yachtsman has to hold a course well past the island before Campbeltown Loch is revealed to the beam. During the eighteen-eighties a young local artist, a man variously named as Archibald or Alexander MacKinnon, painted on the rock face of one of the seven caves on the island a picture of the Crucifixion. As the painter did not admit to his deed, the picture took to itself a certain myth and mystery, given the oddness of its setting. MacKinnon, as an old man in his eighties, returned to Campbeltown in 1934 and repainted much of his earlier work, and since then its continued maintenance has been ensured by a local artist.

Sanda

Sheep Island

Just south-east of the Mull of Kintyre is the small island of Sanda (with its lighthouse), which is a mile long by a quarter wide. Between it and the mainland to the north is Sheep Island, a tiny eight acres (3ha) which, like Sanda, has in the past been used for offshore grazing.

9 The Inner Hebrides

There are between five and six hundred islands in the Hebrides, many more than, by the most generous of counts, England, Wales and the rest of Scotland have around their coasts. Of these, at a rough estimate, perhaps sixty are inhabited. On another count, some 35,000 people exist on 1.7 million acres (0.7 million ha) of land.

By general consensus, the Hebrides are all those islands off the west coast of Scotland, with the exception of the ones in the Firth of Clyde and the Solway and high up the innumerable sea lochs which deeply fray the Scottish coast. Again, it is practice, as well as geographic sense, to think of these Hebrides in two separate groups – the Inner Hebrides, sprawling from Islay in the south to Skye in the north; and the Outer Hebrides, stretching as a distinct chain, and acting as a barrier to the Atlantic storms, over a hundred and thirty miles from Barra Head to the Butt of Lewis. These two great archipelagoes are separated by a stretch of water known variously as the North Minch in the north, the Little Minch to the west of Skye, and further south as the Sea of the Hebrides.

One can then further subdivide the Inner Hebrides into four groups: the isles around Islay and Jura in the south; the isles encircling Mull; the islands in Skye's sea area; and lastly, the less important freckled pattern close to the very north-west coast of the Scottish mainland.

A number of other islands and clusters of islands fail to fit neatly into any of these specific groups. One gathering of small inshore islands which includes Luing and the Garvellachs, otherwise known as the Isles of the Sea, stands separate in the Firth of Lorn. Then out beyond and above the Outer Hebrides are the most far-flung isles of all, the 'Far Isles', including the St Kilda group forty miles out into the Atlantic, with Rockall hundreds of miles beyond that again, and, well to the north of the Butt of

The Calf which hugs the south-west coast of the Isle of Man.

The remains of Bruces's castle stand high on a Rathlin headland.

(Above) *The 'Port of the King' — the sheltered capital, Portree, on the Isle of Skye.*

(Right) *The Storr Rock stands predominate amid Skye's challenging rocky scenery.*

Lewis, the lonely windswept isles of Rona and Sula Sgeir. The fascinating story of these outposts of the British Isles is outlined in a separate section of the book.

As was indicated in the Introduction to this book, in the following description of the Hebrides the Author has been forced by sheer numbers to be very selective about which islands to include. In consequence, some quite sizeable, uninhabited islands, lacking any outstanding features of note, are given only brief mention in the text. Many of the other Western Isles, despite their remoteness from great areas of population, are however blessed with a much fuller descriptive literature about them (particularly subsequent to Dr Johnson's travels) than the majority of islands elsewhere around the British mainland. Their fascination, scenically, culturally and romantically, is extensively documented in other places for those who wish to know more about any individual island.

Geographically and geologically, the inner group of the Western Isles are of every shape and formation, from the great mountain crowns of Skye to the green flats of Coll and Tiree. They are extremely disparate, each one individual to itself. The Outer Hebrides, by contrast, are like a disconnected yet unitary mountain chain, strung out as if they were the vertebrae of some giant of the past. But the scenery of both repeats itself: high rocky outcrops; green and purple hills of heather shot through with bracken; white sandy beaches and rocky foreshores; blankets of Forestry Commission conifers; and, here and there, infrequent signs of human inhabitation, some of it of the present, but more often belonging to the past.

To lovers of wild places, the Hebrides are beautiful at all times, though spring and autumn are the most exciting. This varied and ever-changing mix of land and water – sea and rain, and burns and lochs and pools and mist, and more rain – is swept by an almost constant wind which blows cloudbanks quickly across the skies, producing long hours of sunshine, particularly in the early summer months. Out of reach of the wind, as in the Scilly Islands far to the south, nature blooms; there are, in consequence, famous and long-established subtropical gardens in many a sheltered valley.

Historically and culturally, waves of Stone-, Bronze- and Iron-Age peoples, the Picts, the Celts and the Vikings, came and left their abundant marks. In the years that followed the Battle of Largs the Vikings withdrew for ever, and for the next three hundred years the Hebrides were largely ruled by the Lords of the Isles, who sat in Islay. By a process of gift-giving, war and

The Inner Hebrides

1 *Islay*
2 *Eilean Mór*
3 *Council Isle*
4 *Texa*
5 *Gigha*
6 *Cara*
7 *Jura*
8 *Am Fraoch Eilean*
9 *Brosdale Island*
10 *Small Isles*
11 *Eilean Mór*
12 *Colonsay*
13 *Oronsay*
14 *Scarba*
15 *Luing*
16 *Lunga*
17 *Shuna*
18 *Seil*
19 *Easdale*
20 *The Garvellachs:*
    Eileach an
      Naoimh
    A' Chùli
    Garbh Eileach
    Dùn Chonnuill
21 *Dubh Artach (16*
    miles
    south-west of
    Mull)
22 *Torran Rocks*
23 *Mull*
24 *Calve Island*
25 *Iona*
26 *Erraid*
27 *Erisgeir*
28 *Staffa*
29 *Inch Kenneth*

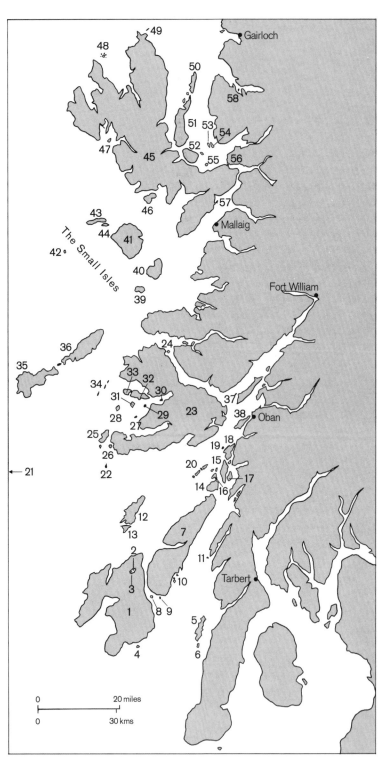

marriage, the Clan Donald came to dominate, and the territory was, to all intents and purposes, a separate kingdom, the subsidiary clan chiefs having more or less absolute power in their own domains.

After many attempts, the kings of Scotland, particularly James IV and James VI, eventually broke the powers of these Lords of the Isles. There followed a period of bitter clan feuding, with, in the eighteenth century, the last great rising of the clans against the Established Crown, culminating in the defeat of Prince Charles Edward Stuart at Culloden in the year 1745. The subsequent systematic destruction of the clan system and the grim nineteenth-century Clearances helped to people the New World. This exodus of many, coupled with religious strife (which eventually had the Free Church predominating in all the islands except South Uist and Barra, where Roman Catholicism still held on), led to a period of great decline.

Only development money and planning in this present century are, in small measure, beginning to reverse this sad trend. For this was a part of the nation that was ignored until comparatively recently by those in the rest of the United Kingdom, who were, at the same time, well-versed and knowledgeable about the wonders of far-flung corners of the globe. (Few travellers of note predated Dr Johnson: he himself paid attention to but two, Dean Monro in 1549, and Martin Martin at the end of the seventeenth century – and Johnson's amanuensis Boswell had plenty of inaccuracies to complain about in the writings of both.) And at a time – up to the middle of the last century – when the British Government and people were bravely waging war on the remnants of the slave trade, forcible depopulation was, incredibly, replacing the indentured labour conditions that had, till then, existed in many parts of the Western Isles. The ruins of countless crofts, overgrown cart tracks and the faint traces of once-cultivated fields are everywhere on these islands as a memorial to this infamous process.

Tragedy and defeat, coupled with the hard ways of life that existed and still do exist in many of these islands, have however left their outstanding mark in the cultural inheritance, particularly the language, the songs and the music of the islands. Gaelic is still the common language of many of them, though almost everyone now speaks English as well. From the lively 'Road to the Isles' to the sweetness of the 'Eriskay Love Lilt' and the great wealth of Jacobite-inspired songs (including, most famous perhaps of all, 'The Skye Boat Song'), music, particularly of the pipes, has had its haunting effect, blurring myth and reality, romanticism and history, into a cultural tradition known the world over.

30 *Eorsa*
31 *Little Colonsay*
32 *Ulva*
33 *Gometra*
34 *Treshnish Isles:*
   Dutchman's Cap
   Cairn na Burgh More
   Cairn na Burgh Beg
   Lunga
   Fladda
   Sgeir an Fheòir
35 *Tiree*
36 *Coll*
37 *Lismore*
38 *Kerrera*
39 *Muck*
40 *Eigg*
41 *Rhum*
42 *Oigh-sgeir*
43 *Canna*
44 *Sanday*
45 *Skye*
46 *Soay*
47 *Wiay*
48 *Ascrib Islands*
49 *Eilean Troddday*
50 *Rona*
51 *Raasay*
52 *Scalpay*
53 *Crowlin Islands*
54 *Eilean Mór*
55 *Pabay*
56 *Eilean Bàn*
57 *Ornsay*
58 *Shieldaig Island*

Islay

Tell me o' lands o' the Orient gay!
Speak o' the riches and joys o' Cathay!
Eh, but it's grand to be walking ilk day
To find yourself nearer to Isla'.

Approached from the south-west, the mercurial island of Islay looks, at a distance, as if it has been split in two. Indeed, the earliest maps, including a famous second-century one by Ptolemy, who doubtless had gained his facts from Roman navigators, show it as two separate islands. Twenty-five miles long and twenty miles wide, it is in fact almost dissected by, in the north, Loch Gruinart and, eating into its south, Loch Indaal. A green and fertile island in general, it has its mountains reaching to a height of 1,610 feet (491m) lying to the south-east. Many of the population of around four thousand are engaged in farming, but, more importantly, there are no less than eight distilleries on the island, which, as any connoisseur knows, is famous for its malts. There is also a well-known creamery which converts the island's milk to cheese. There are two harbours, at Port Ellen and Port Askaig, but the principal village is Bowmore, which boasts a school and a hospital serving the whole island and is the centre of a growing tourist trade. Many visitors come to study the wide varieties of bird life on the island.

Islay has a history dating back to Neolithic times, with evidence of prehistoric villages, Druid or Celtic circles, a vitrified fort and many ancient carved stones, including the exquisitely carved eight-foot (2.5m)-high Kildalton Cross, which is, with the exception of another on Iona, the only early Christian high cross still intact. It would almost certainly have been carved by Columban monks and probably has an eighth-century date.

There are a number of versions of how Islay got its name. One story suggests it comes from the Danish princess Yula, whose grave is said to be marked by two of the standing stones on the island, near Port Ellen.

Eilean Mór

Council Isle

Worth a brief mention, even though it is an 'inland island', is Eilean Mór in Loch Finlaggan; on it stood one of the castle homes of those Lords of the Isles who ruled the Hebrides for three centuries. Fifty yards (45m) south in the loch lies the tiny Council Isle where the fourteen chiefs met in council to advise the Lord of the Isles. In leisurely Bowmore there is an interesting white-walled church, built in circular form so that, according to fable, Satan would have no corner in which to hide. Here too, on a cliff top on the Oa peninsula, is a monument to American soldiers and sailors who were drowned after their ships were torpedoed in February 1918. To the east of the Oa and south-east of Port Ellen

Port Ellen whisky distillery; one of many on the Isle of Islay.

lies the tiny island of Texa, a mile long by just under a third wide. One myth is that it was a rock carelessly dropped by a giant who was making his way from Ireland to raid the Scottish mainland.

Gigha

The happy, charming island of Gigha (meaning 'good island' or 'God's island'), which lies three miles west off the coast of Kintyre and half an hour by ferry from Tayinloan, is six miles long by one and a half at its widest. It has a population of about a hundred and eighty people, mainly engaged in crofting and tenant farming. There is also a small fishing fleet. It is a gracefully fertile island, rising to a height of 331 feet (101m), and claims to have a very high sunshine record. The village at Achamore boasts a small cheese-making industry, and there too, now owned by the National Trust for Scotland, are the colourful gardens of Acha-more House, which have palm trees growing in the open among splendid rhododendrons, azaleas and shrubs of every kind. Created by Sir James Horlick, of malted-milk fame, the gardens are among the finest of their kind in the British Isles. At Ardmin-

The northern end of Gigha viewed from Creag Bhan, the island's highest point.

118

ish there is a church with a stained-glass window commemorating Dr Kenneth MacLeod, who preached there and who helped the famous Marjory Kennedy-Frazer collect so many of the traditional Hebridean folk songs, and who himself wrote the lilt about the call of the Hebrides, 'The Road to the Isles', a song which Sir Harry Lauder was to make his own.

Close beside Gigha, one mile to the south, is Cara, owned since **Cara** the fourteenth century by the Macdonalds of Kintyre. Now uninhabited, it has the ruins of an old chapel on it, though its best-known feature is a prominent stone called the 'Brownie's Chair' which is said to be the seat of a fairy protector of the Macdonald family. Three wishes are granted to the one who sits upon the chair.

Jura

Sailing up the west coast, one has to guard against the danger of running out of superlatives to describe the scenery. Jura, hugging the north-east coast of Islay and six miles west of the Strathclyde coast, is a twin of its neighbour in that it also is almost split in two, with Loch Tarbert cutting the Ardlussa deer forest of the north off from the Jura forest to the south. It is a rugged island with a shoreline of raised beaches and cliffs, and then, beyond, moorland, stretching up to the mountains. The scenery is slowly changing, since several thousand acres of trees have been planted across the island by the Forestry Commission. The entire western half of the island is barren and uninhabited, though the caves that abound there were certainly lived in in prehistoric times.

The most impressive geological features of Jura are the quartzite 'Paps of Jura' which rise, all three peaks, to over 2,400 feet (730m). From the top, on a clear day, one can see, unbelievably, from the Isle of Man in the south, to the Outer Hebrides to the north-west. To the north of the island lies the notorious Gulf of Corryvreckan, a whirlpool in the sea race that separates Jura from the neighbouring island of Scarba. Corryvreckan frequently features in the myths and legends of the Western Isles.

Though Jura is twenty-seven miles long, it is only seven miles at its widest and has only a small population of around two hundred who share the land with an estimated five thousand deer, thereby giving credence to Jura's Viking name of 'Deer Island'. Crofting and whisky-distilling constitute the major part of the island's economy. There are few reminders of the present here, let alone guides to the future: yet it was here that, in the years 1946 to 1949, George Orwell came and, in a lonely croft nine miles from Ardlussa, with no fear of any Big Brother watching him, wrote most of his book *1984*. 'It was a bright cold day in April and the clocks were striking thirteen . . .' was how he began it. Orwell only left the island to die, of tuberculosis, in 1950.

Am Fraoch Eilean

A little island just off the southern shore in the Sound of Islay is called Am Fraoch Eilean and here there are ruins of a castle built by Somerled, king of Argyll in the twelfth century, as a guard for the Sound against the Norse invaders. There are numerous other small islands round Jura, particularly **Brosdale Island** at the southern tip, and a group called the **Small Isles** to the east of Craighouse. East of Jura, in the Sound of Jura and two miles from the entrance to Loch Sween, is another **Eilean Mór**, forty acres (16ha) in size, which has the distinction, along with possessing the remains of hermits' caves and having in the past been a haunt for smugglers, of now being owned by the Scottish National Party, to whom it was recently bequeathed.

The Paps of Jura.

Colonsay

To the west, ten miles from north Jura, are the islands of Colonsay
and Oronsay, joined to each other at low tide by a bar of sand. The
former takes its name from Columba and the latter perhaps from
St Oran, or possibly from an Old Norse word meaning 'tidal isle'.
Oronsay, three miles by one, has but one farm, while the larger
Colonsay, which lies to the north, has a population of around a
hundred. Beautiful islands both, but the sweeping hills of Colonsay are the better known.

Oronsay

Yet Oronsay also has its charm. (There are at least three other
Oronsays in the Western Isles and five Orosays.) Flat and windswept, with fine sheltered and sandy beaches, it was used as a
base by Norsemen and then by Columban monks. Columba
himself is said to have landed here in the year 563, but, because he
could still see Ireland, he insisted on travelling on to the north, to
avoid the temptation to return home. Here are the impressive
ruins of an Augustinian priory built in the mid-fourteenth century, with cloisters, finely carved gravestones, and a beautiful
Celtic altar cross which stands in the reroofed mortuary chapel.
An older, eroded cross on the strand marks the boundary of the
sanctuary within which the monks were permitted to shelter
anyone fleeing justice. A man became free if he stayed within that
sanctuary for a year and a day.

Oronsay also has a large 'midden', dating from the times of the
nomadic Mesolithic food-gatherers, who must have had the
island as one of their frequent camping sites. They lived off
molluscs, crabs and other shellfish, as well as animals and birds,
and they left behind them piles of shells and bones as evidence.
The other 'shells' on Oronsay are of crofts, enduring memories of
the Clearances. And in case one is too fascinated by the past,
Vulcan bombers, like giant rays, frequently roar overhead, hom-
ing in low to their base on the mainland.

Colonsay, sixteen square miles of it, with its low but craggy
protective hills, allows plant growth in the good soil of its sheltered valleys like few other islands on the west coast. The gardens
of Kiloran, which were developed by the late Lord Strathcona
around Colonsay House, contain many tropical and subtropical
plants and emphasise the strange trick of nature that brings little
snow and frost to such an otherwise unpromising terrain. The
west coast of Colonsay is lined with raised beaches and white
sands.

The island has many prehistoric sites, with standing stones,
burial cairns and, in the south, the ruins of a priory matching the
one on Oronsay, dating back to the sixth century. A 'ship-burial'
site, discovered in the sand dunes of Kiloran Bay, contained the

(Right) *The great cross of Oronsay erected to the memory of one of the Abbey priors.*

(Opposite) *The Vale of Kiloran and Colonsay House, Colonsay.*

skeletal remains of a man and his horse, his sword, shield, spear, axe and arrowheads. The skeleton was discovered lying in a crouching position, with a pair of bronze scales between the chin and knees, suggesting that the man may have been a merchant. Coins found at this remarkably rich site dated from the ninth century.

To the north of the Corryvreckan Whirlpool, in the approaches to the Firth of Lorn, lies the almost circular island of Scarba which, with a diameter of only three miles, rises to a height of 1,473 feet (449m). Not only is the Corryvreckan dangerous, but nearly all the waters round Scarba are avoided even by the most expert yachtsmen.   **Scarba**

Two miles to the north-east of Scarba is the island of Luing (pronounced without the 'n'), which has a population of around three hundred, almost all of whom are engaged in agriculture. In the past a slate-cutting industry flourished there, and some of these slates were sent to roof the Abbey of Iona.   **Luing**

To the east and west of Luing lie two other islands: Lunga, one of several of the same name in the isles, and Shuna, with a tiny   **Lunga** **Shuna**

(Right) *Mysterious stone figure, possibly Norse, in a Colonsay field.*

(Opposite) *The Garvellachs viewed from the south.*

Seil

population of around half a dozen who croft on good grazing land. Seil, to the immediate north, four miles by two, hardly deserves the island nomenclature since it is linked to the mainland near Oban by a humpback bridge, known as the Atlantic Bridge, that was designed by Thomas Telford in the year 1792. It has an attractive white-walled village with many holiday cottages. In common with Luing and with Easdale, a further small island a quarter of a mile to the west of Ellanbeich, it has abandoned slate-quarry workings.

Easdale

The Garvellachs

Lying to the west of these inshore islands, in the middle of the approaches to the Firth of Lorn, are the uninhabited Garvellachs, known as the 'Isles of the Sea', a chain of charming small islands stretching for about three miles in a diagonal south-west to north-easterly line. They are well known to archaeologists because two of them are especially rich in prehistoric remains.

On the most southerly, Eileach an Naoimh, the 'Isle of the Saints', there are what may be among the earliest of all Christian settlements in the entire Western Isles. Here are the ruins of beehive cells, one of which has now been fully restored, and an oratory and other early religious buildings, all remains of a monastery probably founded by St Brendan. This island, with its low cliffs, steep rocky beaches and secluded and sheltered valleys, has long been uninhabited, and this may be why the stones of these early buildings have been relatively unpillaged, particularly during those centuries in which respect for the old religious order was at a low ebb. On Eileach an Naoimh too is the reputed grave of St Ethne – Columba's mother – marked by a worn stone cross. This adds credence to a theory that this was Columba's favoured isle of retreat when he needed a physical and spiritual withdrawal from Iona, which lies thirty-odd miles to the west. At the north of the island is a splendid natural sandstone arch, known as 'The Harp', through which one can walk.

Eileach an Naoimh

Moving north-east among these haunting Isles of the Sea, one comes to A' Chùli, where there is the site of a retreat at one time used by St Brendan. He and Columba are only two of the many

A' Chùli

saints, including St Bride and St John, who had connections with these islands.

Garbh Eileach Next in this tiny but fascinating archipelago is Garbh Eileach, one and a half miles long by half a mile wide. It shows signs of fairly recent habitation and has a number of abandoned crofts and a burial ground on it. On the northern cliffs, in the folds of white limestone, innumerable cormorants nest and breed, while above them, in the early summer, corncrakes call amid a mass of wild flowers. Seals breed in large numbers round the Isles of the Sea and may be seen basking on the offshore rocks and skerries.

Dùn Chonnuill Finally, on Dùn Chonnuill (or Chonaill), an island a mile and a quarter long by half a mile wide, are the remains of a castle built in the thirteenth century, on the site of an earlier fort that is said to have been a stronghold of the Dalriadan kings. There is further evidence that this small island was reasonably well populated in early Christian times.

Sailing across the magic blue-green of the Firth of Lorn towards Mull and its satellite islands, one can see over to the west, low against the skyline, the isolated group of rocks known as Dubh **Dubh Artach** Heartach (or Dubh Artach), lying a dozen miles away. Prominent on one of them stands a lighthouse, the foundations of which were first laid down in 1867. Robert Louis Stevenson wrote about the problems of building it in his book *Memories and Portraits*. **Torran Rocks** These rocks are not to be confused with the Torran Rocks which lie close in at the south-west end of Mull, some five miles south of Iona.

Mull

Arriving at the varied island of Mull, round which the second group of islands in the Inner Hebrides is clustered, one discovers a confident, prosperous community including a fair settling of the rich, the wise and the well-born. It is a mountainous island, yet it has more subtlety than is in all the grandeur of Skye; its scenery varies from the high peaks of the south and east (with Ben More the highest at 3,169 feet (966m)) to glens, rough moorland and some of the most beautiful beaches on the entire west coast. Thirty miles from end to end, it is possessed of good roads and other social amenities. The main harbour of Tobermory, shel-**Calve Island** tered as it is by Calve Island, is one of the best protected in the area, and in consequence is very popular with yachtsmen.

The economy of this unrivalled island, with its thousand or two of a population, is centred on sheep, cattle farming and forestry, with sea fishing and tourism as important subsidiary sources of income. Mull has little or no industry, but in the past there was a

quarry just north of Fionnphort, opposite Iona, whose pink granite was, among other things, used for facing the Albert Memorial in London and for building the old Blackfriars Bridge over the Thames. Sadly, the once prosperous fishing fleet based at Tobermory is no more.

Homestead near Lock Scridain with Ardmeanach in the distance, Isle of Mull.

Mull is rich in bird life and has a large fallow-deer population that was reputedly first introduced in the fourteenth century. Geologically interesting are the south coast's Carsaig Arches, sea-sculpted in the basalt rock. Elsewhere are a number of impressive fossil sites, particularly in two areas around Loch Scridain, Ardtun and Ardmeanach, at the last of which the remains of a huge fossilised tree are embedded in the old lava.

The island is also a major focal point in the long history of the Western Isles. There is a wealth of prehistoric sites, including the standing stones at Dervaig, a galleried fort dating from the first century BC near Burg in the north-west, and a number of ruined brochs and Celtic crosses elsewhere around the island. A mile west of Carsaig Bay is the Nun's Cave, where the sisters from Iona took refuge both from the Vikings and, much later, at the grey time of the Reformation.

There are several castles in varying stages of ruin, including one at Aros (a former stronghold of the Lords of the Isles). But the most famous and impressive of them all, and far from a ruin, is the thirteenth-century Duart Castle which faces Loch Linnhe. Taken from Maclean hands in 1691 but bought back and restored in 1912, it is once again the home of the chief of the Clan Maclean. With walls up to twelve feet (3.7m) thick, it is set high on a precipitous and dominating crag, a magnificent and haunting outline against an autumn sunset. It was well placed to be prime among a chain of defensive castles facing the Lorn shore, and beacon signals from it could be relayed thirty-five miles up and down the coast from Mingary on Ardnamurchan to Dunollie by Oban within the space of half an hour. In the castle is a cell where the officers of the Spanish galleon *Florencia* were confined after it sank in Tobermory Bay in the year 1588. Divers still come, hoping to salvage the wreckage and the legendary treasure of thirty million ducats that it carries.

Here too, inevitably, came Dr Johnson and James Boswell in 1773. They landed at Tobermory and rode, with some difficulty 'as bridles were scarce', to visit Sir Alan Maclean on the neighbouring island of Inch Kenneth on the west of Mull. Thomas Campbell wrote his ballad 'The Exile of Erin' when he was a tutor on Mull in 1795, and Keats walked across the island in 1818 with his friend Reynolds, whose spectacles were regarded as a novel curiosity in the remote and backward circumstances of that time.

Mull is an island for the nature-lover, the rambler who likes mountains, sea and open space, and it is unrecognisable as that 'dreary' and 'dolorous' country that Dr Johnson, beset as he was by storms, a tiring journey and the loss of his favourite oaken walking stick, found two hundred-odd years ago.

Iona

Johnson was not renowned for his praise of things Scottish at the best of times, but of Iona (or 'Icolmkill', as he called it) he wrote:

> We were now treading that illustrious Island, which was once the luminary of the Caledonian regions, whence savage clans and roving barbarians derived the benefits of knowledge and the blessings of religion.... That man is little to be envied whose patriotism would not gain force upon the plain of Marathon, or whose piety would not grow warmer among the ruins of Iona!

Despite such magnificent praise, he and his party had, however, to spend the night in a barn, a sad letdown on such a glorious past.

But Johnson would have approved of the present: this most

ancient of Christian settlements in its splendid setting has, after long ages of barbarity, come into its own again in the twentieth century. It is an island of peace set around the perpetual tranquillity of the great abbey, and vulgar cars are banned from disturbing it. Lying three-quarters of a mile off the south-west corner of Mull, it is, for all its fame, only three miles long by one and a half wide. The shores of the island are as splendid as its reputation: dazzling white sands, dashed with dark green pebbles, stretch long and uncrowded. Dùn Hill, at 330 feet (100m), is its highest point, and there is a cairn of stones at the summit, erected in memory of Scotland's favourite saint, Columba.

The centre of the life of this island that is now looked after by the National Trust for Scotland has long been the abbey, which was first founded by Columba after his arrival on Iona in the year 563. It was from here that he and his followers launched their crusade to bring Christianity to Scotland. Ever since then it has been a place of sanctity, pilgrimage and scholarship. While Columba's abbey was destroyed again and again by waves of Norse invaders, it was rebuilt by the chieftain Somerled, in 1203, and a convent was also established there, the ruins of which can still be seen amid the green turf. At the same time, Iona became the sacred burial place for the kings of Scotland, forty-eight of whom, including Macbeth, are interred here on this island that was

Iona Abbey, now largely restored.

declared 'nearest to Heaven'. The Reformation, bitter and harsh, destroyed much of material value on the island, though the eighth-century Book of Kells that was probably compiled there was smuggled out and has survived.

The island really only came back into religious use at the end of the nineteenth century, when the then Duke of Argyll gave the ruined abbey to the Church of Scotland 'for the use of all Christian denominations'. Then, in 1938, the Reverend George MacLeod, now Lord MacLeod of Fuinary, with great vision and perseverance, founded the Iona Community. The buildings were gradually preserved and tastefully restored by the Community to the condition and simple beauty that visitors will find today.

Erraid

> There was no one part of it better than another; it was all
> desolate and rocky; nothing living on it but game birds
> which I lacked the means to kill, and the gulls which
> haunted the outlying rocks in a prodigious number. But
> the creek, or straits, that cut off the isle from the main
> land of the Ross, opened out on the north into a bay and
> the bay again opened into the Sound of Iona. . . .

Thus David Balfour's description of the island of Erraid in Robert Louis Stevenson's *Kidnapped*. Lying close into the Ross of Mull to the south-east of Iona, it was an island the writer knew well, since he came there with his engineer father who was using Erraid as his base-camp for building the Skerryvore and Dubh Heartach lighthouses. As Stevenson reveals, young Balfour need not have been trapped long. From this tiny square-mile island, round whose coast numerous other small islands nestle, one can, at low tide, walk through the sea to Mull.

Erisgeir

Moving northwards through the Sound of Iona towards Staffa, one passes Erisgeir to starboard, a tiny flat-topped islet, two miles off the west coast of Mull. By a complex and none too honest fourteenth-century marriage deal, Erisgeir played its part in the founding of the mixed fortunes of the Clan Maclean.

Staffa

Staffa is one of the geological treasures of Britain, with Fingal's Cave and its magnificently regular hexagonal basalt columns its outstanding feature. The cave, which is 66 feet (20m) high and 227 feet (69m) deep from its entrance to the back, is named after a Scots-Irish folk hero who led the defence of the Isles against the Norsemen and who has also been immortalised in Neil Munro's poem 'Fingal's Weeping':

Because they were so brave and young
Who now are sleeping,
His old heart wrung, his harp unstrung,
Fingal's a-weeping.

They should be mourned by the ocean wave
Round lone isles creeping
But the laughing wave laments no grave
And Fingal's weeping.

A dramatic 19th-century engraving of Fingal's Cave, Staffa.

The name 'Staffa' comes probably from the Vikings calling the island 'Stave Island' after the form of their houses, which were built from vertically set logs. Such harmony, formed in the cooling process of the black basalt after volcanic action (with close comparisons on Rathlin Island and the Giant's Causeway in Northern Ireland), is unique in such scale. The cave was virtually unknown outside the area until a party of scientists visited the island in 1772. Since then, writers (including Scott and Jules Verne), poets (Wordsworth, Keats and Tennyson), painters (such as Turner) and musicians have visited it. All have recorded the event in their own style. Mendelssohn's 'Hebrides' overture, better known as 'Fingal's Cave' overture ('I cannot describe it,' he said, 'only play it'), is one of his best-loved compositions, inspired as it was by what he called this 'cathedral of the sea'.

A mere seventy acres (28ha) of rocky land formed into a rough oval, Staffa is difficult to land on due to the dangers of loose cliff rocks. To visit it in the manner of nineteenth-century travellers (including Queen Victoria herself in the year 1847) is best – by small boat, complete with a piper standing and playing at the prow. The music reverberates with the sea as they break together into the fluted cave. Besides Fingal's Cave, there are numerous other caves and rock formations, including a Giant's Causeway in miniature (often called 'the other end of the Giant's Causeway'). Here too is a pothole, called Gunna Mor (Big Gun Cave), that emits a heavy thudding noise each time a westerly gale blows up, causing a large boulder in it to move and crash against its walls. Two years ago it was bought by a retired chartered accountant from Yorkshire for £100,000. It is reported that he receives partial return on his capital from selling the franchise for Staffa's own issue of stamps, which nets him £5,500 a year. By contrast, he receives a mere £60 for the grazing rights.

Inch Kenneth

After Iona and Staffa, it is difficult not to turn away from the use of superlatives as one sails east again towards Mull, and to the little island of Inch Kenneth that sits less than a mile off its shore. Yet this tiny 200-acre (81ha) island, named after one of Columba's colleagues, has a valuable history and there has long been a Christian settlement on it. Here are the remains of the twelfth-century chapel beside which clan chiefs and others would be buried when the crossing to saintly Iona was too stormy. Of a much later date is the cottage in which Johnson and Boswell stayed in 1773 while visiting the then chief of the Clan Maclean on his 'pretty' island. In recent years it was owned by Lord Redesdale, and was much visited by his family, including the well-known Mitford sisters.

Eorsa

Little Colonsay

Ulva

Passing to the west of the sheep-grazing island of Eorsa that lies in the centre of Loch na Keal, and with, on the port bow, the green island of Little Colonsay (one of so many totally depopulated during the Clearances), we reach Ulva or Wolf Island. Four miles by two, Ulva is the largest of the islands hugging the west coast of Mull. Mainly moorland and rising to a height of over a thousand feet (300m) in the west, it provided the setting in which the chief of the Clan MacQuarrie entertained those indefatigable travellers Johnson and his colleague. The father of the explorer and missionary David Livingstone came from here, as did one of the most famous of the founding fathers of Australia, Lachlan MacQuarrie. Ulva once had a population of six hundred, engaged in crofting and in the ill-fated kelp industry that produced chemicals, including iodine, out of burnt seaweed. Now it has less than forty inhabitants. It was to Ulva that Lord Ullin's daughter was fleeing in Thomas Campbell's romantic ballad, until, in Loch na Keal and to her father's horror:

The waters wild went o'er his child
And he was left lamenting.

Turning west again, towards the sunset, we pass the island of Gometra to starboard. It is a wild rocky mass with an inhospitable-looking coastline, though in fact it is comfortably connected to Ulva by an unlikely bridge. Next landfall further to the west are the uninhabited Treshnish Isles, a group of a dozen or so islets and skerries that lie in a broken arc streaming out towards Coll and Tiree four miles out from Mull. They are best known for their variety of curious shapes, their bird life, and as a major breeding ground for seals. At the south of the fragmented string is the thinly grassed Dutchman's Cap, that indeed lives up to its name, with a humped centre and flat brim. Further up the line are the flat-topped Cairn na Burgh More and Cairn na Burgh Beg (there are various spellings), both of which have ruined forts on them.

Gometra

Treshnish Isles

Dutchman's Cap

Cairn na Burgh More
Cairn na Burgh Beg

Lunga, the largest of the group, was much used for sheep grazing. It rises to a height of 337 feet (103m), dominating its less prominent neighbours. Here and there among the bracken and rocks can be seen clusters of ruined crofts, abandoned over a century ago in a surrender to a mix of poverty and promise. Next to Lunga in size is the flat, green-topped Fladda, and between the two is Sgeir an Fheòir, on which many different types of seabirds, including puffins, breed. The whole group, now a nature sanctuary, is teeming with bird life, the deposit from which fertilises the top of the islands (as with so many islets throughout the Western Isles), thereby producing, across the years, lush green caps of grass on what would otherwise be barren and inhospitable rock.

Lunga

Fladda
Sgeir an Fheòir

Coll and Tiree

A journey to the west again, some ten to fifteen miles, and, parallelling the Treshnish Isles, the two large islands of Tiree and, to its north-east, Coll show up low along the horizon.

Tiree

Enchanting Tiree, sometimes spelt 'Tyree', is the furthest west of all the Inner Hebrides. Twelve miles long and six miles at its widest, it lies fifty miles west of Oban on the mainland. It is a flat low island with a mild climate, long hours of summer sun, and a seemingly unceasing wind, which has given it the Gaelic nickname 'the land whose peaks are lower than the waves'. It was also known as the 'Isle of Grain', supplying, by tradition, the monks of Iona with food. Nowadays crofting, cattle farming and fishing occupy the eight hundred or so Gaelic-speaking inhabitants. The main village, Scarinish, has benefited from an increased annual influx of tourists, enticed by a golf course or attracted by excellent fishing and by quiet beaches of soft sand.

Tiree long belonged to the Lords of the Isles, and then, as their successors, to the Macleans of Duart, before eventually becoming Campbell territory. There are a number of prehistoric brochs, forts or 'duns' on the island, as testimony to fairly heavy early settlement, so much so that on some parts of the coast nearly every headland has its faint ruins of past defences. At the time of his visit, Dr Johnson said that a popular funeral feast on Tiree would 'bring out over nine hundred men'.

Coll   Two miles to the north-east of Tiree is Coll; due west, America. As a result, these islands are exposed to the Atlantic gales, yet at times can carry a surprising air of tranquillity about them. Of the two, Coll is less prosperous, with a population of only a hundred and twenty and sharing with its neighbour one policeman who has little traffic, few parking problems and an insubstantial crime rate to trouble his year. The main village is Arinagour on the east coast, whose inhabitants benefit from the growing tourism.

Coll is treeless; its landscape is undulating stone-flecked moorland, fringed by beautiful beaches and bays. At its highest point, it reaches only about 330 feet (100m). Its inhabitants are almost entirely involved in crofting. This is just what they were doing in the year 1841, when the landlord, having gone almost bankrupt buying grain for his tenants during the potato famine, decided that half of the some eight hundred souls should be transported to America. There are numerous signs of earlier generations still: the ruins of small forts or 'duns' built on tiny islets in the many inland lochs and a larger castle at the south of the island that was built for the Lords of the Isles and later became a Maclean stronghold. Beside it now stands an eighteenth-century mock castle of a strange architectural mix, which Dr Johnson, when visiting the island with his amanuensis (they had not intended to go there but were blown ashore in a storm while *en route* from Skye to Mull), dubbed 'neat and new', but nonetheless a 'tradesman's box'. At Arnabost there is, by a ruined schoolhouse, an underground 'earth house' of an ancient style that was reached by an underground passage some forty feet (12m) long. Here, too, are great mystic stones, burial cairns and cists standing amid the wind-bent grass and rocky moorland of this sadly beautiful outpost of the Inner Hebrides.

Before voyaging north towards the romantic and mist-blended mountains of Skye, we have to turn back round the northern point of Mull and down in a south-easterly direction along the beautiful Sound of Mull to Loch Linnhe. There, opposite Duart Castle and parallel to the shores of the loch, is the long, thin, treeless isle of Lismore. Dominated and sheltered by the historic **Lismore** and mystical peaks of Appin and Morvern, it was once the site of a major Christian settlement, a fact reflected in the meaning of its name, 'great enclosure'. Here, in this powerfully framed setting, St Moluag, a contemporary and rival of Columba (for he was a Pict and Columba a Celt), based himself; later, in the thirteenth century, a cathedral was built on the isle. It must have been small in dimensions and only a few dubiously verified stones now remain in the choir of the parish church. On the west side of the island is the ruined castle of Auchindown, once a bishop's palace, while at the south, as a marker to the loch, a lighthouse stands white against the green of the bracken.

James Macpherson, the poet who 'invented' and 'translated' the poems of Ossian, a mythical third-century Gaelic bard, used the discovery of *The Book of the Dean of Lismore*, a collection of Celtic and English poems gathered by a cleric who died in 1551, to try and substantiate his claim that Ossian was a genuine part of the Celtic tradition.

Home to three hundred or so inhabitants, Lismore is a fertile, sheltered island, the low green hills splashed with the white of neatly kept crofts and small farms.

There is one last island to visit before sailing back north up the Sound of Mull to Skye. Kerrera is the valuable shelter to the **Kerrera** harbour of Oban, that prosperous town that is central to Scotland's sea communications with all the Western Isles. Three-quarters of a mile from the town foreshore, Kerrera nowadays has a peaceful farming community, but it was here that, in the thirteenth century, the Viking fleet anchored on its fateful way to its last battle at Largs. Here too, in the year 1249, King Alexander II of Scotland died of a fever after fighting the Vikings. High on a precipitous ivy-covered crag stands that ancient ruined fortress of both Norseman and Scot, Gylen Castle, stronghold latterly of the Clan MacDougall, still staring, crumbling but defiant, out across the blue-grey waters of the Firth of Lorn.

The Small Isles

Muck, known best for its strangely unappealing name, should **Muck** really be called 'Muic', meaning the 'Isle of the Sow', or pig: not a particularly happy alternative. It is one of the group of four, Rhum, Eigg and Canna being the others, known collectively as the 'Small Isles', whose famous names are distorted into convoluted sentences in many a Scottish schoolboy joke. These four

The Scuir of Eigg, which stands nearly 1,300 feet high.

scatter themselves across the otherwise empty sea space between the Ardnamurchan peninsula in the south and the indented coast of Skye to the north.

Muck, only two miles long, is the most fertile of the Small Isles and is known for its bird life and the abundance of its wild flowers. It now has a tiny population of around twenty, crofting, lobster fishing and estate working, though there are many traces of much greater numbers of inhabitants in past generations. It is an island with a serrated shore, flat, but with one hill, 451 feet (137m) high, at the west side.

Eigg

Each of the other Small Isles has its distinctive shape. Eigg, formed like a backwards 'L', has a great glen that almost cuts its five-mile length in half. Then, at the south end, there is the sudden and spectacular pinnacled dome called the Scuir or An Sgurr, 1,289 feet (393m) high, at the top of which, as the result of some ancient volcanic eruption, there is a huge 400-foot (122m) block of lava in which many fossils have been found. The Scuir, towering above the patches of purple and green moor, the yellow cornfields and the white-walled crofts, is one of the most extraordinary sights, at times sparkling, at times menacing and seeming to overhang the whole island.

Landing on Eigg, as on Muck, is by small boat from the larger ferry, a boat shared with sheep and cattle being sent to and from the mainland. Two other features of Eigg to note are the singing sands of Laig Bay, silver beach sand that does indeed squeak musically underfoot as one walks along. And then, from a more tragic past, the cave, half a mile away from Galmisdale, in which the entire population of the island, 395 Macdonalds, were suffocated by smoke from the fire which a raiding party of MacLeods from Skye lit outside their refuge. Exaggerated the story may be, but about two hundred years later Sir Walter Scott, visiting Eigg in 1814, found skeletons in that very cave. Close by is a second cave, known as 'The Cathedral', where, after the Reformation, priests came to take secret mass.

Eigg is currently the site of an experiment by its Yorkshire-businessman owner to change it from its old ways, from being a place of crofting and dwindling population, into something lively and modern. There is praise and equal criticism for the owner's attempt to inject new life without endangering the island's inherited charms.

Rhum

Four or five miles to the north-east is the much larger island of Rhum (or Rum), a distorted square, eight miles by eight, edged by high sea cliffs and rising in the south to mountains of over 2,500 feet (750m). This mass of island has a tiny population of forty who are mainly estate workers for the Nature Conservancy. A group of research students, carrying out long-term studies of

the large red-deer population, is also based there. The deer were among the inspirations for these lines from Will Ogilvie's 'The Kingship of the Hills'.

Here in the pride of all high-born things
The red deer go with the gait of kings.
And only a step from their cottage doors,
The rough hill-shepherds are emperors.

The story of the island is a sad one. It was always poor, and from here, with the help of the then owners, the Macleans of Coll, around four hundred crofters, almost the entire population, emigrated voluntarily to Canada in the year 1826. Sheep grazing followed, to be replaced latterly by the deer. This mass exodus is evidenced today by the abandoned villages near Kinloch and at Kilmory. Most of the buildings here and elsewhere were so-called 'black houses', two simple rooms built round a fire, the smoke of which escaped through a hole in the roof.

Kinloch Castle, built in 1902 by the then owner of Rhum, was taken over along with the island itself by the Nature Conservancy in 1957. For many years before then Rhum had the reputation of being very much a 'forbidden' island, but now, while permission is required in order to land, the Conservancy, who use the island as a 'living laboratory', encourage interested visitors, particularly botanists and geologists, to follow the nature trails round the island and see some of their development schemes. These include a long-term project for reafforestation. The special breed of Rhum ponies that grow to a height of only fourteen hands are said to be descendants of survivors from a galleon of the Spanish Armada wrecked on the coast in 1588.

On the two and a half miles by boat to Canna, one sees, eight miles to the south-west, the thin white lighthouse marking a group of rocks called Oigh-sgeir. Canna itself, highly recognisable by its shape – a platform of rock lava that slopes from a height of about 400 feet (120m) to 690 (210m) – is the most seaward of all the Small Isles. It is favoured by being the only one with a sheltered harbour, to which the mail boat from Mallaig calls three times a week. Five miles long, it is in fact two islands, Canna to the north and Sanday, connected to it by a bridge at the south-east end. With a total population of less than thirty, these are green isles, a happy mixture of cattle farm, crofts and wildlife sanctuary. This is largely due to the foresight and care of the present owners, who have made Canna worthy of its title 'Garden of the Hebrides'. This was an appellation that, even in the late eighteenth century, was felt to be fully justified by one traveller, who called it 'rich, verdant and covered with hundreds of cattle'.

Oigh-sgeir
Canna

Sanday

At the north-east end of Canna is Compass Hill, a landmark well known to navigators since it is supposed to affect the magnetic compasses of passing ships. From here the views of the Hebrides, and in particular of Skye, are unsurpassed. There are a number of historic sites on the island, including the ruins of a nunnery on the south shore. To the east of the island there is a strange pillar of rock over 100 feet (30m) high, on top of which is a ruined prison of the Clan Ranald where one of the clan chiefs, in a fit of jealousy, is said to have incarcerated his wayward wife.

Ponies on the foreshore of Rhum.

Skye

Sing me a song of a lad that is gone,
Say, could that lad be I?
Merry of soul, he sailed on a day
Over the sea to Skye.

Mull was astern, Rhum on the port,
Eigg on the starboard bow;

Glory of youth glowed in his soul.
Where is that glory now?

So wrote Robert Louis Stevenson in his *Songs of Travel*. From Canna, whichever way we sail – east, north-east or north – we too reach perhaps the most famous of all the Scottish islands, Skye, the 'Winged Isle' to the Celts, and to the Vikings the 'Isle of Clouds'. Skye is the romantic's delight, the mountaineer's paradise, 'home of the thousand beauties', and many things more. It is, to an imaginative eye, shaped like an eagle poised for flight, with each wing and talon different, stretching in its own separate way out into the seas.

By far the largest of all the isles, Skye deserves and has a library of its own; these few following pages serve only to whet the appetite for what it offers the visitor. Although the island is sixty miles long and twenty-five miles at its widest, because of its indented, spectacular and cliff-bounded shoreline, it is never possible to be further than five miles from the sea. Generally one approaches Skye from the south, via Sleat, either by car ferry from Mallaig to Armadale or from Kyle of Lochalsh to Kyleakin, but the land to the south-east is the less dramatic and the majority of the population of eight thousand live to the north and west where both soil and climate are better. The largely Gaelic-speaking people are crofters; their patchwork fields lie gentle, dwarfed as they are by Skye's unique magnificence, the Cuillins. These mountains, beloved of climbers and less energetic visitors alike, have been likened to a crown for Skye, fifteen rock peaks, decked with cloud and reaching to a height of over 3,000 feet (900m). But it is not only the Cuillins that are superb in scenic terms. In the north-west, around Dunvegan, the variety and mixture of scenery, moor and mountain and the mottle of croft and farm, all of this ringed by the sea, is an unforgettable expression of natural beauty. In the northern peninsula is a ten-mile ridge of mountain, the highest point of which is the Storr, with its famous landmark, the 160-foot (49m)-high pinnacle of lava rock which is known as the Old Man of Storr, in this small space all a rock-climber could wish for.

The capital of the island, with a population of two thousand, is Portree ('The Port of the King'), which is now the administrative centre for the whole district. It sits in a bay, sheltered by the neighbouring island of Raasay, which lies to the east side of Skye. A neat and attractive town of whitewashed houses, Portree benefits from the tourism which has been generated, in Skye more than in any of the other Western Isles, over the past century. It makes an excellent base from where to see something of the island's many fascinations. The people are friendly and

Fishing salmon in a small boat off the Isle of Skye.

140

generous; all they ask in return is that the visitor respect their customs, particularly the keeping of the Sabbath.

To the north-west stands the most famous castle of a total of five on the island, Dunvegan, home of the MacLeods. It sternly overlooks a deep sea loch filled with a multitude of islands. Some parts of the castle date from as far back as the ninth century; there is a fifteenth-century dungeon and other much later additions; and the building as a whole is said to be the oldest inhabited castle still in the hands of the original family. One of the treasures there is the 'faery flag' believed to have been captured and brought back by a MacLeod chief from the Crusades. One of the most

142

The great mountain crown of the Isle of Skye.

prominent recent owners of Dunvegan was the late Dame Flora MacLeod, who died there in 1976 at the ripe age of ninety-nine. She was, among many other things, an ardent bagpipe-music enthusiast, as befitted the chief of the clan that has its own subsidiary clan of hereditary pipers – the MacCrimmons.

Skye's history is a long and convoluted one: Celts, then Norsemen, came and went. Ever since the Battle of Largs, when King Haakon's Scottish empire was finally shattered, the isle has been ruled to a greater or lesser degree by the Dunvegan Mac-Leods and, in the south, by the Macdonalds of Sleat. But, after the Jacobite uprising of 1745 and the escape to Skye of Prince

143

Charles Edward Stuart (disguised as a maidservant to the famous Flora Macdonald), the island was put firmly on the map of history. This was helped by much embroidered romantic legend and by evocative song.

> Speed, bonny boat, like a bird on the wing,
> 'Onward' the sailors cry.
> Carry a lad that's born to be King
> Over the Sea to Skye.

Boswell and Johnson were much impressed by actually meeting and staying with Flora Macdonald, 'a little woman, of a mild and genteel appearance, mighty soft and well-bred', an occasion when she told them about her journeys with Bonnie Prince Charlie. To his further satisfaction, Johnson himself ended the night of their meeting by sleeping in the Prince's bed. They also stayed an agreeable ten days with the MacLeods at Dunvegan, where Johnson was offered by his host one of the offshore islands for his very own, if he would only promise to spend a month of every year there.

The eighteenth-century Clearances left an indelible mark on the island, a subject on which Boswell and Johnson left their views after their visit there in the year 1773. Over a hundred years later the opposition of some of the Skye crofters to the worst excesses of the Clearances, and their eventual confrontation with the sheriff's officers, led in no small measure to the passing of the first Acts of Parliament in the year 1886 to protect their rights of tenure on their traditional lands. Now, after years of decline, even the old culture and language are being re-established and invigorated. In 1972 a Gaelic College was founded at Sleat, near Armadale, which, hopefully, will open the way to more understanding of the past but not at the expense of the future of this most spectacular isle.

Soay

Crofters grinding corn on the Isle of Skye, Note the simple black house with its roof held down with weighted stones.

Sailing clockwise round the western seaboard of Skye from the southern tip, one comes, first, to the three and a half mile long island of Soay, whose Norse name means 'Isle of Sheep'. This is not to be confused with the more famous Solay in the St Kilda group; the latter island is the home of the brown-haired, agile, rock-climbing Soay sheep. Skye's Soay has a tiny population of around fifty, who are mainly lobster fishermen, though, in recent years, a small artists' colony has flourished on the island. Here Gavin Maxwell, the writer, lived and was involved in launching a doomed shark-fishing industry, an enterprise that he described in his book *Harpoon at a Venture*. The island, less than a mile off Skye's shore, is flat, but at one point it rises to a height of 463 feet (141m). As with so many islands here, the first sight that strikes

144

the casual visitor is that sad and repeated one of deserted, ruined crofts littered all too numerously across the landscape.

Wiay

Passing the mile-wide isle of Wiay, among a group of three or four others in Loch Bracadale which are now only used for summer grazing, we turn round the north-west cape of Skye at Dunvegan Head. There are many islands and rocky islets in sight in the two arms of Loch Dunvegan, and then, round Waternish Point, comes a further tiny archipelago, the Ascrib Islands (only five of them of any size), two and a half miles off the coast at the entrance to Loch Snizort. These too have occasional sheep grazing as their only use. There is a large puffin colony there, burrowed into the grassy tops of the cliffs. At the peak of the topmost wing of Skye is tiny Eilean Trodday, and then, passing another patchwork of islets off Staffin, we move south again to the ghost island of Rona and to Raasay, by the Sound of Raasay, the water that lies between Skye and the village of Applecross on the mainland.

Ascrib Islands

Eilean Trodday

Rona

Rona (not to be confused with the remote far-northern Rona) was notorious in the seventeenth and eighteenth centuries as the place of the 'Broken Men', who were renegades, owing allegiance to no clan. From their base there, 'The Port of Robbers', they pirated and pillaged the surrounding islands and the defenceless communities on the mainland, raiding ships and stealing fish cargoes at liberty. On the island, high on a hillside, is the so-called 'Warriors Cave', possibly used as a secret church; inside, stones to seat forty or fifty are set in rows around a stone altar or font. Rona is now only populated by three honest men who man the lighthouse at the northern tip of the island.

Raasay

The elongated fourteen-mile-long island of Raasay is much overshadowed by the Cuillins, which lie across the Sound to the west. It has a generally precipitous and barren seaboard, with crofts, green fields and woods only to the south, where most of the population of around a hundred and thirty live. It is serviced by a daily boat from Portree. Here, during the First World War, an iron-ore mine flourished briefly at the southern tip, perched on the slopes of the 1,456-foot (444m) Dun Caan hill, with German prisoners of war used as labour to extract the ore. Since then, Raasay and its community have fallen on hard times. The aura of the island is sadly and strangely remote from that prevalent on the day in 1773 when Johnson and friend came and were so hospitably looked after at Raasay House in Clachan. On that occasion Boswell took it upon himself to 'dance a jig for joy' and cavorted the night away with the many unmarried daughters of his host. Raasay House, like so much all round the island, is now mouldering and abandoned.

Neil Munro wrote of the island:

Gone in the mist the brave Macleods of Raasay
Far forth from fortune sundered from their lands,
And now the last grey stone of Castle Raasay
Lies level with the sands.

A winter's day on the Isle of Skye.

A sad story, made even sadder by present-day controversy and neglect.

Scalpay

To the south of unfortunate Raasay lies Scalpay, an egg-shaped island four miles long and three wide that stands half a mile from the shore of Skye, by Loch Ainort. Lacking any modern facilities, its tiny population maintains contact with its large neighbour Skye by small boat. Very different from the isle of the same name which lies off Harris in the Outer Hebrides, it has deer, sheep grazing and a wide variety of bird life. In earlier times there was a larger population here too. The ruins of a chapel are to be found near Scalpay House at the south-east end of the island.

Crowlin Islands
Eilean Mór

Pabay

Over towards the mainland, to the south of Applecross, are a group of islands and reefs known as the Crowlin Islands, with Eilean Mór as the largest. On it stand the ruins of a chapel and oratory, reputedly dedicated to St Cormac. South again, two miles off Broadford on Skye, is Pabay, like Rona a past refuge for the 'Broken Men', pirates and robbers. This island is not to be confused with the Pabbay in the Outer Isles.

147

Eilean Bàn

In the narrow stretch of water which separates Skye at Kyleakin from the mainland at Kyle of Lochalsh is the tiny Eilean Bàn. It is also known as 'White Island' because, though it is only twelve acres (5ha) in area, it has an incredible beauty, with wide stretches of the whitest of white sands, a sight that John Buchan described so well in his book *Prince of the Captivity*. Here, too, came the writer Gavin Maxwell, and bought the island with the intention of converting it into a naturally bounded zoo, populated specifically by West Highland mammals and birds. The project ended with his early death. His partner, John Lister-Kaye, wrote a book about both island and the now-abandoned project which he named after the island.

Ornsay

Finally down the Sound of Sleat, in which there are many other named and unnamed islands, islets and rocky reefs, is the tiny island of Ornsay, which, like the others of the same name, takes its title from St Oran, who was one of the followers of Columba. Here are the scant remains of his chapel and the more modern structure of a lighthouse that marks the channel for shipping.

Shieldaig Island

One last island, not forgotten but buried in Loch Shieldaig to the east of Rona, is Shieldaig Island, which is owned by the National Trust for Scotland. Together with the Nature Conservancy, it is afforesting the island in order to preserve and develop its natural character.

10 The Outer Hebrides

Frequently when there is talk of the 'Western Isles', what will be meant by the speaker will be the Outer Hebrides, that 140-mile-long chain of islands which stretches north-north-east from the Barra Isles in the south to the Butt of Lewis in the north. Popularly known, because they are in so many ways a compact and unbroken chain, as the 'Long Island', they have, nonetheless, a subtle range of geology, spirit and culture, the breadth of which becomes apparent as one moves from island to island. Here are sea, mountain and, above all, space, in a unique Gaelic setting. And Gaelic it is that is first language of the people, though inevitably in recent years it is on the wane through the increasingly omnipotent presence of radio and television. Here too is a mix of religion, Roman Catholic on one isle, staunch Protestant on its neighbour. All these factors, those arising from both tradition and setting, blend to give a character to these islands and their people that is unique.

The Outer Hebrides undoubtedly give to some visitors an overall impression of charm and timelessness. Others find that a tired, uncaring vacancy, a sort of sleeping sickness, hangs in the air and in the spirit of many of the inhabitants. There is, sadly, squalor beside the beauty, a lack of concern for the environment, and at times a bitter overconcentration, not on self-help, but on what the Government is or is not doing to rectify the perennial problems of living a hard life under even harder conditions. New and vigorous life there is, but one is constantly reminded at the same time that the best of past generations often left for the more hopeful pastures of new worlds.

These outer islands divide themselves into three general groups, those of the Barra Isles to the south, the Uists in the centre (which include North and South Uist, Benbecula and Eriskay), and thirdly, the northern group around the large siamese twin of an island, Lewis and Harris.

149

The Outer Hebrides

1 *Berneray*
2 *Mingulay*
3 *Pabbay*
4 *Sandray*
5 *Vatersay*
6 *Barra*
7 *Fiaray*
8 *Fuday*
9 *Hellisay*
10 *Eriskay*
11 *Stack Island*
12 *South Uist*
13 *Calvay*
14 *Benbecula*
15 *Grimsay*
16 *Wiay*
17 *North Uist*
18 *Ronay*
19 *Oronsay*
20 *Monach Isles*
21 *Haskeir Islands*
22 *Harris with*
   Lewis
23 *Boreray*
24 *Berneray*
25 *Pabbay*
26 *Shillay*
27 *Ensay*
28 *Hermetray*
29 *Taransay*
30 *Scarp*
31 *Bearasay*
32 *Great Bernera*
33 *Luchruban*
34 *Shiant Isles*
35 *Eilean Chaluim*
   Chille
36 *Scalpay*

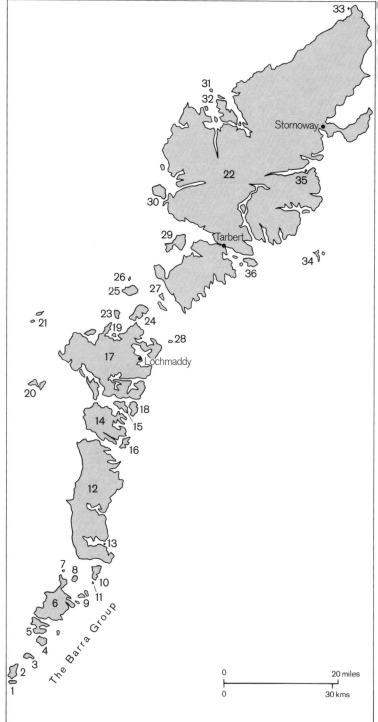

The Barra Group

First of all, of the twenty or so islands known as the Barra group, which include Vatersay, Sandray, Pabbay, Mingulay, Berneray and Barra, only Vatersay and Barra itself are now inhabited, though even on them the population is still drastically on the wane. But new developments, and the creation of a Central Islands Authority to run them, have introduced many hopeful signs of rebirth. Education programmes, development plans and the involvement of the churches (whatever the religion) in what is being done are gradually encouraging the people who left the Isles to return and improve their homelands, but not at the expense of their Gaelic culture, language and heritage.

The most southerly point on the band of all these outer isles is the Barra Head rock, with, at its peak, a lighthouse atop a 600-foot (180m) cliff. It is the last barrier to the Atlantic, and such are the storms here that it is not uncommon for fish to be washed up and stranded by breakers on the turf around the light itself. North of it is the rest of the storm-battered island of Berneray, one of several **Berneray** of that name in the Isles, and then comes the empty island of Mingulay that only eighty years ago had a population of around a **Mingulay** hundred and thirty on a land area only two and a half miles by one. Sailing today into Mingulay Bay, edged by its white sands, one sees the deserted village with its long-neglected fields stretching up the slopes behind.

> Wives are waiting on the bank
> Or looking seaward from the heather;
> Pull her round boys! and we'll anchor,
> Ere the sun sets at Mingulay.

This is the island of the other famous boat song, a land of constant winds, blowing the fine sand in a gentle hiss across the shore. This fact, along with the lack of any reasonable harbour, must have been one of the main causes for the final abandonment of Mingulay in 1908. The inhabitants left *en masse* to squat on neighbouring Vatersay, eventually being imprisoned for trying to escape from their devastating poverty. In the long run, however, their perseverance achieved advances for crofters throughout the Western Isles.

Mingulay's astonishing and spectacular attraction is its cliffs, teeming with a bird life that is breathtaking both for its variety and the sheer weight of numbers. This has earned it the nickname 'Bird Island'. Ornithologists come annually to study, in particular, the myriad auks and kittiwakes that breed on the cliff ledges. Above the ruins of the village, a climb up the slope will take one to the brink of these cliffs which stand a giddy 750 feet (230m) above sea level. Here too are magnificent rock formations, including one huge natural bridge on the west side of the island, through which a small boat may pass. To the north of the island is the highest point, known as Macphee's Hill, named after an unfortunate servant of the MacNeil of Barra who had sent him to find out why his tenants on Mingulay were so behind in paying their rents. Put ashore from a small boat, Macphee entered croft after croft and found all the inhabitants dead of the plague. The boatmen with him, fearful of infection, abandoned the unfortunate man on the island, where he was left to fend for himself for a whole year before he was rescued. Eventually Macphee came back and settled on the island permanently; so his exile must have had some attraction for him.

In these seas there are many other isles and islets that, if they have ever had a name, are now abandoned, anonymous and forgotten. But, moving north-north-east for one and a half miles, **Pabbay** one reaches another almost deserted island, Pabbay, on which a number of ancient Pictish stones have been discovered, and where there is also an ancient burial mound, of unknown origins. (Another better known Pabbay is to the north, in the Sound of Harris.)

Sandray Next in the long chain comes Sandray, a flat desolate island about one and a half miles square which is occasionally used for sheep grazing and is noted for its wide variety of wild flowers. To the north of it, and half a mile off the south shore of Barra itself, is **Vatersay** the strange 'H'-shaped island of Vatersay, which still holds on to a Gaelic-speaking Roman Catholic population of about eighty, many of them descendants of the so-called 'Vatersay Raiders' who settled there in 1908 to avoid starvation on neighbouring Mingulay. At that time there was only one farm on the island, so the squatters built themselves shanty huts of wood and prepared to stay. Charged with land-grabbing, they were sentenced to a short term in prison. But they became local heroes through standing up to the absentee landlord of the day, who had never even visited the island over which they were taken to court.

On Vatersay, with its barren rocks and white sands, stands the sad memorial to over two hundred passengers and crew of the emigrant ship the *Annie Jane* which, on its way from Liverpool to Quebec in Canada, sank there in 1853.

Vatersay's economy is based on fishing and crofting. It has a tiny school, church and post office, and one short stretch of tarmac road connecting these buildings with the landing pier where the ferry from Castlebay on Barra comes when the vagaries of the weather allow.

Barra The scenery of the island of Barra itself seems to change round every corner, for, while the interior is rocky and mountainous, its coastline has sheltered green bays with beautiful beaches in between. It is a lively island, eight miles long by four to five miles wide, with a population of one and a half thousand. They are mainly Gaelic-speaking and Catholic, and they have a tradition of making the growing number of tourists very welcome with their dances and *ceilidhs*. Here too, crofting and fishing are the mainstays of the economy. At Castlebay, the principal town, there is a modern fishing fleet, and at North Bay there is a fish-processing plant. More surprisingly, a perfume factory flourishes on the island, and a number of other incipient craft and more modern industries are being encouraged. There is even a plant to crush cockleshells for facing the outsides of buildings. This is one island of very few where it is worth arriving by air. The plane lands on a great stretch of beach known as Tràigh Mhór or the Cockle Strand, which is washed daily by the tides, and the wheels of the plane send up a great spray as it taxis in to a stop.

Castlebay itself is a scatter of white houses round the shore. In the centre of the bay and a few yards offshore is the squat form of Kisimul Castle on an islet of the same name. It dates from the fifteenth century and is the home of the chief of the Clan MacNeil,

Barra's beautiful 'airfield' — Tràigh Mhor.

153

now an American, who has had a modern home constructed inside the walls. It was from the walls of this castle that, it is said, the self-proud chiefs would have a trumpeter sound and announce to the world: 'Hear, o ye people, and listen, o ye nations. The great MacNeil of Barra having finished his meal, the princes of the earth may dine.' But they were benevolently paternalistic, these MacNeils, and they had a long and good reputation for looking after their kinsfolk in a crisis. Without the MacNeils to lead them, the people of the island were lost, and on Barra some of the worst scenes of the Clearances were enacted. The then owner, a Colonel John Gordon, had the population forceably expelled, most of the Barra men being put on the emigrant ships in chains.

One can drive the fourteen miles round the island, at the northern tip of which there is a church dedicated to St Findbarr of Cork, a sixth-century monk who is said to have given his name to the island. There are many other Celtic remains, cairns, standing stones and brochs, scattered across the island. Here too are a number of spectacular hills, including the highest, the Heaval, at 1,260 feet (383m). From the top of it there are panoramic views across to the Inner Hebrides and to the mountains of the mainland.

Since the war, Barra has gained some considerable fame as the setting for Compton Mackenzie's *Whisky Galore*, which was based on the real wreck of the SS *Politician* off the north shore of the island. When that ship went down, loaded with a cargo of whisky, only some of its precious hoard of 20,000 crates was salvaged. Compton Mackenzie himself lived on the island until he left for one of those other of Britain's offshore isles, right at the furthest extremity, in the warmth of the Channel Islands. But it was to Barra that his body was brought for burial.

Fiaray

Fuday

Hellisay

To the north of Barra are a scattered group of islands, including Fiaray (or Fuiary), Fuday and Hellisay. Fiaray is known for its barnacle geese and as the home of a fairy woman who is seen from time to time by passing fishermen from their boats. On Fuday there are numerous burial chambers, and it was here that one of the previous MacNeils of Barra is said to have hurled the heads of his Viking enemies into one of the island's wells. Hellisay, too, is an island of myth and of fairies, and Alasdair Alpin MacGregor, among the greatest of the writers about these islands, tells many strange and delightful stories of fairy weddings and other happenings there.

Eriskay

Moving northwards again, off the south coast of South Uist we come to the isle with the haunting name, Eriskay. Only three and a half miles long by one and a half wide, this soft and beautiful isle

154

'Prince Charlie's Flower' — the sea convolvulous (Calystegia soldanella).

with its colourful cottages has a sizeable population of close to two hundred people. This by itself has Eriskay singled out from all its neighbours. As late as the mid-nineteenth century it had a tiny population and it was settled thereafter by some of the luckier crofters who had been brutally expelled from Hellisay and South Uist. Until then, Eriskay had been considered too barren 'even to support sheep'. But these hardy pioneers, who were generously allowed to stay, layered the rocky land, using sea-weed as fertiliser on which to base the precious soil, and culti-vated strips of land to produce potatoes, off which they were able to live and flourish. Here is found a breed of sure-footed but unshod ponies, indigenous to the island, that are used to this day for bringing in the peats from the moors. And the smell of burn-ing peat is a memory of this and so many others of these island communities.

Eriskay's name in history comes from the fact that here, on the white sands of Prince's Beach (Coilleag a' Phrionnsa), Prince Charles Edward Stuart made his first landing on Scottish soil, on 23 July 1745. He received a less than warm welcome from the local laird, who bluntly suggested that he return to France. By tradition, the Prince, undaunted, planted some seeds of *Calystegia soldanella*, the sea convolvulus, known to this day as 'Prince Charlie's Flower', to celebrate his arrival. It still flourishes there.

Eriskay's Gaelic-speaking, Catholic community are crofters; the men also go out with the herring fishing fleet and the lobster boats, while the women knit shawls and jerseys to patterns that are unique to Eriskay. A more dubious claim to fame is that it was here that Drambuie was first drunk on Scottish soil. From Eriskay, preserved by the late Father Allan MacDonald, some of the best loved of all the Gaelic songs come, including 'The Eriskay Love Lilt'.

Thou'rt the music of my heart,
Harp of joy, oh, *chruit mo chridhe* [Harp of my heart],
Moon of guidance by night,
Strength and light thou'rt to me.

Here too is St Michael's Church, built in 1903, which contains a fine painting of the baptism of Christ by John Duncan, the artist who once made Eriskay his home. The church's bell is an old ship's bell from a German warship that was sunk in Scapa Flow.

The 'tangle' — piles of seaweed drying at a factory in Uist.

At the time of writing Eriskay is on the market and various plans are being discussed to enable it to be bought for the islanders themselves. On the islet of Stack Island at the south are the ruins of a castle once used by outlawed pirates of the MacNeil clan who held out there and ravaged this coast.

Stack Island

South Uist

Moving due north again, we come, after a two-hour journey by ferry, within sight of the mountains and sea lochs of South Uist, a large island with well over two thousand inhabitants. It and its two northern neighbours, Benbecula and North Uist, are now linked by a causeway. Here is a major Ministry of Defence rocket base, which has brought certain disputed economic advantages to the island, though crofting is still the mainstay of the economy. In consequence, modern buildings and thatched crofts stand close together. The land rises to a height of over two thousand feet (610m), offering, with some superb cliffs, a great challenge to rock- and mountain-climbers alike. The north of the island, which is in all twenty miles long by six wide, is generally desolate and uninhabited, though there are traces of early occupation. Loch Druidibeg, a large freshwater loch, is part of a new nature reserve set up and run by the Nature Conservancy at the time of the rocket range's establishment, as a project to help allay fears that local wildlife would be threatened. It is a major breeding ground for the greylag goose.

At Corodale Bay to the east, Prince Charles Edward Stuart landed in 1746 after his flight from Culloden, and the island was the scene of many of his subsequent wanderings. Here also his rescuer, Flora Macdonald, was born. Lochboisdale, the main village on South Uist, makes an attractive base for the excellent sea and loch fishing that is to be had there; it is also the ferry point for boats to Barra and the mainland. On the tiny island of Calvay, at the mouth of the loch, the Prince spent a night before setting off with Flora Macdonald for Skye.

Calvay

The unhurried people here are all Gaelic-speaking; there are four Roman Catholic churches to only one of the Church of Scotland. To emphasise this latter fact, there is a striking thirty-foot (9m) statue to 'Our Lady of the Isles' which stands on a rocky hill to the north of the island and acts as a major landmark for navigators. Here are many relics of an earlier age as well. At Howmore are the ancient graves of the chiefs of Clanranald, while further south are the ruins of Ormaclete Castle, a Clanranald fort that was burned down, not by enemies, but by a venison-roasting fire that got out of hand. Ruined crofts are everywhere, testimony to the brutal fact that over sixteen hundred people were cleared to Canada during the eighteen-fifties by South Uist's notorious landlord of the day.

Benbecula

Benbecula is the 'Mountain of the Fords', though these fords to the north and to the south have, through the efforts and because of the needs of the Ministry of Defence, now been replaced by a causeway and bridges via the lobster-rich island of Grimsay off the north-east coast. It is now possible to drive from the north of North Uist, through Benbecula, to the south of South Uist along the A865, a convenience, since the airport for these three islands is here at the centre. Benbecula is called a mountain, but it is a pretty flat one, of moors and machair (the name for the long island sands, bound with couch grass and wild flowers); its myriad of lochs make an angler's paradise. The community here, too, is principally a crofting and farming one, a mixed group who, like the island itself, act as a bridge between the strongly Protestant North Uist and the almost entirely Catholic South, and have Gaelic as their common language, one that knows few religious barriers. This cultural tradition is strongly shared; in the music of the songs and of the bagpipes, the past glories and sorrows are relived, enjoyed and mourned over with equal feeling.

Grimsay

Here too, at Balivanich, a further Army rocket range has appeared, and the military presence has given, despite the antagonisms and opposition that the range reaped at the beginning, a considerable and lasting impetus to the local economy. Around the island are some of the most peaceful and beautiful beaches in the Western Isles, while offshore are a maze of tiny satellite islands, some tidal, some remote. Most are unnamed and anonymous, and not many are much more than a few acres in size; but they all contribute to this unique pattern of nature. One off the south-east coast, the uninhabited Wiay, recently found itself in the news headlines when a large brown bear made its home there after escaping from a filming session on Benbecula by swimming the short distance between the two islands. He was recaptured on North Uist twenty-two days later.

Wiay

North Uist

The northernmost of the middle cluster of islands in the Outer Hebrides is North Uist, which is separated from Harris by an eight-mile stretch of sea. It has, religiously if nothing else, more in keeping with the northern group because from here north live the Protestant community; as we have seen, they only cohabit alongside Catholics to a sizeable extent on Benbecula. This stress on the religious affiliations of the islanders is in no way meant to suggest any tendency to a situation of conflict; all is harmony in these isles. In the past any lack of social harmony came, not from

Traditional crofts, North Uist. The only visible 'modern' developments are the chimneys.

religion, but from the overenthusiastic pursuit of certain sports. Horse racing was popular here but led to conflict, and as for golf and football, as an Act of the Scottish Parliament had decreed in 1457, they were both to be discouraged and banned, since 'golf led to archery being neglected', while football led to 'riot'.

North Uist, twelve miles by sixteen, is, like Benbecula, a mecca for anglers, since it is well endowed with freshwater lochs. It is a much less mountainous island than its southern namesake though reaching over one thousand feet (300m) at its highest point. Along with the crofting, which occupies a majority of the population of around two and a half thousand, catering to anglers from the mainland contributes considerably to the economy.

Here too, with its resident warden, is a noted nature and bird reserve at Balranald. For archaeologists, North Uist offers a wealth of prehistoric sites, duns or early forts, circles of standing stones, burial cairns, and, at Carinish, the 'Trinity Temple', two vaulted chapels dating from the thirteenth century. The capital of North Uist, with around four hundred inhabitants, is Lochmaddy, which, set on the shores of a winding loch of the same name, is served by ferries from Harris and the mainland. Near here there is an alginate factory where seaweed products are produced, and the mild climate has even allowed commercial bulb-growing to be developed on the west of the island.

Around the island are a myriad of small isles, which are scattered across this entire sea area. On one or two of them such as **Ronay** to the south-east, and **Oronsay** to the north, tiny crofting communities still survive, but otherwise they are barren, deserted and often lack even a name, though they may well have been home to past generations.

Monach Isles   Across the Sound of Monach, the Monach Isles lie six miles to the west of North Uist. There are five or six flat islands in all, two of which are of substantial size, with, on one, an abandoned lighthouse, school, church and post office. None rise to more than fifty feet (15m) above sea level. From here, the majority of the population of around a hundred emigrated, mainly to Canada, in the last century. From then the decline was steady and the last two families finally left the islands in 1942. At an earlier age there was a nunnery (linked to Iona) on one of the islands. The nuns, not surprisingly in such an environment, had a reputation of Amazonian dimensions. Today, summer grazing and lobster fishing round the coasts are the only signs of human activity.

Haskeir Islands   North of the Monach Isles are the Haskeir Islands, one main island surrounded by a group of barren rocks, which are of note as a breeding ground for seals.

Harris with Lewis

Though frequently listed as two separate islands, Harris and Lewis are one landmass, sixty miles long, connected very firmly by a neck of terrain several miles wide. But there are two good reasons for thinking of them as largely separate entities. One is that they have, in the past, been treated as such in terms of administrative overlordship. Secondly and more importantly, they are very different both geographically and socially. Harris is generally speaking mountainous, while Lewis is, for the most part, barren moorland, and the two are separated by a sort of natural barrier from Loch Resort in the west to Loch Seaforth in the east. Experts argue that this has led to different characteristics and even speech forms in the inhabitants of the two parts, but such differences are, for the casual visitor, unnoticeable and irrelevant.

Harris to the south is itself divided into two, at the isthmus of Tarbert, where there is a prosperous village of the same name and to and from which the car ferry plies. ('Tarbert', incidentally, means a narrow neck between two waters, which is why it appears frequently as a place name in the West Highlands.) North Harris is particularly mountainous, with the peak of Clisham, at 2,622 feet (799m), the highest peak in the Western Isles; and there are a number of other summits challenging to the rock-climber. Here, too, are well-stocked lochs and rivers and equally thriving deer forests. Pleasant, quiet beaches, a mix of prosperous and long-abandoned crofts, all these contribute to the character of the land. The inhabitants of Harris are mainly crofters and estate workers, though weaving (of the famous Orb-symbolled Harris Tweed) and fishing offer subsidiary employment. The ancestors of Harris men were less troubled by Norse invasion than those of Lewis, but throughout recent history the blight of absentee landlordism has left its mark.

For the historian there is much to fascinate: there are a number of duns, particularly at Borve, near the west coast, and Rodel at

A crofter weaving the famous Harris Tweed.

the south-east corner of the island. Some of these ancient forts have been built on islets and are reached by the curiously subtle method of treading a series of underwater stepping stones. At Rodel too, on a hill overlooking the bay, is the architecturally superb cruciform church of St Clement. Dating from the year 1500, it contains some outstanding stone carvings and, as an ancient burial place for the MacLeods, a highly decorated and canopied tomb that is rich in Celtic design. There are also two sandstone panels of a man and a woman in sexually explicit poses, symbolising fertility. The carving of the male has been mutilated, reputedly in a fit of morality by the lady who most recently paid for the restoration of the chapel.

To the south-west of Harris is the small port of Leverburgh, named after the late Lord Leverhulme, who, as the landlord who bought both Lewis and Harris in 1918, made strenuous, if not always welcome, efforts to try and develop the island. He built and improved the pier, the housing and the amenities there, but died before he could realise his aims for the scheme and for the island people. To the east, where the soil is poor and scarce, the 'lazybed' system has long been employed (as on Eriskay and elsewhere). Lazybeds are narrow ribbed strips of land, one to three yards (1–3m) wide, built up between the rocks with peat, seaweed as fertiliser, and sometimes crushed shell, which, layered and improved across the centuries, can produce creditable crops of potato, barley or oats. This form of agriculture was given an impetus by the Clearances, when crofters were driven from more profitable land to fend as they could on otherwise barren ground.

Lewis too is a community of crofters, Harris Tweed weavers and fishermen. But something of a new, mainland-type prosperity has come to the northern part of this Siamese-twin island, through the development of its capital, Stornoway, into a modern small town, with a population of around six thousand. Lewis, unlike Harris, is mainly flat, sullen moorland, with the highest hill reaching to only eight hundred or so feet (250m); thus it lacks some of the scenic character of the other islands to the south. Many of the villages, however, are attractive and colourful, such as Port of Ness where the houses are brightly painted in Scandinavian style. It is from this village that young men set sail to Sula Sgeir to reap their annual harvest of Solan geese (gannets) or 'gugas' which, when salted, are still considered much of a delicacy in the isles. Apart from Stornoway, most of the population, among them many strict Sabbatarians, live in scattered communities or 'townships' that, by tradition, had a less outward-going and welcoming aspect than the rest of the Isles. But, just as the largely croft-based weavers are being forced to come to terms

Cutting and drying peat on Lewis.

162

with the competition from cheap artificial textiles and move towards communal weaving ventures, so the community at large is having to adapt to an influx of modern ideas and more relaxed social attitudes.

Stornoway, the capital of the Western Isles, is, like so many communities in the Orkneys and Shetlands, changing very fast, due to the influx of oil-based industry, which is particularly looking to those oil fields in the sea areas to the north and west of the British Isles. But the sheltered harbour of the only 'town' in the Outer Hebrides still has its powerful white-fish fishing fleet; and there is in consequence no problem about diversification. It is also the main harbour for ferries to the other isles and to the mainland, and the town's new airport is not only a valuable communications link, but also a NATO base. At the entrance to the harbour is a rock on which, tragically, an Admiralty vessel was sunk on New Year's Day, 1919; two hundred soldiers and sailors, returning home from the war, were drowned there within sight of their homes. Here are an excellent secondary school, a training college and a hospital, all of which cater to the needs of all the Outer Islands' people. Like Harris, Stornoway was a site for the much-maligned efforts of Lord Leverhulme; at the expense of a reputed million pounds, he tried to inject new economic life and energy into the community. The castle and its adjacent grounds were given to the town and stand as a permanent memorial to his unmatched energy and drive.

Much of that perseverance which Leverhulme looked for must have gone with the thousands who were forced to leave during the Clearances and with those with the initiative to leave voluntarily at other times. One of the most famous of the groups of involuntary exiles was that which went with the Reverend Norman Macleod in the eighteen-twenties, first to Nova Scotia and then, when that settlement failed, on to an eventually prosperous life in New Zealand. Traces of the life they left behind can be seen, for example, at Arnol on the west coast, where one of the basic but traditional 'black houses', a dry-stone and turf bothy, is now a museum.

At Callanish, thirteen miles west of Stornoway on Loch Roag, is a remarkable series or 'henge' of megaliths which probably date from between 1500 and 2000 BC. This circle, which against a darkening sky could easily be thought to conjure up spirits, is second only in size to Stonehenge, and it stands dramatically on a promontory which reaches out into the loch. In the centre is a chambered cairn which it is thought may well have been a sacrificial altar connected with sun-worship. There is a long avenue of megaliths leading to it, some of them an enormous seventeen feet (5m) high, adding to the mystery of the place itself, and posing

Lewis: machair, sky and sea.

165

A happy wedding procession on Pabbay.

the problem of how they could have been erected without mechanical assistance. Until the last century their true size and magnificence were hidden under a blanket of peat, five and a half feet (1.7m) deep, which was removed at that time.

One of the most famous of all historical finds in Lewis is of very much smaller dimensions: the seventy-seven ivory chessmen dating from around AD 1200 which were unearthed in 1831. They are beautifully carved and must be among the oldest found in Europe: now they are frequently reproduced in modern editions.

Off the coast of Harris and Lewis in the Sound of Harris there are a number of important smaller islands of varying degrees of prosperity, size and population. To the south-west is the island of **Boreray**, until recently the home of but a single crofting family. By **Berneray** comparison, close by is Berneray, only three miles long by one and a half wide, but with a population of around three hundred **Pabbay** farmers and fishermen. The adjacent oval island of Pabbay, five miles west of Harris, is about the same size as Berneray, but it manages to support only one farm. At one time it, too, was home to over four hundred people as well as a flourishing whisky distillery but, as with a number of other isles, lack of resolution combined with economic adversity led to rapid and increasingly accelerated decline. Also in the Sound of Harris are a number of small grazing islands, including Shillay, Ensay (barely populated) and Hermetray, which are known as breeding grounds for the grey seal.

Shillay
Ensay
Hermetray

Up the west coast, two miles west of Harris, is the bleak island of Taransay which has a tiny population living in simple stone houses, with crofting and lobster fishing as employment. Further up, off Hushinish Point, is Scarp (or Scarpay), with a population of around a hundred; then, in Loch Roag, Bearasay, once the stronghold of the outlaw Neil MacLeod, a seventeenth-century pirate, who had a long and violent life before he was eventually caught and executed. Nearby is Great Bernera, since 1953 connected to Lewis by the 'Bridge across the Atlantic'. It is now not an 'island' by the definitions of this book, but it has all the characteristics of a separate entity. Its sizeable population is engaged in crofting and lobster fishing. The lobsters are 'stored' in large ponds until needed for export.

Taransay

Scarp
Bearasay

Great Bernera

To the south-west of the Butt of Lewis is Luchruban (or Luchubran) which, according to an old tale, was once inhabited by pigmies, a story given substance in the sixteenth-century writings of Dean Monro. Later researches seemed to back this up and there were reputed 'finds' of small human bones and skulls buried round a ruined kirk on the island. Recent researches, sadly, seem to have disproved this quaint story. The bones are thought to be of animals: the food of some unknown hermit of a forgotten era. On the summit of the island is a ruined stone cell of this nameless hermit, who must have lived a hard life on this island which is constantly battered by Atlantic storms.

Luchruban

Turning back down the east coast of Lewis and Harris, about twelve miles east of East Loch Tarbert one comes to the uninhabited Shiant Isles, high cliff-bound and haunting islands, only three of which even merit a name; two of them are Siamese, joined by a spit of land. Sir Compton Mackenzie, whose name frequently appears in this book as a renowned 'islomane', once owned the group which is often described, in Gaelic, as 'The Enchanted Isles'. Here is splendid rocky scenery, the cliffs rising dramatically to a height of four hundred feet (120m). They stand splendid, with a fantastic range of seabirds wheeling round them. The Shiants are still privately owned, but they can, with permission, be visited, though for many months of the year the weather makes landing very difficult. There is one roofed house

Shiant Isles

Eilean Chaluim Chille

Scalpay

The haunting and uninhabited Shiant Isles, known as the 'Enchanted Isles'.

on these islands, but there are many ruins to prove that once they, too, were well inhabited by man.

At the entrance of Loch Erisort is St Columba's Isle, or Eilean Chaluim Chille, which has at its south end the ruins of a chapel dedicated to the saint. Finally, close by Harris, one comes to Scalpay, one of over twenty islands sheltering in the entrance to East Loch Tarbert. Three miles by one and a half, it has, remarkably, a population of five hundred, who are engaged in white-fish and lobster fishing; its fleet was recently assisted to its now prosperous size by money from the Highlands and Islands Development Board. Here the practice of lazybed farming is as widespread as anywhere in the Western Isles. It was also among the remote places where Prince Charles Edward Stuart found brief refuge.

11 The Far Isles

From the Butt of Lewis one has a choice: to travel inland towards the islands that hug the extreme north-west coast of Scotland; to go north to the remote island of Rona, west to the mysterious Flannan Isles, or even further west to those ultimate outposts, the St Kilda group, and away on out towards the New World, to the remotest of them all – Rockall. We go north, then west, then east.

Rona (usually known as North Rona), forty-four miles north-north-east of the Butt, is 300 acres (120ha) of inaccessibility. One early nineteenth-century traveller pointed out that he discovered Rona some thirteen miles to the north of where most maps had it; an amusing sidelight on the attention paid to these islands at a time when the rest of the world was being mapped by the British in the greatest detail. That is until one finds that, even on today's maps, it varies its position alarmingly, where it is marked at all. It takes its name from St Ronan (as does its namesake to the east of Skye), whose ruined chapel is still visible. (As *'ron'* is Gaelic for 'grey seal', this is a highly plausible alternative source for the name.) It was populated until fairly recent times, at its peak having nearly thirty inhabitants. But towards the end of the seventeenth century, a plague of rats destroyed the economy by eating the crops and thus bringing starvation to the inhabitants. In addition, the crew of a visiting Spanish ship landed and, demanding hospitality, succeeded in having the island's only bull slaughtered: thus no more calves and no more milk – or so the story goes. In the year 1844 its then owner offered it as a penal settlement, an offer that was refused. Now faint ruins of primitive underground dwellings comprising a series of chambers connected by passages, along with the more visible walls of the chapel, are all that are left to indicate that men once lived there.

 To the west, about forty miles north of the Butt of Lewis, is the tiny island, half a mile long by only a few hundred yards wide, of

Rona

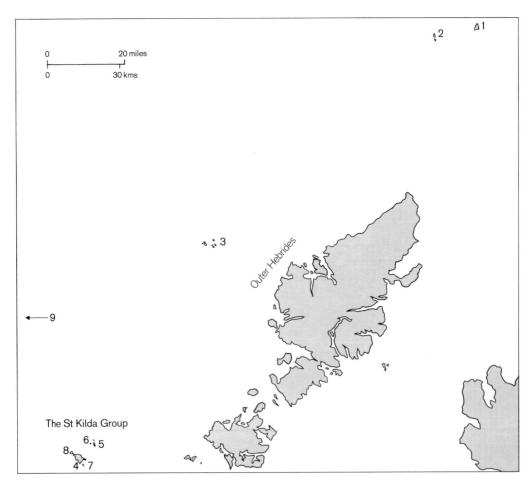

Sula Sgeir

The Far Isles

1 *Rona*
2 *Sula Sgeir*
3 *The Flannan Isles*
4 *Hirta*
5 *Boreray*
6 *Stac Lee*
7 *Dun*
8 *Soay*
9 *Rockall (186 miles west of St Kilda)*

Sula Sgeir. Here, unbelievably, are Christian remains as well: a tiny ruined chapel stands on it. It is now, with its many satellite islets and reefs, a nature reserve, the breeding ground for puffins, gannets and fulmars. Among the rocks and cliffs, there is a cave that runs the whole length of the island. Despite the fact that Sula Sgeir is a nature reserve under the Nature Conservancy Council, it is the traditional right of the men of Ness on Lewis to harvest the gannets there. The resulting 'guga', a boned and lightly smoked young bird, is exported widely to expatriate Lewismen. (The use of the word 'harvest' is precise since it has been carried out for centuries without any visible decrease in the gannet population.) In the middle of 1980 the Government announced plans to curb this culling, by introducing a system of licences which would be issued on a nontransferable basis, so that when the holders die, the practice will gradually cease. Needless to say, the men of Ness are resolved to fight this threat.

170

South-west we sail to the holy yet haunted Flannan Isles, a group of seven, lying fifteen miles to the west of Lewis. Like Rona, Sula Sgeir, and other remote isles, they have a large amount to interest the naturalist. At an earlier age they were the refuge for hermits who lived there in 'beehive' cells. They are now uninhabited.

A famous manned lighthouse was built on the Flannan Isles in 1899, and the year following, at Christmas time, all three lighthouse-keepers mysteriously disappeared one stormy night. This incident became the subject of a poem by Wilfrid Wilson Gibson, who tells how other men went to find out why the lamp on Flannan Isle was not lit, and discovered no sign of the keepers. And though they searched from shore to shore,

The Flannan Isles

> In every cranny, cleft or nook
> That might have hid a bird or mouse . . .
> Of the three men's fate we found no trace
> Of any kind in any place,
> But a door ajar, and an untouch'd meal,
> And an overtoppled chair.

Filled with dread, they recalled the misfortune that was said to come to all who kept the Flannan light:

> We seem'd to stand for an endless while,
> Though still no word was said,
> Three men alive on Flannan Isle,
> Who thought on three men dead.

The St Kilda Group

While, by the way this book is structured, the journey round the coasts of Britain is still far from complete, the author left the writing of the following section on the St Kilda group to the very last. This was not just because these islands are the most remote of all, nor because of the varied fascination they have for so many, but because a study of them, as was indicated in the Introduction, seems to offer some sort of conclusion, an encapsulated analysis of the problems of so many isolated communities around our coasts. The life and death and artificial rebirth of St Kilda as a military base is a case study of important dimensions, in that it tells us a great deal about the history, sociology and geography of the United Kingdom. Not surprisingly, there is a sizeable library of books on this group alone.

St Kilda (the origin of the name is obscure, since there is no saint of that name) is often thought of as one island; in fact it is a group of islands with wild geological structures which thrust themselves dramatically out of the sea fifty miles out into the Atlantic to the west of Harris. The four main islands are Hirta, Boreray, Dun and Soay. Hirta rises to a splendid 1,400 feet (430m)

171

and falls to the western side with a cliff that is the highest sheer drop in the United Kingdom, while Boreray, teeming with wild birds, is a jagged pile of massive proportions. All these islands were bequeathed to the National Trust for Scotland by the Marquess of Bute in 1957, and were subsequently leased to the Nature Conservancy, who carry out research into the interesting, and in many respects unique, natural history of St Kilda.

Hirta
Hirta, two and a half square miles in area, is the largest island in the group and is topped by the Conachair peak. Its westwards-facing coastline of spectacular cliffs is full of great caves, some of which extend several hundred feet into the depths of the island.

The main settlement was round the small pier at Village Bay and here and across the island there are the remains of the dwellings and stone houses of countless generations of inhabitants. It is the tragic story of this population, akin to the more recent fate of those other islanders from far-off Tristan da Cunha, that has, perhaps more than any other single factor, caused St Kilda to make its mark on history. At the end of the seventeenth century there were some hundred and eighty inhabitants, who annually paid a rent in kind to the MacLeod of MacLeod. This chief would send his bailiff there to pick up a consignment of bird feathers, and many other simple commodities; but during the subsequent century deprivation in a variety of forms led to the population steadily declining, with at one stage plans being made to have the entire population emigrate to Canada. Nineteenth-century tourist excursions to see the 'wild people' of Hirta contributed to this, and also brought disease, notably the 'boat cough' that followed the arrival of every group of visitors, and from then on, the unique life style on the island was rapidly eroded. By 1929 the economy of the island, with a population of only thirty-seven, had virtually collapsed, and in the following year its people petitioned the Secretary of State for Scotland, asking for help to leave the island 'and to find homes and occupations for us on the mainland'. On 29 August they were finally evacuated by naval ship to Oban, most of them eventually settling in Morven. Film of the evacuation which has recently come to light shows in sad detail the human problems of this final act.

There is much to study about the previous history and administration of the island. The community had its own 'Parliament', comprising all adult males. The Calvinistic forms of religion practised there led to the minister of the day having considerable legal powers over the islanders, including the right to impose fines and penalties for a wide range of both valid and strange faults.

Nowadays, landing at Village Bay, where the green slopes stretch up behind the ruined settlement, one finds modern developments close to hand. Ever since 1957, when the British Government set up a rocket range on South Uist, there has been a military tracking station on Hirta. This has led to the erection of new buildings, a radar station and living accommodation for the twenty to thirty men who are stationed there. The men of this loneliest of garrisons have been of considerable assistance to the National Trust over the years in the latter's efforts to preserve something of what Hirta used to be like, and in its programme of repairing some of the old buildings. The Nature Conservancy Council has its own projects as well, in its ecological study of this island. For there is much to investigate. Here is one of the major seabird breeding grounds in Britain – for puffin, gannet, razorbill, fulmar, many varieties that were once the only source of food and income for the inhabitants (fulmars for oil, gannets for meat and puffins for feathers). They caught the birds by standing dramatically at the cliff edges wielding long nets. Here too are a number of unique species, such as the St Kilda wren and a distinctive type of mouse. The great auk, now extinct, was once common here. Unable to fly with its vestigial wings, it proved too good for eating to survive.

The other islands in the group include 'the gannets' isle',

A group of inhabitants of St Kilda.

(Opposite) *Modern St Kilda, showing the radar station and army camp close by the neat ruins of Village Bay.*

(Left) *The Union Jack flies dramatically over Rockall for the first time in 1955.*

Boreray, with its thousand-foot (300m) cliffs which make it extremely difficult to effect a landing. It, too, had its inhabitants once, and there is a strange semi-subterranean house on the island, called Staller's House, which is sunk into the ground and was fortress to an outlawed individual who took refuge there. Nearby, a third of a mile away to the west, is Stac Lee, a huge, 564-foot (172m) rock that stands magnificently out of the sea. Separated by a narrow stretch of water from Hirta is Dun, another massive island rising precipitously from the sea, which the inhabitants of Hirta once used for grazing. Last, and about a quarter of a mile off Hirta, is Soay, a mere 240 acres (97ha) – a sort of escarpment of high cliffs topped with succulent turf, on which breed the wild Soay sheep, goatlike, nimble and unique.

Boreray

Stac Lee

Dun

Soay

On a calm day the St Kilda group is, as photographs tell in a way that simple words cannot, geologically spellbinding. With a high sea running and crashing against these great guano-laden cliffs, sending clouds of gannets, puffins and fulmars cascading into the grey skies, the wonder is that, in the past, people cut off from the world for so many months of every year could have survived there as long as they did. That they succeeded on an almost entirely 'bird-based' economy, clinging to their homeland to the bitter last, is an indication of how rugged and determined these loneliest of Britain's island-dwellers were.

Rockall   Rockall, 190 miles to the west of St Kilda and 230 long miles from North Uist, is, in one sense, the most recent part of the British Isles, as well as being by far the most westerly and inaccessible. A Royal Navy landing party, with difficulty, planted a flag on it in 1955, but it was not until 1972 that, under the terms of the Island of Rockall Act, it became legally part of the United Kingdom.

Rising a sheer seventy feet (20m), it has a tiny top which measures only one hundred by eighty feet (30 × 25m). Crowning it, and the only sign of man-made civilisation, is an automatic navigation light. The island gives its name to the sea area around it and stands steadfast in the midst of valuable fishing grounds and, who knows, on a potentially oil-rich seabed.

176

Sweeping beaches at Traigh Seilebost, on Harris, the Outer Hebrides.

A northern challenge to Stonehenge: the dramatic Standing Stones of Callanish, Loch Roag, Lewis.

(Top) *Maintaining Britain's highest landbuilt light, North Ronaldsay, Orkney.*
(Above) *Built by prisoners of war, the Nissen-hut Italian Chapel on Lamb Holm, Orkney.*

180

12 The Islands of the North-West and North Coasts of Scotland

Off the west coast of Highland Region, the uninhabited isle of Longa lies at the mouth of Loch Gairloch, less than a mile from shore. It covers an area of 360 acres (145ha). Round the next northern headland, right in the middle of Loch Ewe, is the scarcely inhabited Isle of Ewe, which during the Second World War was at the centre of an important naval base. It is a low island of grass and bracken, privately owned and now used for farming. Round to the north again, in Gruinard Bay, is the strangely forbidden island of Gruinard. During the war, because of its isolated yet accessible situation, it was used for secret biological-warfare experimentation. As a sad and long-lasting result, it became contaminated with anthrax, and it is still inspected every year to see whether this remains the case. Warning notices are prominently displayed and access is strictly forbidden, giving it the status of perhaps the only really unvisitable island in this book.

Journeying north, we come next to the Summer Isles, an archipelago of a dozen islands of many shapes and sizes which are scattered at the entrance to Loch Broom. Summer is their season, when all the flowers are in bloom. The main isles are Tanera Mór, Tanera Beg, Priest Island, Horse Island, Isle Ristol and Isle Martin, which latter island lies much higher up Loch Broom. A subgroup of five of them, about five miles west of the mainland, are known as the Carn Isles. Some of them were once inhabited but now, with few exceptions and discounting a handful of seasonal residents, this is no longer the case. Ristol and Isle Martin even had herring-curing 'factories' on them which operated in the eighteenth century, benefiting from the excellent fishing in the loch. This declined in the latter part of the last century. On Tanera Mór, Dr Frazer Darling, the well-known naturalist who wrote the book *The Natural History of the Highlands and Islands*, lived for some time and wrote about the Summer Isles

Longa

Isle of Ewe

Gruinard

The Summer Isles

Tanera Mór
Tanera Beg
Priest Island
Horse Island
Isle Ristol
Isle Martin

The Carn Isles

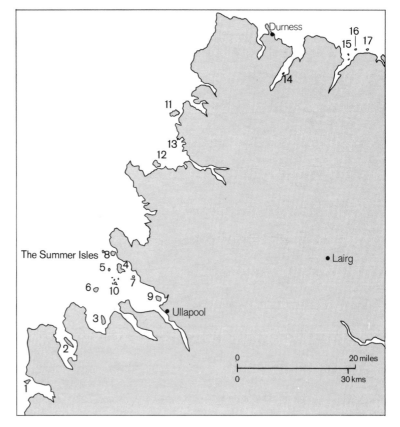

The Northen Coasts of Scotland

1   *Longa*
2   *Isle of Ewe*
3   *Gruinard*
4   *Tanera Mór*
5   *Tanera Beg*
6   *Priest Island*
7   *Horse Island*
8   *Isle Ristol*
9   *Isle Martin*
10 *The Carn Isles*
11 *Handa*
12 *Oldany*
13 *Badcall*
14 *Eilean Choraidh*
15 *Rabbit Islands*
16 *Eilean nan Ròn*
17 *Neave Island*

Handa
Oldany
Badcall

in another book, *Island Years*. Horse Island has no horses, but there is a herd of wild goats to companion its noted bird life.

Turning north past Enard Bay and Loch Inver and into Eddrachillis Bay (with coastal islets all the way), we come, surprisingly, to thirty to forty islands, with, among the most prominent, Handa, Oldany and the Badcall group, the latter a cluster of islets, rocks and skerries about two miles from Badcall village to the north end of the bay. Oldany, which is the second largest of the Eddrachillis Bay islands, is two miles long by one and a half wide, and has been used for grazing.

In 1962 the Royal Society for the Protection of Birds established Handa (with 766 acres (310ha), the largest of the group) as a bird reserve, and refurbished the only habitable building on the island to make a base for its members. There is no pier on the island, and the lobster fishermen, making the two-mile journey from Tarbet on the mainland, beach their boats on the white sand. The island used to be well populated and there are many ruins of former crofts to be seen everywhere. The graveyard is also extensive since, according to one story, it was the custom of mainlanders to

182

bring their dead to the island to prevent the corpses being disturbed by wolves. Thousands of seabirds nest on the cliffs to the north-west, where stands the precipitous Stack of Handa.

The island of Handa, which is a notable bird reserve.

Moving north from Handa towards Cape Wrath, we find numerous little islands, mostly unnamed, particularly in Loch Laxford. Eastwards along the north coast of Scotland, the many more islands there include some buried deep in sea lochs, like the mile-long Eilean Choraidh in Loch Eriboll, an island also known locally as Chorrie Island. In the mouth of the Kyle of Tongue are a number of other islands, including the Rabbit Islands and Eilean nan Ròn, or Roan, which is a mile long by half a mile wide. To the east of the Kyle is Neave Island, also known as Coomb Island. None of these islands have any significant distinguishing features.

Eilean Choraidh

Rabbit Islands
Eilean nan Ròn

Neave Island

13 The Orkney Islands

When I began researching the section on the Orkneys, the so-called 'Isles of the Grey Winds', I started by trying to marshal a few basic statistical facts. Consulting the well-known texts on this group, I was told, variously, that there were fifty-nine, sixty-seven or around a hundred islands, of which, according to source, between eighteen and twenty-four were inhabited. Once again definitions are called in to help. But how much land does that proverbial sheep need to survive (very little if one takes the isle of North Ronaldsay where they are walled-off on to the shore to eat only seaweed)? And is an island with only lighthouse-keepers or a summer bird-warden inhabited or not?

This book lists and describes thirty-three of the more sizeable or interesting islands; the rest must remain an anonymous and disputable statistic. In all, about eighteen of them are inhabited by a determined, hardy and friendly people, possessively proud of their turbulent history. They are more Norse than Scots, as a result of their six centuries as a Norwegian earldom. Indeed, until only two centuries ago they spoke a Norse dialect called Norn.

A brief seven miles north of John o' Groats, the Orkneys are, above all, a storehouse of archaeological and historical treasures, from the well-preserved Stone-Age settlement of Skara Brae, the mysteries of the standing stones of Stenness, the brochs, through to the more recent but still ancient splendour of St Magnus's Cathedral in Kirkwall. The long period of Norwegian/Danish domination, which ended only with the pledging of the islands as dowry for Margaret of Norway in the year 1468, is still very much part of their inheritance. There is indeed one well-argued case that they are still technically only in pawn to Scotland. The Norwegians voted to stay out of the European Community; so did Orkney.

For such a sea-bound people – numbering around nineteen thousand – remarkably few of them turn to the sea for their livelihood. Unlike Shetlanders, the self-contained Orcadians are 'farmers with boats'. They may catch lobster, but their prosperity comes from dairy and egg farming. And then of course came oil, with all its attendant economic stimulants and its threats to established life styles.

The people of Orkney keep to themselves. The 'outside world' means as much mainland Britain to the south as Scandinavia. The Orkney candidate for the British Civil Service was, proverbially, offered a railway warrant to travel to London for the qualifying exam. To the request 'Give nearest railway station', he replied 'Bergen'. Not quite true, but . . .

The Orkneys divide themselves into three groups: the South Isles, Mainland, which accounts for half the land area, and the North Isles. Together they are enclosed within a square of sea fifty miles by fifty. Kirkwall is the major town, with a population of around four and a half thousand inhabitants; the only other sizeable community is at the town of Stromness on the southwest tip of Mainland.

On the way north from John o' Groats in Highland Region, the first island we encounter is that of Stroma, a ghost island now,

The Muckle Skerry lighthouse that stands in the Pentland Firth, between John o' Groats and the Orkneys.

Stroma

185

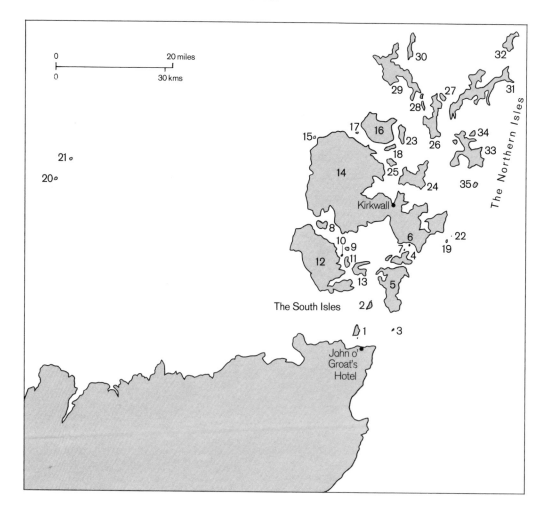

and one of the worst recent examples of depopulation in the northern isles. A few years ago it was offered as a prize in a US television contest but this scheme was abandoned after massive national protest. Close by is the two-mile-long island of Swona, also now near to being uninhabited, and a group of four small uninhabited islets known as the Pentland Skerries, on the largest of which stands a lighthouse.

Swona

Pentland Skerries

The South Isles

South of Mainland, which is sometimes inaccurately called Pomona, the South Isles include the major islands of South Ronaldsay and Hoy. Together they enclose the famous and historic area of water known as Scapa Flow, where the British fleet was based in two world wars. The Grand Fleet sailed from there

The climbers ultimate challenge: the Old Man of Hoy.

The Orkney Islands

 1 Stroma
 2 Swona
 3 Pentland Skerries
 4 Burray
 5 South Ronaldsay
 6 Lamb Holm
 7 Glims Holm
 8 Graemsay
 9 Cava
10 Rysa Little
11 Fara
12 Hoy
13 Flotta
14 Mainland
15 Brough of Birsay
16 Rousay
17 Eynhallow
18 Wyre
19 Copinsay
20 Stack Skerry
21 Sule Skerry
22 Horse of
     Copinsay
23 Egilsay
24 Shapinsay
25 Gairsay
26 Eday
27 Calf of Eday
28 Faray
29 Westray
30 Papa Westray
31 Sanday
32 North Ronaldsay
33 Stronsay
34 Papa Stronsay
35 Auskerry

in 1916 to put an end to the Kaiser's maritime power at the Battle of Jutland, and it was there too that the German navy scuttled seventy-four of their ships after their final surrender in 1918. In the Second World War this was the site for the tragic torpedoing of the battleship the *Royal Oak* by the German U-boat which had slipped through the Scapa defences, causing the deaths of over eight hundred men. Now it is a huge natural naval memorial to the dead, as well as an anchorage for the new oil-based activity.

The isles of Burray and South Ronaldsay are technically no longer islands since they are connected to the east of Mainland by the four 'Churchill Barriers' – artificial causeways of concrete blocks. They have a road running along them which passes through the uninhabited isles of Lamb Holm and Glims (or Glimpse) Holm and thence to Burray. They were built as part of the defences of Scapa Flow after the *Royal Oak* disaster. This area

Burray
South Ronaldsay
Lamb Holm
Glims Holm

was once the centre of a busy herring-fishing industry. Now the skeletons of the old boats show up through the sands. On Lamb Holm is the Italian Chapel built and decorated inside a Nissen hut by the Italian prisoners of war who had been brought to Orkney to build the Churchill Causeways. This 'road across the sea' leads on to South Ronaldsay with its tiny village of St Margaret's Hope. The farms that line the shores here are gradually regaining some of the prosperity that was lost, largely due to bad land-management, in the nineteenth century.

On the west side of Scapa Flow there are no Churchill Causeways and access between Hoy and Mainland is by boat. Between them lies the green island of Graemsay with its two lighthouses, while down the east coast of Hoy are the little islands of Cava, Rysa Little, Fara and Flotta, all known too well by two generations of servicemen.

Graemsay
Cava
Rysa Little
Fara

Hoy itself, the second largest island, is the most hilly island in the Orkneys; it also has cliffs like none elsewhere. Here is the famous stack, the Old Man of Hoy, a perpendicular column of red sandstone which, 450 feet (137m) high, lies offshore, north of Rora Head, as a perpetual challenge to rock-climbers.

Hoy

In a glen under the shadow of the 1,570-foot (479m) Ward Hill is the Dwarfie Stone, a huge sandstone boulder, its interior carved out and with only a small entrance: a unique, four-thousand-year-old tomb. East, on the shores of the Flow, is the strange modern ghost town of Lyness, twice the hyperactive centre of a great naval base. Now, only the scarred hillsides recall the memory of countless huts and shelters for thousands of men. Beyond and to the south, on the peninsula of South Walls, which is connected by a narrow isthmus to Hoy, are the whitewashed walls of the proud village of Longhope with its memorial to the men of the Longhope lifeboat which was lost with all its crew in 1969.

A famous and dramatic photograph of the German Fleet anchored in Scapa Flow in 1918.

Offshore to the south of Scapa Flow the strategic isle of Flotta was, in the years after 1945, largely returning to nature with an increasingly diminishing and ageing population. Now, Flotta has taken on a new and important role as an oil-terminal base. The oil company concerned is making a considerable effort (still much criticised) to preserve something of the natural environment, as Flotta is precipitately launched into the technological age.

Flotta

Mainland

A hundred years ago there were some thirty thousand people on the islands; now the figure is around nineteen thousand. Only the capital town, Kirkwall, has increased in size and now accommodates around a third of the entire Orkney population. The so-called 'drift from the isles' continues unabated. Kirkwall itself, with its narrow flagstoned streets and crow-stepped house roofs, is clustered around the eight-hundred-year-old St Magnus's Cathedral, the tower of which can be seen from many miles away. Interestingly, the cathedral is owned by the town and not by the Church of Scotland. Stromness, Mainland's second town, is built along a series of little quays, behind which narrow lanes and closes link up to the stone-flagged main street.

Mainland divides itself carefully into west and east at the Scapa isthmus. The west has magnificent cliffs and rock scenery. It also has the important prehistoric village of Skara Brae, which was uncovered last century when a gale shifted the sands and revealed seven dwellings with interconnecting corridors and stone 'furniture'. Here too, just north-east of Stromness, is Maeshowe, another antiquarian treasure, with its two-thousand-year-old chambered tomb made of gigantic stones, rich with later runic inscriptions. At Stenness there is also a magnificent northern Stonehenge.

To the north-west, at Marwick Head, is a modern square tower erected in memory of Lord Kitchener who was drowned when his ship struck a German mine off there in 1916.

Monoliths, brochs and other monuments to the past are com-

Brough of Birsay

Rousay
Eynhallow

Wyre

Copinsay

Stack Skerry
Sule Skerry

mon on Mainland. Off Birsay at the north-western tip is the tidal island of the Brough of Birsay on which there are other fascinating traces of early Christian and Norse occupation. These include an eleventh-century church and graveyard. East along the coast is the hilly island of Rousay, with, between it and west Mainland, the haunted island of Eynhallow, which carries the faint ruins of a church. Rousay, too, is rich in archaeological sites, brochs and cairns, a mysterious island where the past lingers still. Perhaps most impressive and sinister is Mid Howe Cairn, which has been described as a 'great ship of death', a seventy-five-foot (23m)-long chamber divided into twelve separate funeral compartments. To the south is the small island of Wyre with a twelfth-century chapel and castle dating from the time of the Norse occupation.

East Mainland is, by contrast, less spectacular but has some very intensive dairy farming. The farmers live mainly on their land, scattered and independent, rather than together in villages.

Off the east coast is the 200-acre (80ha) island of Copinsay which now has a bird sanctuary named after the famous naturalist James Fisher. Its sharp cliffs to the east and gentle slopes to the west are home for a vast variety of birds.

Forty miles to the west of Stromness are the two remote islets of Stack Skerry and Sule Skerry, the former like a starkly exposed mountain peak, inhabited only by a myriad of gannets, while the latter carries a lighthouse and a huge puffin colony.

The Northern Isles

As well as Rousay and Wyre, the Northern Isles include, among others, Gairsay, Egilsay, Shapinsay, Westray, Papa Westray, Faray (or Fara), Eday, Sanday, Stronsay, Papa Stronsay, North Ronaldsay and the uninhabited Auskerry. Many of these can be visited by steamer from Kirkwall, a round-trip journey that lasts eight hours. A number of these islands have little islets close beside them. Some are called 'The Calf of . . .'; others have equally

(Opposite) *The magnificent building skills of the past at Skara Brae, Orkney.*

(Below) *Standing stones amid a hayfield at Stenness, on Orkney's Mainland.*

Horse of Copinsay quaint animal names such as the memorable Horse of Copinsay.

Egilsay Egilsay, with the remains of its splendid round-towered church marking the site of St Magnus's martyrdom (he was ritually murdered by Earl Haakon in the year 1116), still has a tiny **Shapinsay** community living on it. To the south, Shapinsay (sometimes spelt Shapansay), one of the few islands with any trees on it, is so close to Kirkwall that it is known locally as the 'suburban' island. **Gairsay** Between it and Mainland is Gairsay, shaped like a flat cone. It was once home to the 'Last Viking', Sweyn Asleifsson. It is now uninhabited.

Eday The black hills of the largely depopulated Eday lie to the north-east. Eday is famous for its thick layers of peat. Beside it is **Calf of Eday** the uninhabited Calf of Eday, where the notorious eighteenth-century pirate Gow was finally captured. On it too is a notable chambered cairn.

Faray Faray (or Fara), with its roofless and windowless crofts, lies a mile due west of Eday. It was finally evacuated in 1947, though it is still occasionally used for grazing. Beyond, to the north-west, is Westray, with the stone-flagged roofs of Pierowall. A village with *The gannets wheel* strong Jacobite traditions, it is overshadowed by the grim ruins of *round remote Stack* the fifteenth-century Noltland (or Northland) Castle. Westray *Skerry.* has currently a population of around seven hundred and, con-

trary to the situation on most of the other islands, this is increasing, due in part to the thriving fishing fleet and the lobster- and crab-processing plant. On Papa Westray to the north-east, a small moorland island four miles long by a mile wide, there is a fascinating dwelling, said to be around five thousand years old. Here too are a number of other prehistoric and early Christian sites. (The pre-name 'Papa' on a number of Orkney's islands comes from the Celtic word for a priest, *'papae'*. Once again, as we have found elsewhere around Britain, the early religious and monastic communities tended to live away from the larger population groups.) Off the coast here is an islet said to be the last home of the now extinct great auk. **Westray**

Papa Westray

Low-lying and indeed sandy, Sanday is one of Orkney's larger isles. Fourteen miles long, it is an island with great vistas of sea and sky, and with long beaches on which the winter seas can pile seaweed in great heaps. Once there was only farming and fishing. Now a modern electronics industry and a cottage-based co-operative knitting venture have added their impetus to the island's economy. **Sanday**

Due north, North Ronaldsay, low-lying and gale-swept, is the most northerly island in the group. A stone dyke has been built right round its edge to keep its small brown sheep to the shore, obliging them to feed on the seaweed, the land being considered too valuable for mere grazing. There are many prehistoric sites and the highest land-built lighthouse in Britain on this relatively well-populated island. **North Ronaldsay**

Stronsay, four miles south of Sanday, is low, flat and much indented by three great bays. With its tiny neighbour Papa Stronsay, it was once the centre of Sanday's herring and fish-curing industry. It is now almost entirely agricultural, with a population of around four hundred. Finally, the uninhabited island of Auskerry, which lies two miles to the south of Stronsay, has a lighthouse at its southernmost point, acting as warning outrider to this group of individualistic and increasingly thriving islands. **Stronsay**
Papa Stronsay

Auskerry

193

14 The Shetland Isles

Surrounded though the Shetland Isles are by so much excitingly new, oil-based wealth, the inhabitants of many of the remoter islands, and even the not so remote, can still be seen out on the moors cutting their peat. Old and new exist side by side, not always comfortably.

If anything, Shetland is more Scandinavian, more Norwegian, than it is Scots. It is not too dangerous a statement to say that the population of around eighteen and a half thousand, a third of whom live in the capital Lerwick, think of themselves as just as different from the Scots as do the English or Welsh. Even the scenery is wilder, more Norse, in contrast with Orkney which has much more in keeping with the comfortable Scottish mainland, though there is one striking difference from Norwegian scenery: here there are almost no trees. One is constantly reminded that north of the Shetlands there is only Spitzbergen until one reaches the Pole. And while the Orcadians are farmers and to a surprising extent ignore the sea, the Shetlanders, never more than three miles from it, are first and foremost seafarers. They are cautious people too, as their material, if suspicious, approach to the new North Sea wealth demonstrates. They, not the oil companies, control development at Sullom Voe and have, with difficulty, made certain that a fair share of the oil money stays firmly in Shetland to ensure that their community is not too badly or lastingly damaged. The oil barons know they have a match in the islands' councils.

There are around a hundred Shetland islands, of which between seventeen and twenty are inhabited permanently. By far the largest of them is Mainland, fifty-four miles from north to south, an island deeply indented, of magnificent cliff scenery and voes or sea lochs. Together these make for a strong blend of wild land and wilder sea. Geographically as well as historically, the Shetlands are closer to Bergen in Norway than to Aberdeen in

Scotland. Their problem is, as with so many islands around the coast, that of depopulation, relentlessly advancing. But North Sea oil has arrived to halt this trend and has moved the reputation of the islands away from the traditional knitted shawls and Shetland ponies.

As with Orkney (with which they have little else in common, separated as they are by a fifty-mile stretch of rugged seas), their five centuries of Norse tradition, which ended only in 1469, are very strong in place names, in attitudes, and even in speech. Here too the old dialect was called Norn, and Norse law-forms lingered for centuries after the Vikings departed. Before the Vikings came, there were two tribes, so they said: the 'Picts and the Papae', the Christian priests. From all three of these groups there is a strong archaeological inheritance.

It was a commonplace of writers of books about the Shetlands to complain that these most northerly parts of Britain were ignored. On maps they were (and are) always an insert, geographically and educationally confusing, particularly when they are inset on a different scale. More commonly on maps today, they are simply left out altogether. But Britain's answer to the

The future: the giant Sullom Voe oil terminal.

The Shetland Isles

1 *Mainland*
2 *St Ninian's Isle*
3 *South Havra*
4 *Burra*
5 *Papa*
6 *Oxna*
7 *Trondra*
8 *Hildasay*
9 *Vaila*
10 *Linga*
11 *Papa Stour*
12 *Vementry*
13 *Papa Little*
14 *Muckle Roe*
15 *Egilsay*
16 *Lamba*
17 *Whalsay*
18 *Bressay*
19 *Noss*
20 *Mousa*
21 *Yell*
22 *Fetlar*
23 *Unst*
24 *Uyea*
25 *Haaf Gruney*
26 *Balta*
27 *Muckle Flugga*
28 *Out Stack*
29 *Bruray*
30 *Housay*
31 *Foula*
32 *Fair Isle*

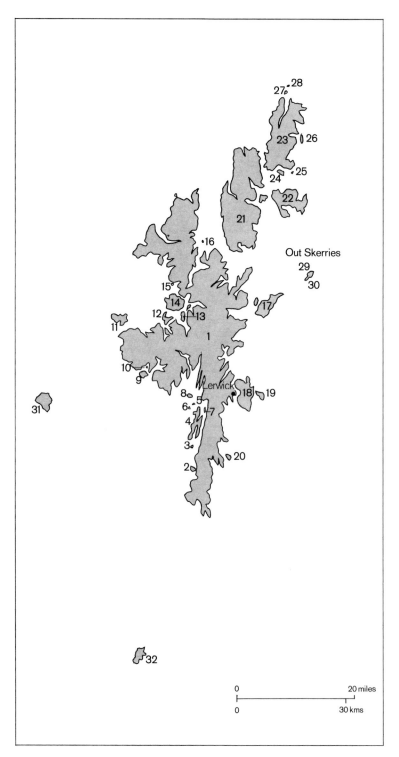

energy crisis is changing this fast, as the numerous oil-rig helicopters at Lerwick's Sumburgh airport and the massive oil-related activity in the harbour immediately indicate to the arriving visitor.

The depleted fishing fleet sheltering in Lerwick Harbour, Shetland.

We can usefully look at the Shetlands in three separate groups. First, Mainland and its adjacent islands; second, the so-called North Isles grouped round Yell, Unst and Fetlar; and third, the distant islands, Foula, lying in the Atlantic twenty-six miles west of Scalloway, and the remote Fair Isle, halfway between Shetland and Orkney but within the former's domain.

Mainland

The capital of Mainland is Lerwick, where half the island's inhabitants live. The second largest village or township is Scalloway on the west coast. Lerwick itself is becoming increasingly prosperous, almost a boom town, with an excellent harbour and a thriving fishing industry, as well as the new oil-based economy. Here the famous January festival of Up-Helly-Aa is held, which recalls the Shetlands' Viking past and culminates in a large crowd bearing a Norse longship through the town. They eventually

The magnificent prehistoric subterranean dwellings at Jarlshof.

launch it and throw burning torches on to it, until the galley itself is ablaze. Dressed in horned helmets, they sing the Up-Helly-Aa song:

> From grand old Viking centuries, Up-Helly-Aa has come,
> Then light the torch and form the march and sound the rolling drum . . .

Scalloway was base for the 'Shetland Bus' saga in the Second World War, when spies, refugees and partisans were smuggled in and out of German-occupied Norway by the Norwegian resistance movement. Here there is a seventeenth-century castle, and on a small offshore island nearby an open-air parliament (such as on the Isle of Man) used to be held. The dull and almost treeless scenery of Mainland is enlivened in the west by well-stocked land and sea lochs (known as 'voes') and towering cliffs, particularly at Esha Ness in the far north-west, where the rock formations are striking. The rest of the north is bleak and somewhat desolate. Back in the south there are many rich archaeological sites, particularly at Jarlshof, where a group of prehistoric wheel-houses, circular habitations of stone built round an open central hearth, has been excavated.

In the north, almost dissecting Mainland, is Sullom Voe, a deep, well-sheltered sea loch. It was a major wartime naval base and is now the biggest oil port in Britain, able to accommodate the largest tankers in existence. Finally, worth brief mention is the township of Weisdale in central Mainland, the birthplace in 1786 of that famous islander, John Clunies Ross, who travelled thousands of miles away to settle with his family and become 'king' of the Cocos Islands in the far Pacific.

St Ninian's Isle Sailing clockwise round and up the west coast of Mainland, the first island of note we come to is the delightful St Ninian's Isle, which is not properly independent as it is joined to the mainland, but beautifully, by a spit of white sand to the north of Rerwick. Here is the site of one of the earliest Celtic churches in Shetland, which was only disinterred, by a party from Aberdeen University, as late as 1958. During the excavations a local schoolboy who was helping with the dig levered up a stone slab to reveal the fabulous St Ninian's Treasure, silver bowls, brooches, and many other ornaments, buried probably by St Ninian's monks to preserve them from the invading Vikings.

South Havra To the north, beyond the 150-acre (60ha) island of South Havra which was inhabited until the beginning of this century, are the **Burra** long green 'twin' islands of Burra (now joined by a bridge) which have a population of around six hundred who mainly live in the picturesque fishing village of Hamnavoe. There are a number of sculptured stones on 'the Burras' dating from early Christian

Ferrying sheep at Tingwall, the Shetlands.

times. One of two fine ones found there and called the Papil Stones is now in the National Museum of Antiquities in Edinburgh. At one time the island had a splendid high-towered Roman Catholic church, but this was demolished in the early nineteenth century in an attempt to stamp out the old religion (and also to provide stone for the bleak kirk that replaced it). Knitwear, produced by the wives of Burra, supplements the economy of the island which is mainly based on fishing. Nearby

Papa is the uninhabited island of Papa, its name obviously recording its
Oxna Christian past, and the 180 acres (73ha) of Oxna, now also uninhabited. There are a number of other sizeable but uninhabited islands in this area which lack any particular distinguishing features, though undoubtedly most of them were once occupied. No one can doubt that on them there are still substantial archaeological finds to be made.

Trondra The green but bleak isle of Trondra, with its tiny and sadly decreasing population, provides shelter for the harbour at Scal-

200

loway. Though lacking a harbour itself, it is now linked to both Burra and Mainland by a system of bridges. Hildasay, now also abandoned to nature, was once the site of a quarry where an attractive red and greenish granite was, at the end of the last century, excavated and exported to be used for ornamental building work in the south.

Hildasay

Vaila, with its watchtower, is the island that shelters the harbour of the township of Walls. It too is now left with a tiny population. But in the eighteen-thirties it was the site of an early fish-curing station, started by Arthur Anderson, one of the co-founders of the P & O Shipping Company. Beside it nestles the tiny island of Linga, one of at least three of that name in the Shetlands.

Vaila

Linga

The recent history of Papa Stour, the 'Big Isle of the Priests', tells the same forlorn story of a small and diminishing population, though there has been a slight turn for the better over the last few years with the arrival of a few younger families to settle there. Three miles long and a little less in breadth, it is bleak and unattractive. Its one major delight is its sea caves, particularly one called Francie's Hole whose green and red walls glisten and whose serrated ceilings are like those of some subterranean church. These caves, which one can best see by boat, entranced the early Victorian traveller John Tudor, who argued that there were none like them elsewhere in the British Isles. Others who came later moderated that claim by arguing that only Fingal's Cave on Staffa surpassed them. In the seventeenth and eighteenth centuries scurvy was rampant in the Shetland Islands, and those with it were frequently expelled from the mainland to a 'leper colony' outside the walls of the villages of Papa Stour. The island has inherited its own special sword dance, performed by seven men representing the seven saints of Christendom, who jig to very Scandinavian-sounding music.

Papa Stour

Vementry is the largest uninhabited island in all the Shetlands. But it was not always so, and there are many ruined brochs, burial cairns and even gun-emplacements, complete with their great guns dating from the First World War, which still point menacingly out across St Magnus Bay. Nearby is the 500-acre (202ha) island of Papa Little at the head of Aith Voe, once also a Christian settlement. It remained inhabited until the middle of the nineteenth century. Linked by an iron bridge to Mainland ever since 1905, the almost circular island of Muckle Roe, guarding Olna Firth, is home to a farming community of around a hundred. It is surrounded by high, reddish, volcanic cliffs and the scenery and views are particularly impressive. Nearby are the fifty-four uninhabited acres (22ha) of Egilsay, named after one of the great Icelandic sagas, a lesser namesake to the one in Orkney.

Vementry

Papa Little

Muckle Roe

Egilsay

Turning south round the top of Mainland, we come across a number of islands scattered in the sound between it and Yell. **Lamba** Lamba, now deserted, was once the home of a witch who sold 'fair winds' to sailors. The others, some of which are quite large and which used to be cultivated, have little of note available to record about them.

Whalsay Dropping down further south, three miles east of Mainland one reaches the large island of Whalsay. Five miles long by two wide, it has a population of around eight hundred; it also boasts a regular car-ferry service. Surrounded by many subsidiary islets and studded with lochs, Whalsay is an important fishing centre, largely turning its back on the possibilities for agriculture. One peculiar historic building is at Symbister – a so-called Hanseatic booth, dating from the times when Shetland's trade was with the Hanseatic ports of Bremen and Hamburg. The German merchants built such 'booths' in which to store their merchandise. This one, though five centuries old, remains well preserved. Off the coast of Whalsay a Dutch East Indiaman was wrecked in the year 1664. It was reputedly carrying a cargo of golden guilders, and though some of them have been washed ashore over the years, attempts to discover the rest of the hoard have so far been unsuccessful. Here too, at Symbister, is a strange nineteenth-century folly of a house built by an eccentric laird in his own memory, to use up his fortune and deprive his detested relations of their inheritance.

Bressay Bressay island is Lerwick harbour's shelter and has become almost a suburb of the town. It is a highly fertile island, six miles long, with the conically shaped Ward Hill at its highest point. Near to the southernmost tip is the Cave of the Bard (which one is not recorded). There are no poems or prophesies, only stalactites and resounding echoes. Unlike many of the Shetland Isles, Bressay is well farmed, with Lerwick as its marketplace, and there is also a thriving fishmeal factory. Known nowadays for its bird life, it was used in the last century for breeding Shetland ponies, which were of particular value in working the satanic coalmines of the south. Nearby, in Bressay Sound, the English fleet defeated the Dutch in a skirmish in the year 1665.

Noss Close to the east shore of Bressay are the high cliffs of the small island of Noss, which is a noted seabird sanctuary and is also used for sheep-grazing. Such is the density of the bird population that when they are disturbed on their packed cliffside perches and nests, the birds rise to blacken, or rather whiten, the skies in a vast feathered stormcloud. On the east of the island one cliff, the Noup, rises spectacularly to 594 feet (181m). Now uninhabited, a hundred years ago it had a sizeable community, but the drift to Mainland and other parts of Britain was inevitable.

Spinning of wool on Shetland. The end product has a warmth and lightness of texture which is unique.

The fertile island of Unst.

Mousa Before we turn to the North Islands, one last island on the east coast is worth a mention: Mousa. A mile and a half long, it has an example of an almost perfect broch or Pictish castle, which is estimated to be about eighteen hundred years old. It is of a different build from the other brochs, in that, in a feat of primitive architecture, the round wall has been made to overhang outwards near the top, making it impossible to scale. The island, now uninhabited except by wild sheep and wilder ponies, is privately owned.

Yell We move north of Mainland now to the isle of Yell and beyond. Yell is the second largest of the isles of Shetland, some seventeen miles long and seven wide, rectangular in shape and almost bisected by two deep voes. With a population of around one thousand, for the most part it is bleak neglected moorland, large expanses of it now totally depopulated. With the exception of its areas of voe and cliff scenery, it is a melancholy place. Even lovers

204

of the isles like Eric Linklater found it hard to use words of enthusiasm for it, as it lies, almost abandoned, under its thick blanket of peat. He aptly named it 'the problem child of the archipelago', and it has long had such a reputation. Thus the sixteenth-century traveller Buchanan: 'So uncouth a place that no creature can live therein, except such as are born there.' But, courtesy of the Highlands and Islands Development Board, there is now investment money and, as a result, greater hope for the future.

Next, by contrast, comes the potentially fertile island of Fetlar, **Fetlar** two and a half miles to the east of Yell. It is rich in strange prehistoric sites, some of which have on them large rings of stone up to ninety feet (27m) across. Lacking a good harbour, it has had its constant problems throughout the ages. In consequence it also is in rapid decline, with a population now of well under a hundred inhabitants, a tenth of what it had in the eighteen-fifties. It was once the only known nesting place in Britain of snowy owls

205

(in recent years they have visited but not nested on Fetlar). Nowadays (despite, or perhaps because of, its lack of a harbour) it is a favourite spot for Russian fishing boats and factory ships to shelter off in bad weather.

Unst Unst is the third largest island of the archipelago and the most northerly, with only Muckle Flugga above it. It is eleven miles from north to south and about four miles across. It, like Fetlar, is a fertile island, and inland from its bird-filled cliffs, it has some prosperous farms and crofts. There are three villages, one of which, Haroldswick, has the distinction of having Britain's most northerly post office.

It is a well-developed island of a thousand inhabitants and with much for the visitor to see, including the still dignified ruins of a sixteenth-century castle at Muness and some Viking settlements. At the northern tip, alongside modern radar masts, is Hermaness, which is a nature reserve and a breeding ground for the great skua. Here on Unst is a plethora of ruined churches – twenty-two of them at one count – as well as many cairns and standing stones. Along the shores there are other, more modern, skeletons of the past, the rotting wrecks of a once proud fishing industry, though fishing, crofting and weaving are still the mainstays of the economy today.

Uyea Close by, at the southern end, is the little island of Uyea, where once too there was a church with a little community clustered around it. At an earlier time it was also the site of a Norse settlement. Further along the coast and two miles to the south- **Haaf Gruney** east is the little island of Haaf Gruney where there was once a chromite quarry and where there is now a nature reserve. Up the east coast, sheltering Balta Sound, which is all it now does, is the **Balta** deserted two-mile-long island of Balta.

Then north once again, to the real top of these British Isles, **Muckle Flugga** Muckle Flugga, with its seal colony and its manned white lighthouse pinnacled above it. It is surrounded by strangely named **Out Stack** skerries, like the Rumblings and Tipta, with Out Stack as the ultimate sea-washed rock of all.

Out Skerries Five miles north-east of Whalsay lie the Out Skerries, a fascinating group of several surprisingly well-populated islets covering in all a bare square mile of inhospitable rock. They include **Bruray** Bruray and Housay, which are linked by a bridge. The hardy **Housay** inhabitants, over a hundred of them, live amid a well-stocked fishing ground. Because of this and their having an excellent natural harbour, despite the distance there is to their markets, the population is the only one in the Shetlands to have increased over the last century. Severe cliffs surround this tiny world, but by the sheltered harbour, with its small but modern fishing fleet, the

houses are brightly painted and neat and on a good day it all looks charming. In a storm, however, the waves and spray break all around the islands, and over the years many vessels, including a Dutch treasure ship, have been wrecked there. The elements are not the only danger; in the Second World War the lighthouse station was bombed and a keeper's wife killed. Pleasures are few; weddings, for example, are kept to the winter months, but then the whole community is invited to the festivities, which may last continuously for several days and nights.

The northernmost British isle of all: Muckle Flugga.

One of the remotest populated islands in Britain is Foula, some thirty miles west of Lerwick. Its additional problem is that it is very exposed and has no sheltered harbour and thus can be cut off for weeks at a time during the long winter months. The most striking geographical feature of the island is the Kame, the cliff at the north-west end of the island which has a sheer drop of 1,250 feet (380m) to the sea. The varied bird population includes a large colony of great and arctic skuas, which are aggressive birds, even attacking humans, particularly during the nesting season.

Foula

207

One of the deceptive Fair Isle's many wrecks.

At the beginning of the century there were around two hundred inhabitants of Foula; now there are around forty, a third of them old-age pensioners. Here is no hotel, pub, shop or accommodation, and visitors have to make travel plans long in advance. It is a place so remote that it was used as the setting for the film *The Edge of the World*, which was based on the story of the evacuation of St Kilda. Here too are old traditions, such as celebrating Christmas and the New Year according to the old Julian calendar, with New Year on the thirteenth of January. Given the feeling of total isolation that exists as the old pass on, it is not altogether surprising that very few if any young people come to replace them.

In 1914 the liner *Oceanic* was wrecked on Foula's notorious Hœvdi Reef. It happened on a calm day and for some time the ship remained upright, allowing the passengers and crew to get off and the men of Foula to go on board and see the sort of luxury that was beyond the comprehension of people accustomed to

208

their simple life style. Even today there are many pieces of furniture and a myriad of other fittings on Foula which originated in the staterooms of the *Oceanic*.

Last but far from least in these twin northern archipelagos of Orkney and Shetland is Fair Isle. Covering less than six square miles, it lies midway between the two groups but comes into Shetland's domain. Its name is best known for the particular design of its knitting patterns which, with their use of homespun and dyed wool, are reputed to have originated from patterns brought ashore by Spanish seamen wrecked after the defeat of the Armada in 1588. More likely they are Scandinavian in origin. Spaniards there were however. From one galleon alone, the crew of about two hundred spent six weeks on the island, causing near famine among the inhabitants, until some were, so it is said, thrown over the cliffs, and the rest pointedly asked to leave for the Shetland mainland.

Fair Isle

    The population of Fair Isle was decreasing steadily until recent years. But the trend reversed after the island was bought by the National Trust for Scotland in 1954. The Trust have introduced and financed schemes to improve housing and other amenities, and the process of regeneration of the social economy of the island is well under way.

    The island has two lighthouses and an important bird observatory which was established in 1948. Since then this latter has become world-famous; over three hundred different species of bird have been observed there. Equally well known is the Fair Isle lifeboat, which has been in operation since 1878 and has saved many lives across those last hundred years.

The Orkneys and Shetlands, these 180-odd islands scattered so anonymously in the sea areas north of the British mainland, are poised precariously between the old and the new. Where such ancient history and rugged geography blend together, it is not an uncommon sight to find a track of sodden moorland and a stretch of sea with, as the only signs of human life, a two-thousand-year-old broch, a group of desolate standing stones, and beyond, a tangle of oil rigs and other prosperous marks of the most modern of the world's technologies. And, in between, an old man with cap, boots and knee-protectors, standing on a grey windswept moor, is cutting peats for his fire. The tide of fortune of the islands is changing fast; with care it will be to the good.

15 The Islands of the East Coast of Scotland

Mugdrum

There are few islands down the east coast of Scotland until one reaches the Firth of Forth, on the north bank of which, at Largo, perhaps the most famous islander of all time, Alexander Selkirk or Robinson Crusoe, was born in the year 1676. One exception is the thirty-five-acre (14ha) island of Mugdrum deep in the Firth of Tay, opposite the ancient and royal borough of Newburgh. It is used as arable farmland. Other exceptions are the new, man-made islands – the oil rigs.

Bell Rock

Before turning the corner south round Fife Ness, it is also worth briefly noting the Bell or Inchcape Rock, twelve miles off the Tayside coast, a dangerous reef barely uncovered at low water. On it now stands a lighthouse built by Robert Stevenson, the grandfather of Robert Louis Stevenson. R. M. Ballantyne spent some time there researching a book, but it is best known for the ballad about it written by Robert Southey, which tells the fate of the pirate, Ralph the Rover, who cut the rope of the warning bell on the rock.

> The worthy Abbot of Aberbrothok
> Had placed that bell on the Inchcape Rock;
> On a buoy in the storm it floated and swung
> And over the waves its warning rung.

> When the rock was hid by the surge's swell,
> The mariners heard the warning bell;
> And then they knew the perilous rock,
> And blest the Abbot of Aberbrothok.

Isle of May

The historic Isle of May that stands at the north-east entrance to the Firth of Forth.

In the outer reaches of the Firth of Forth is the Isle of May, 126 acres (51ha) on which there is a lighthouse and a particularly important bird observatory, since it lies on a main migration route south. Here, according to legend, St Adrian had his base when he was converting the peoples of Fife and it was here too that he was murdered by Norse invaders. A ruined chapel, built to his memory in the thirteenth century, can be seen on the island.

210

The East Coast of Scotland

1 *Mugdrum*
2 *Bell Rock*
3 *Isle of May*
4 *The Bass Rock*
5 *Craigleith*
6 *Fidra*
7 *Lamb Islet*
8 *Inchkeith*
9 *Inchmickery*
10 *Inchcolm*
11 *Cramond Island*

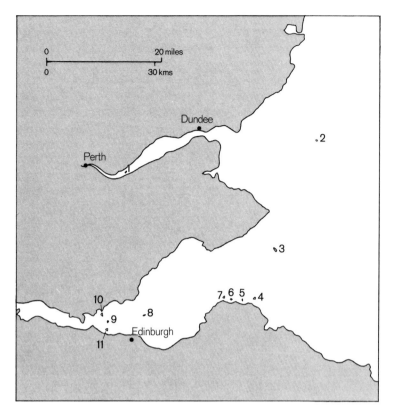

The Bass Rock

Approached by sea, the Bass Rock, which acts as southern gate-post to the inner harbours of the Firth of Forth, looks completely out of place standing close to the comfortable Lothian shoreline with its rich farms and well-populated golf courses. This glowering and extravagant basalt plug, with its high, bird-dropping-grey walls looming over 350 feet (107m) above the sea, would be much more at home facing the Atlantic breakers far to the west. The cliffs, pierced by a huge natural tunnel, break down to the water's edge only at the south-west corner, and there the ruins of an old fort guard the sole route to the top. The rest is sheer.

The National Trust for Scotland now owns the island, which is home to a myriad of gannets, one of the largest and oldest recorded colonies in Britain. (The Latin name for the gannet is *Sula bassana*, after the Rock.) Until the end of the eighteenth century the gannets were harvested and sold in the streets of Edinburgh; they were considered good eating before the domestically reared chicken supplanted them, their feathers were highly praised for bedding, and their fat was used both as a medicine and for waterproofing boots – a veritable panacea.

212

(Top) *The island of Papa Stour, Shetlands.*
(Above) *Granite strength — the 350ft-high Bass Rock stands at the mouth of the Firth of Forth.*

213

Remotest Britain — one of the few remaining inhabitants of Foula, which lies thirty miles west of Lerwick.

On its turret of rock, Lindisfarne Castle, Holy Island, Northumberland.

When the culling stopped, the colonies expanded rapidly, and now, unless one is a determined bird-lover, they and their smell present the most immediately unattractive aspect of life on the island as far as visitors are concerned.

In the cliff face, just above where the lighthouse now stands, are the remains of a seventh-century hermitage where, by tradition, the monk St Baldred lived out his life. There too are the ruins of a dry-stone chapel, built in memory of the saint some eight hundred years later. In the seventeenth century the Rock served as a sort of bleak Scottish Alcatraz, where Covenanters were left to rot with only the sea to guard them. In the same century many Jacobite prisoners were also held there, and in 1691 some Jacobite officers seized the prison when the guards were out on a working party with the other prisoners. They drove the guards from the island and, flying the Scottish lion of the usurped James VII (James II of Great Britain), held out for three whole years before being rewarded for their perseverance with their liberty. Doubtless this gave Stevenson his idea for making the Rock prison to David Balfour in his book *Catriona*. There is also the tale that from time to time mainland people hear, from across the waters of a dark night, Covenanter prisoners – the 'Sweet Singers' they are called – still chanting their psalms to a world beyond the Rock.

Off North Berwick in Lothian are a group of islands, Craigleith and Fidra being the most important. Craigleith is also known as Lamb Island, which can be confusing since there is also a Lamb Islet close to North Berwick; both possibly take their names from their shape and from the whitish colour of their rocks, caused by the deposit of seabirds. On Fidra there are the remains of a burial ground and a chapel dedicated to St Nicholas, and also a lighthouse. There is a natural bridge right through the island which is meant to be shaped like a veiled female figure, and is, in consequence, known as the White Lady of Fidra. Remains of other buildings on the island are reputed to be on the site of a hospital or refuge dating from times of the plague. It is supposedly the island that inspired Robert Louis Stevenson to write his book *Treasure Island*. Certainly that author was fascinated by Fidra and he has James Balfour describe it in the book *Catriona* as:

> a strange grey islet of two humps, made more conspicuous by a piece of ruin: and I mind that (as we drew closer to it) by some door or window of these ruins, the sea peeped through like a man's eye. Under the lee of Fidra, there is a good anchorage in westerly winds ...

Craigleith
Fidra
Lamb Islet

Then come three islands all with the prefix 'Inch': Inchkeith, Inchmickery and Inchcolm. Inchkeith, with its lighthouse, stands

Inchkeith

Inchkeith, with the symmetrical Paps of Fife in the background.

in the middle of the Firth of Forth and consequently has long been regarded as of considerable strategic importance in the defence of the Scottish capital. The island was garrisoned in the sixteenth century by the French soldiers of the Queen Regent, Mary of Lorraine, who stayed loyal to her daughter, Mary Queen of Scots. In later wars, including the Napoleonic and the First and Second World Wars, it was again well fortified. It was on this island that King James IV was said to have carried out the strange experiment of putting two babies on the island in the care of a deaf-and-dumb nurse, to discover what language they would learn to speak. According to the legend they were found years later to speak 'passable Hebrew'.

Inchmickery

Inchmickery, two and a half miles from Cramond, consists of about thirty acres (12ha) of poor land on which there is a standing stone known as the Mickery Stone. The island was almost entirely built over with Second World War fortifications. It is now a bird sanctuary and is a noted breeding spot for the roseate tern.

Inchcolm

Inchcolm, on the north side of the Forth, a mile long by a half wide, has been called the 'Iona of the East' because King Alexander I, having taken refuge on it in a storm, was well looked after by a hermit who was living on the isle. In gratitude the King built an Augustinian abbey on the island, which became a place of great sanctity to pilgrims. The well-preserved ruins of the buildings, including a thirteenth-century octagonal chapter house, are now in the care of the Department of the Environment. This was

Cramond Island with the outskirts of Edinburgh visible in the background.

one of many islands on which to be buried was 'to be close to heaven', and it was so well known that Shakespeare referred to it in *Macbeth*. In Act I Scene II Ross tells King Duncan:

> That now
> Sweno, the Norways' king, craves composition;
> Nor would we deign him burial of his men
> Till he disbursed at Saint Colme's inch
> Ten thousand dollars to our general use.

Cramond Island   The last island of any note, the eighty-odd acres (30ha) of Cramond Island, can be reached on foot at low tide from that popular suburb of Edinburgh, Cramond itself.

220

16 The Islands of the East Coast of England

Lindisfarne, known also as Holy Island, is perhaps the most romantic of all the islands along the east coast of the British Isles. In terms of definition, this island, which is six miles to the north-west of Bamburgh and close to Beal, is really not a permanent one, since there is a causeway, marked by tall wooden posts, where it is possible to cross except at high tide. It is a place of very strong religious connections which have lasted since the beginnings of Christianity in Britain. Perhaps the only other islands to rival it in terms of monastic associations are the islands of Iona and Caldey and St Michael's Mount.

Lindisfarne has been a place of pilgrimage throughout the centuries; it has a monastery which was founded by St Aidan, who came from Iona, summoned by King Oswald, to be the first bishop of Lindisfarne, in the year 634. At those earliest times it would have been but a collection of huts and an oratory with a defensive wall around them. From the monastery monks would set out, prepared with the gospel, to proselytise the nearby mainland areas. St Cuthbert, as a young shepherd in the hills, heard of Aidan's death and himself turned to the Church and its austerity. He later became closely associated with the development of the monastery and was perhaps the most famous of all Lindisfarne's bishops.

Many other saints have had connections with Holy Island across the centuries, and it was here that one of the finest early English manuscripts, the so-called 'Lindisfarne Gospels', was produced. It is now in the British Museum. Illuminated by monks in about the year 700, it includes some of the best-preserved and richest pages in the entire history of religious literature. In 793 the monastery was sacked by the Vikings and most of the monks slain, but the treasured Gospels were saved for posterity.

Today the monastery and the priory that succeeded it are mainly ruins, but the walls and west front of the Norman church

Lindisfarne

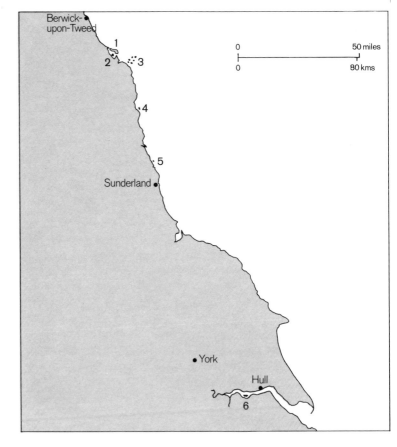

The East Coast of
England

1 *Lindisfarne*
2 *St Cuthbert's*
   Island
3 *The Farne*
   Islands:
   Megstones
   Crumstones
   Knivestone
   Longstone
   Big Harcar
   The Wamses
   Brownsman
   Staple Island
   Farne Island
4 *Coquet Island*
5 *St Mary's*
6 *Read's Island*

still stand impressively, as they did in 1830 when Turner came to paint them. Even today, pilgrims, as many as two thousand at a time, cross to the island from the mainland to worship at the parish church of St Mary which dates from the thirteenth century. Of one such pilgrimage to Lindisfarne, Sir Walter Scott wrote:

> With the flow and ebb its style
> Varies from continent to isle,
> Dry shod o'er sands twice every day,
> The pilgrims to the shrine find way;
> Twice every day the waves efface
> Of staves and sandal'd feet the trace.

Lindisfarne today even has a cottage industry with religious connections: Lindisfarne Liqueur, supposedly made on the basis of recipes used by monks of old, is produced there. Otherwise, the main income of the islanders comes from the tourist trade.

There are many fables and superstitions relating to life on the island, some undoubtedly retained in order to assist with that

222

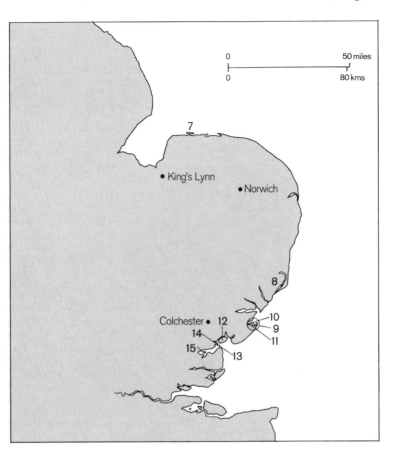

7   Scolt Head
8   Havergate
9   Hamford Water
     Islands
     (including
     Havergate)
10 Horsey
11 Skipper's Island
12 Mersea Island
13 Cobmarsh
14 Sunken Island
15 Osea

tourist trade. These include one relating to the famous Petting Stone, close to the church, over which brides have to jump to ensure a happy marriage. One modern phenomenon is that a community of under two hundred is served by no less than four public houses.

Lindisfarne has been threatened by invaders throughout the ages and in the sixteenth century it was a stronghold against the Scots. More recently, during the Second World War, it became an RAF training base, though post-war attempts to retain it as such for use by the Ministry of Defence were strongly defeated. On the south-east of the island is the dramatic castle of Lindisfarne which is sited on the top of a high conical rock overlooking the harbour. Dating from around the year 1550, it was briefly seized by the Stuarts in 1715 but after 1819 it fell into disuse. Edward Hudson, the founder of *Country Life*, bought it in 1902 and found it in very poor condition. He had it extensively refurbished by Lutyens, the man who built New Delhi for the British Raj, and now it is a charming miniature castle that has been described as

223

having 'romance without period'. The castle and much of the land round about it is now owned by the National Trust.

St Cuthbert's Island

Near the harbour, some two hundred yards (200m) from the shore, is a flat grassy islet known as St Cuthbert's Island, on which ruins of a retreat said to have been used by the saint are visible. It is here that the legend of St Cuthbert's beads – fossilised bones, the joints of encrinites (otherwise called 'stone lilies') which are found here – has its place.

> St Cuthbert sits and toils to frame
> The sea-born beads that bear his name.

The Farne Islands

While the west coast of the United Kingdom has by far the majority of the most spectacular and interesting of the islands with which this book is concerned, a compelling exception is the group of barren, treeless islands known as the Farne Islands which lie off the northern coast of Northumberland. There are

The Megstones
The Crumstones

two main clusters of them: the so-called Megstones lying to the west and the Crumstones to the east, around thirty islands in all. Some of these are only visible at low tide. The whole group were bought for the National Trust by public subscription in the year

1925. They now constitute one of the most important bird reserves in the east of the British Isles. As a result, special permission is needed before visitors can land on them.

The Farnes are an extremely dramatic group, with high cliffs on the south and west, all deeply lined and scarred, and white with the sediment of the teeming bird life that haunts the islands. Particularly common are shag, fulmar and petrel, and the eider, or St Cuthbert's, duck. There is also a large grey-seal colony which has had such a massive population explosion over recent years that there are frequent and strong demands for culling.

Taking these islands in turn and moving from the north inwards in a south-westerly direction, we reach first the most remote of the islands, Knivestone. This is a low-tide island and is particularly renowned for the number of shipwrecks it has caused over the centuries. Next to it is the island of Longstone, where the heroine Grace Darling lived with her lighthouse-keeper father. In September of the year 1838 she and her father rowed out to a ship that was in danger of being wrecked on a rock, called Big Harcar,

(Opposite) *The so-called Ship Room in the reconstructed Lindisfarne Castle.*

(Below) *Aerial view of the National Trust owned Farne Islands off the Northumberland coast.*

Knivestone

Longstone

Big Harcar

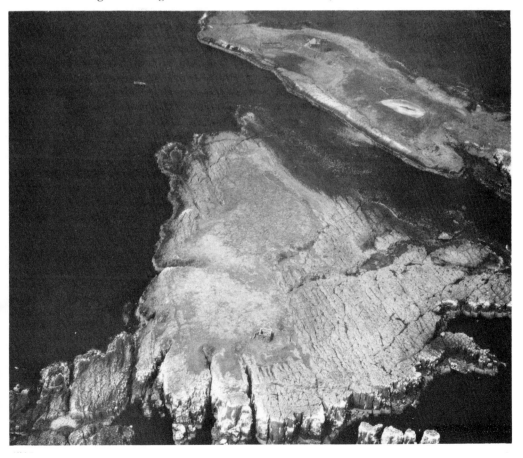

Cliffs known as the Pinnacles, on Staple Island in the Farnes.

a mile and a half away. Despite the fierce gales, they rescued a number of people from the wreck and Grace Darling herself became a national folk heroine, with many stories, plays and songs written about her. There are in fact two Harcar islands, which are today known as major breeding grounds for cormorants. Passing two further rocky islands called the Wamses, the next substantial piece of land we come to is the seven acres (3ha) of Brownsman, on which are two ruined lighthouses, and which carries a nature observatory, manned only during the summer.

The Wamses

Brownsman

Staple Island

Further in towards the mainland is Staple Island, which is major seal-breeding ground. Its cliffs are a remarkable sight at certain seasons of the year, when they are a teeming mass of seabirds.

Farne Island

Some two and a half miles off the Northumberland coast, south-east of the Megstone group of islands, lies Farne Island itself, which, at sixteen acres (6ha), is the largest of all the Farne Islands. It is the only one with enough soil to allow for any proper vegetation. St Cuthbert made his extremely austere retreat here from Lindisfarne in the seventh century. He lived in a primitive cell, a dedication to the hereafter which, with the chapel dating

226

from 1370 which marks the spot (also containing a memorial to Grace Darling), has attracted many pilgrims to the Farnes throughout the ages. It is a dramatic little island which rises clear tỏ a height of sixty feet (18m). On it is the Inner Farne Light, a major warning to shipping on that part of the coast. The lighthouse's predecessor was a tower of grey stone which still stands; on top of it a fire used to be lit in times of bad weather. As poor visibility and storms are far from uncommon there, the system must have been demanding in terms of fuel supply, which would have to have been ferried to the island to supplement what driftwood landed on the otherwise barren shores.

Coquet Island

One mile off the Northumberland coast, beyond the expanse of Alnmouth Bay and at the mouth of the river of the same name, is Coquet Island, a flat, grass-coated island which, geologically, is interesting in that its foundations are mainly of coal. It is a bleak and barren little place of some sixteen acres (6ha) and is favoured by the eider duck. Its lighthouse is the only other distinguishing feature. Eighty foot (24m) high, it was built in 1841; the remains of a chapel and a priest's cell are incorporated into the lighthouse-keeper's cottage.

Coquet's past was of certain interest; it had inhabitants in Roman times and, as with so many of the other islands around the British Isles, there are traces of there having been a small monastery, dating from the seventh century, which St Cuthbert is reputed to have had within his bishopric. The island is named after and was the setting for the self-imposed exile of one St Henry of Coquet, a Danish nobleman who, acting as the result of a vision he had, became a hermit there rather than enter into an arranged marriage. Growing his own food on the island, he is said to have performed miracles and died there alone in January 1127. A monk on the island, living in a cell that was part of Tynemouth Priory, heard the saint's bell ringing. On arriving at his colleague's hermitage, he found Henry already dead, with a candle beside him and one hand still clutching the bell rope.

St Mary's

Half a mile off Whitley Bay in Northumberland is St Mary's, also known as Bait Island, which is linked to the mainland by a causeway at low tide. Almost all its surface area is taken up by the tall white lighthouse and the two adjacent houses maintained by Trinity House. There was once a chapel on the island and there was also a cemetery whose main clients were drowned or plague-stricken sailors. While the lighthouse was being built, the inhabitants of the cemetery had to go, and the remains were reinterred on the mainland. The name St Mary's comes probably from the light which was kept burning in the chapel as an early form of lighthouse, to warn passing ships of the dangers of the island's rocks. It is an attractive, rocky island with a few tiny beaches.

Read's Island

East of the mouth of the river Humber is Read's Island, which has marginal qualifications for an entry in this book, since it is no more than a silted and come-up-in-the-world sandbank. According to one story, it built itself up round the wreck of a French cargo boat early in the last century; now grass-covered, it is used for sheep-grazing and is a valuable wildlife sanctuary. The island is privately owned and there is no public access to it.

Scolt Head

On the most northerly part of the coast of Norfolk, separated from the mainland by a narrow silted channel, lies the four-mile-long by half a mile wide island of Scolt Head, which shelters the small natural harbour of Brancaster Staithe, making the area a popular sailing centre. It is a flat, marshy and shingle-ridged island with dunes and sandflats, and there is no regular ferry to it. The seaward coast with its long sand beach is, when seen from the air, curved gracefully like some medieval bow. Bathing can be dangerous due to strong tidal currents.

There is a wide range of bird life on its sand dunes, and it is a happy hunting ground for wildfowlers. Hundreds of different types of birds, including sandwich terns, redshanks and arctic skuas, have been seen on the island. Scolt Head has, as one can see by comparing its form with old charts, changed in shape considerably over the decades, the sand dunes shifting visibly from year to year. However, the vegetation, which includes the hardier strains of sea grass, is beginning to compact the island into a more stable mass. During the war it was an artillery range. Now most of it, and the whole area around, is under the care of the National Trust, who bought it in 1923 with funds raised by local naturalists. The eastern tip of the island is owned by the Norfolk Naturalists' Trust.

Havergate

The Inner Farne light.

In the middle of the river Ore, in Suffolk, is the lonely and uninhabited island of Havergate, a nature reserve and bird

228

sanctuary since 1947, noted as the breeding ground for that graceful wader, the avocet, which for many years had not been seen in Britain. These birds can, with permission, be studied from special hides provided by the Royal Society for the Protection of Birds, which has a warden on Havergate. The northern tip of the island relates to another type of bird – Cuckold's Point.

Hamford Water Islands

On the Essex coast by Stone Point and two miles from Walton on the Naze lie a group of more than ten low-lying islands, the Hamford Water Islands. They are separated by a maze of winding channels and reed-banked streams. One or two of them have farmhouses on them and there is some good grazing among the **Horsey** marshland. The largest of the group is called Horsey Island (Arab stallions are bred on a farm here). The whole area, marshland, islands and creeks, has been designated a site of special scientific interest by the Nature Conservancy Council. Skipper's Island, which is a nature reserve administered by the Essex Naturalists' **Skipper's Island** Trust, is part of the reserve. Skipper's Island consists of clay, covered in rough pasture, and scrub. The more low-lying land on this and on the other islands reverts from time to time to salt-marsh, as the sea walls are breached. The inner sea wall round Skipper's Island has been repaired, and walks and firebreaks have now been forced through the undergrowth of bush and bramble that once totally dominated it.

Mersea Islands

Mersea Island The main Mersea Island, a low hump five miles long and two across, lies off the Essex coast to the south-west of Brightlingsea. It is no longer a real island, since it is connected to the mainland by a permanent road. It is well populated. Its two smaller com-**Cobmarsh** panions, Cobmarsh, a quarter of a mile from West Mersea, and **Sunken Island** Sunken Island, in the Salcott Channel west of Cobmarsh, are, however, only accessible by boat. The whole area is a famous yachting centre. Cobmarsh has traces of a medieval fort while Sunken Island is mainly a bird sanctuary. The islands are a mix of saltmarsh and mudflat, half land and half water.

Osea

Finally in this book is the island of Osea, in the Blackwater Estuary about three and a half miles from Maldon. Surrounded by flats of mud and sand, and connected to the north bank by a mile-long causeway at low water, it is all privately owned, and some would argue that it hardly deserves being classified as an island at all. Well known as a yachting centre, it now has over 300 acres (120ha) of good agricultural land on it. Defoe wrote about it, saying it was well known for its wildfowl in his day too, and it was mentioned in the Domesday Book as home for a fisherman and three serfs 'and pasture for sixty sheep'. Around here are ancient saltpans which were used in Roman times. At one stage at the beginning of this century Osea was owned by a temperance fanatic (a Mr Charrington of the brewing family) who was intent on establishing a community where no alcoholic drink would be permitted. A convalescent home on the island was picturesquely advertised as an 'inebriates' retreat', conveniently and healthily surrounded by the sea, 'an ideal home for Ladies and Gentlemen suffering from the baneful effects of Alcohol and Narcotics ... lighted throughout with Acetylene gas, and replete with every comfort'. Happily, the scheme was abandoned.

Afterthought

These are a few hundred of the thousands of islands that form an intrinsic part of the British national archipelago. Among those not listed and described are many anonymous ones that may, one day, prove to have an important contribution to make to our historic and natural heritage. Some of those, which lack even a name and which are seldom if ever visited by man, may at a later, more informed date reveal evidence of a rich past inhabitation and a new wealth of interest to natural historians. After all, the mainlanders' knowledge of the majority of Britain's offshore islands is still proportionately scanty and slight. Dr Johnson, after his celebrated tour, pointed out that though the British had circumnavigated and explored the globe, they often knew little of the geography or social conditions of what was on their own doorstep. This remains true today.

Of all the signs for the future of the majority of these islands, the question of depopulation is one of the most telling and inevitable. This problem is still to the forefront since the root causes of it continue, explaining to us something fundamental about island ways of life. The sense of isolation (the root of that word is, after all, the same as for the word 'island') makes social as much as economic reasons predominate in this continuing trend; the decision to leave, when it comes, is usually to do with an awareness of the lack of social benefits which exist elsewhere. It is not so much isolation by distance that matters, as isolation from material prosperity and the chance to gain it, heightened by the scene of others leaving from around one in order to seek it.

The poet Cowper expressed the dilemma of islanders in the words he attributed to the original of Robinson Crusoe in his poem 'Verses Supposed to be Written by Alexander Selkirk'. It begins well:

I am monarch of all I survey,
My right there is none to dispute;

From the centre all round to the sea
I am lord of the fowl and the brute.

but it ends with the bitter cry of a man alone:

Oh, solitude! where are the charms
That sages have seen in thy face?
Better dwell in the midst of alarms,
Than reign in this horrible place.

There is considerable evidence to prove that there is a cut-off or critical point for any island population. In other words, if the number of inhabitants drops below a certain minimum figure (as in any community, but emphasised by the geographical nature of an island), the social infrastructure of modern life becomes difficult to support. This will vary of course, in terms of the degree of isolation, the relative prosperity and the determination of the inhabitants. Medical services and modern communications (such as a post office) must generally be justified by numbers, and by a good age balance in the community, and there is a point where local authorities, quite apart from commercial interests, are forced, for example, to stop subsidising a ferry service or to close a school.

The problem is exaggerated by the fact that those who emigrate voluntarily are often the younger, the fitter, the more enterprising, the more adventurous. They leave behind (as a harsh yet undisputed reality) the aged and less fit, both socially and economically. But there are also hopeful signs: a growing awareness by central and local government of the need and their duty to look after remote and isolated small communities everywhere. And then there is rebirth – oil, tourism and the return of the native, determined to make his island thrive, determined to return to where there are other qualities of life– peace, nature and contentment.

For islands will continue to keep their fascination for man, not only for the reasons given elsewhere in this book, but also on more subtle and emotional grounds. One of these is the implicit reciprocal to that most famous of all quotations about islands – that by John Donne: 'No man is an Island, entire of itself; every man is a piece of the Continent, a part of the main.' This is a self-evident truth. Yet Donne would, equally, have argued that each and every one of us has, to some extent, secret 'island' qualities in our make-up: we are all individual, with separate characteristics, faults and qualities, even though, inevitably, we share common aspects of personal geography, heredity and environment. For that very reason of differentness yet of community, islands will offer an alternative way of life and living that will be envied and sought after by those who live elsewhere.

Additional Islands

The following islands are listed for the record. No substantial information has been found on them, or they are disbarred for other reasons from the text.

England

Flory Island North Devon. Also known as Black Humphrey's Rock (Humphrey was a local smuggler and wrecker.)

Fowley Island In the Swale, south of the Isle of Sheppey.

Hayling Island By Portsmouth. Permanently connected to the mainland.

Medway Islands Burntwick Island, etc., in the River Medway.

Northey Island River Blackwater. Inland from Osea Island.

Purbeck, Isle of Not an island, but a peninsula in Dorset.

Northern Ireland

Bird Island East of the Ards Peninsula.

Scotland

Carna Uninhabited island at entrance of Loch Sunart.

Danna Island Not an island but a peninsula between Loch Sween and the Sound of Jura.

Fladday/Flodday/Floday There are six or seven islands with these names in the Inner and Outer Hebrides.

Innis Bheag At the entrance to the Dornoch Firth

Innis Mhor At the entrance to the Dornoch Firth.

Insh Island Uninhabited island in the Firth of Lorn, one mile west of Seil.

Kishorn Island In Loch Kishorn, near the oil-rig construction site.

Longay Between Scalpay and the Crowlin Islands to the east of Skye.

Nave Island Uninhabited island off the north-west coast of Islay.

Oronsay Uninhabited island at entrance to Loch Sunart.

Wales

Barry Island Not a proper island. Part of the docks of Barry in South Glamorgan.

Dee Island At mouth of River Dee near Hilbre Point.

Sully Island Small tidal island near Sully in South Glamorgan. Has remains of fort on it.

A Note on Island Wildlife

by Patrick Roper

Most naturalists are fascinated by islands, partly because they represent a kind of outdoor laboratory with a conveniently defined boundary. Often they have unique species or subspecies of plants and animals and, because of their isolation, they usually provide a sanctuary for wildlife of a kind that has become rare on the mainland. Britain's offshore islands have all of these elements and, in terms of conservation, are a wonderful asset in our over-populated, industrialised country. Many islands are now carefully preserved and managed as nature reserves at local or national level and two of these reserves are of international importance, putting them on a par with some of the remaining wilderness areas of the world. These two are the Grogarry Lochs on South Uist and the St Kilda archipelago, both of which have the resounding designation of UNESCO Biosphere Reserves.

The biology of any of our islands could occupy a whole book in itself. For the purposes of this chapter I have, however, concentrated on the unique aspects of island life; on the things that either cannot be seen, or are only rarely seen, on the mainland. In some senses this might give a slightly false impression as the more commonplace is usually represented on our islands and often in a particularly impressive way. Few, perhaps, would imagine that the banks of Primroses on Barra in the Outer Hebrides are arguably the finest displays of this delightful flower anywhere in the kingdom.

Mammals

Our largest island animal is the Red Deer, found on fifteen of the islands off the west coast of Scotland from the Outer Hebrides to Arran. The animals on Rhum have been intensively studied and a good deal of our knowledge of the habits and behaviour of the species is derived from the observations made here over many years. Pioneer work on Red Deer was done on Jura by Henry Evans in the last century.

Red Deer are good swimmers, as debunkers of the Loch Ness Monster argument have frequently pointed out, and they probably arrived on most islands by water and under their own steam. Being fairly long-lived, the high chance of a member of the opposite sex reaching the same island by a similar route would have ensured that a breeding population was established. Stating the facts like that, however, somehow seems to demean the extraordinary will to survive shown by a hind or stag driven into the sea by wolves, or maybe human hunters, on the west coast of Scotland, finally to land on the Outer Hebrides after who knows how many hours or days struggling alone through the rough and icy currents of the Minches.

Our other native deer, the small and nimble Roe, is found only on Bute, Islay and Seil, but several other species have been introduced, both on the mainland and on offshore islands. The Fallow Deer brought to Britain from the Mediterranean, probably during Roman times, is established on Islay, Mull and Scarba. The somewhat similar Japanese Sika Deer from eastern Asia occurs on Lundy and, within the last decade, tiny Muntjac Deer from China – they bark like dogs as well as looking slightly like them from a distance – have been taken to Steep Holm.

Rather few of the predatory animals from the mainland are found on offshore islands and the absence of foxes, badgers, wild cats and weasels has undoubtedly helped isolated populations of mice, voles and shrews. Because they breed quickly, evolution among small animals takes place at a relatively fast rate and many of our island rodents have distinctive characteristics. At the turn of the century this sent British mammalogists into a frenzy of naming, and innumerable island species and subspecies were described, commemorating the men who named them just as much as the mice. Conferring instant rarity on an animal by calling it the Guernsey Vole or St Kilda Mouse undoubtedly adds a little more glamour both to zoology and the study of islands, but most of these animals are now considered to be forms of the mainland stock that have evolved slightly away from their nearest neighbours through many generations in isolation.

The story of island mice is, however, a fascinating one as it now seems evident that the majority were introduced by humans, often in the distant past. Until the nineteen-seventies it was thought that natural events since the ice age receded after the last glaciation accounted for the peculiar patterns of distribution that put the Common Vole on Guernsey and Orkney but not on the mainland, European species of shrew on the Scilly Isles and the Channel Islands, and different strains of Wood Mice on many islands off north-west Scotland. Various land bridges were postulated and internecine strife between different species so that they died out in one place but not in another.

In proposing these elaborate and ingenious hypotheses, the earlier naturalists were unaware of an important genetic phenomenon without which the argument for the introduction of these mice, etc., to islands by humans is difficult to justify. This key factor is broadly as follows: if an island has no mice (shrews or voles) of a given species and some are introduced they will, provided conditions are suitable for survival at all, breed until the population reaches a level that is broadly sustainable. Since this population originated from one introduction the characteristics of every individual will be genetically derived from the first arrivals and, over many generations, the exigencies of life on the island in question may favour the development of some distinctive modifications. So far so good; but what happens if further introductions of the same species are made? Recent work has shown that nothing will happen: the new arrivals may breed with the existing population, but the smaller group will quite quickly lose any characteristics it may possess to the larger. In other words, the first arrivals on any small island will retain their original characteristics regardless of later introductions.

The fascinating story of British island mice has been elaborated, using this knowledge, by Professor R. J. Berry in his book *Inheritance and Natural History* (Collins, London, 1977). It started on Skokholm Island where he studied the House Mice that lived in the cliffs and was able to show that they most nearly resembled examples from the Welsh mainland some distance from the point closest to Skokholm. It could then be shown that these mice had been introduced with fodder for the island animals in the last century. Further work led Berry to the conclusion that Hebridean mice had been brought down by the Vikings in the Dark Ages. From initial landings on a few of the islands, they had later been spread to others and created many of the so-called subspecies.

The story of the voles was even more dramatic. The Common Vole is abundant on the Continent, but in Britain occurs only on Guernsey and Orkney, as subspecies of the typical European stock. The Guernsey Vole shows a clear correlation with its French neighbours and an introduction from France seems reasonable. But what about Orkney? Bones of the Orkney Vole have been found deeply buried at the prehistoric site of Skara Brae and Orkney Voles most closely resemble European examples from Yugoslavia. The clear inference is that these little creatures travelled in the boats of the Skara Brae people when they made their long migration from the eastern Mediterranean to the north.

238

Berry's findings can apply to any animal as far as is known, and the newer genetic theories will enable us to learn a good deal about early human migration. Apart from anything else, this reinforces a point about conservation – twenty years ago it could not have been known that the Orkney Vole or Skokholm House Mouse could be highly relevant to the study of human migration and some may have been tempted to say that their continued survival could have no bearing on human affairs.

As for the mice themselves, the most widespread on offshore islands is the Wood Mouse, *Apodemus sylvaticus*, which, thanks to transport provided by the Viking longboats, flourishes on places as remote as Foula, St Kilda and Fair Isle. The House Mouse also reached St Kilda, probably via the Vikings, where it was isolated long enough to form a subspecies, *Mus musculus muralis*. Unfortunately it became extinct after the St Kilda people left in 1930: it seems that it simply could not compete with the local Wood Mice that moved into the abandoned houses. The St Kilda House Mouse was larger and paler than its mainland relatives.

The voles that live on Guernsey and Orkney are both subspecies of the so-called Common Vole, *Microtus arvalis*, whose typical form does not occur in Britain at all – it is a Continental creature. The Guernsey Vole has been named *Microtus arvalis sarnius*, while in Orkney two subspecies have been described, the typical *M. arvalis orcadensis* and the paler Sanday Orkney Vole, *M. arvalis sandayensis*, which is confined to Sanday and Westray. Hitching a ride with the Skara Brae people was a bold move for these little creatures, but life on Orkney is far from a bed of roses as the voles make excellent eating for Hen Harriers and Short-eared Owls. If the Snowy Owls move south from Shetland, the voles will no doubt have to devote more practice to their running.

The Field Vole, *Microtus agrestis*, and the Bank Vole, *Clethrionomys glareolus*, are both common on the mainland. The first has reached many islands. On Islay, Field Voles have much darker fur on their undersides and are considered a good subspecies under the name of *M. agrestis macgillivrayi*. The Bank Vole has reached nine offshore islands and evolved distinctive races on Raasay and Jersey. On Skomer it is very much heavier and more sluggish than its mainland neighbours and has been accorded subspecific rank as the Skomer Vole, *C. glareolus skomerensis*.

Shrews are not closely related to mice but, because they are similar in size to mice and voles and occupy a similar position in the ecosystem of any given place, they are conveniently considered under the same heading. Of greatest interest so far as islands are concerned are the White-toothed Shrews (thus named because the commoner types of shrew have red-tipped teeth).

These predominantly western and southern European species have just managed to reach, and survive in, our most benign climates – those of the Isles of Scilly and the Channel Islands – perhaps naturally, more probably as very early introductions. In the Channel Islands both the Greater and Lesser White-toothed Shrews are found, but not on the same islands. The Greater White-toothed, *Crocidura russula*, occurs on Alderney, Guernsey and Herm, while the Lesser White-toothed, *Crocidura suaveolens*, favours Jersey and Sark and is also found on the Scilly Isles. On the Continent *C. russula* is known as the House Shrew because it seems to enjoy living near buildings. The Guernsey Greater White-tooths were once given subspecific status as *C. russula peta*, while the smaller species in its Scilly form was named *C. suaveolens cassiteridum*, but these taxonomic distinctions have now been withdrawn.

The Common Shrew is abundant on the British mainland and is represented in Jersey by the subspecies *Sorex araneus fretalis*, which has a blunter snout than normal, while a second sub-species, *Sorex araneus granti*, with greyer flanks than the mainland animals, occurs on Islay. Like the Water Vole, the Water Shrew, *Neomys fodiens*, seems less of a traveller than some of its relatives, but it does have an insular form on southern Shuna with the fur on its underparts of a pale grey colour.

Neither of our two species of British rat, the Black or Ship Rat, *Rattus rattus*, and the Brown Rat, *Rattus norvegicus*, are native animals, but they have been spread far and wide through mercantile activity and can wreak havoc among wildlife as well as being a major pest to humans. The Black Rat, the one that brought the Plague, cannot compete with the Brown and is now quite rare. It still occurs on Alderney, Sark, Lundy, the Shiants and Westray, but its future must be in some doubt. The Brown Rat is one of the world's greatest survivors and is firmly entrenched on too many of our offshore islands.

Another introduction that has proved more of a nuisance than an asset is the Grey Squirrel, *Sciurus carolinensis*. As well as damaging trees, the Grey was once thought to have driven out the more attractive Red Squirrel, which has suffered a severe decline over the last century. It now seems, however, that the Reds are dying from a flu-like disease and Greys simply fill up the vacated territory. Whether or not it is because of lack of disease or competition from a stronger species, Red Squirrels have survived in the south much more successfully on offshore islands. Their tree-top antics can still be enjoyed on the Isle of Wight, Brownsea Island and Jersey.

The tiny Scilly Islands shrew.

One of the few British carnivores that has successfully invaded a number of offshore islands is the Stoat, *Mustela erminea*. On Jura

240

and Islay, stoats have slightly oddly shaped heads and small ears. This minor distinction has led to their being rather dubiously awarded subspecific status under the name *Mustela erminea ricinae*.

With its special stoats and subspecies of shrew and vole, Islay has a lot of interest so far as mammals are concerned. Another distinction of the island is that its Mountain Hares are of the Irish rather than the Scottish race, which only gets as far south as Jura.

Apart from whales and dolphins, three of our native mammals are quite at home in the sea and in consequence are regular visitors to offshore islands. Otters have reached most Hebridean and many other islands, and the Grey and the less common Common Seal have their breeding strongholds on our offshore islands, particularly in the west. Grey Seals prefer rocky coasts with cliffs and caves, while the Common Seal favours gently shelving beaches and is seen in northern shallows and estuaries.

Despite the fact that they can fly, bats, generally speaking, are not great visitors to islands. Bat-lovers will be pleased to note, however, that the only British record of the central European Parti-coloured Bat, *Vespertilio murinus*, is from Shetland.

All the mammals considered so far have either reached the offshore islands under their own steam or have been unwittingly introduced through human activity. There are, however, several species whose introduction has been more deliberate, although usually a very mixed blessing.

Wild Goats (i.e. domesticated goats that have escaped) are found on several Hebridean islands, on Anglesey, Skokholm, Man, Lundy and Rathlin. Many of these are relatively recent arrivals, but in the Hebrides there are herds of white animals that are thought to be descended from goats brought by the Vikings, although on Cara, in Strathclyde, local legend has it that the stock originated from animals that came ashore from a wrecked Armada galleon.

The fascinating Soay Sheep are justly famed as a Bronze-Age or Viking survival on the St Kilda group, but less well known are the Loghtan Sheep from the Isle of Man, not dissimilar to the Soays, and also of ancient stock. Small flocks are carefully conserved at Cregneish and on the Calf of Man. Like that of the Soay Sheep, the tough Loghtan wool is a brownish colour, but unlike Soay rams, many of the Loghtan ones have two pairs of horns, making them look particularly fierce.

Rabbits have been introduced to innumerable islands (one notable exception being Tiree, which seems never to have had any), often as a source of food in the first instance. In fact the first records of rabbits in Britain were from Scilly, Lundy and the Isle of White in the twelfth century, while on the mainland bones

found in kitchen middens in Essex may have originated from warrens deliberately set up on some of the coastal islands. It seems that those responsible for the introduction of the animal were aware of its rapid breeding and destructive capacities and therefore confined the rabbits to islands, where they would also receive less attention from predators. Innumerable offshore islands have, at one time or another, been used for rabbit-breeding, and the relative newness of the conservation movement is highlighted by the fact that rabbits were deliberately established on Rathlin Island in 1911 – a step that would never be contemplated today. Myxomatosis has reduced their numbers in some places, but they are still one of the most active (i.e. destructive) biotic agents in Britain, whole landscapes being altered by their attentions.

Usually rabbits cause nothing but destruction; in one or two places, though, their presence has actually helped conserve rare plants. In the Channel Islands, for instance, some of the tiny

The Atlantic or Grey seal with its calf (Halichoerus grypus).

243

coastal plants with a very restricted range soon get crowded out by coarse grasses if rabbit grazing ceases (as it did after myxomatosis).

In order to catch renegade rabbits man has made use of ferrets from time immemorial and, not surprisingly, these have occasionally escaped on offshore islands and settled down to a life of peace and plenty. Thriving colonies of Polecat Ferrets are known from the Isle of Man, Mull, Lewis, Arran and Bute. On Arran mink have also escaped to join the ferrets, while the Monach Isles have a colony of feral cats ('feral' meaning animals that were formerly domestic but are now living wild).

The most recent mammalian introduction to our offshore islands is the Mongolian Gerbil, *Meriones unguiculatus,* which has established itself since 1973 near Fishbourne on the Isle of Wight.

A discussion of island mammals inevitably leads one to speculate about human parallels. It must immediately be pointed out that Britain's offshore islands do not have any special races resident upon them: all our islanders are, so far as anthropologists can tell, of straightforward Indo-European stock, like the rest of us in Britain, although somewhat more Celtic or more Norse and so on in different places. We do not have the equivalents of the Guanches, a fair-haired, blue-eyed people exterminated by the Spaniards in the Canary Islands, or of the Tasmanians, a race quite unlike the Australian aborigines, exterminated by ourselves in the last century, or the hairy Ainu who still survive in small numbers on Hokkaido and a few other north Japanese islands. Any differences among our island people stem largely from historic and cultural factors coupled with small, inbreeding populations possessed of what, for lack of a better term, might be called an 'island psychology' that, in some ways, makes them sometimes seem different.

Many islands have been populated, abandoned and populated again, by different people down the centuries. Unless they were forced to go there one must, to some extent, consider this tendency as a romantic aberration of a few members of a larger community. What on earth could have taken folk willingly out to remote St Kilda when the whole of Scotland was covered in game-rich forest and contained a population of only a few thousand souls at the very most? Why were the Scillies abandoned, then repopulated? Why did a handful of Norman French choose to live on storm-girt Alderney rather than the fat pastures of the French mainland?

In modern society people are still doing this sort of thing – looking for places where they are physically separated from social pressures with which they feel they cannot cope. An island can represent the ideal community, separated by sea, virtually self-

governing but, most of all, relatively less accessible to 'cultural pollution' from the surrounding world. It is simply twentieth-century arrogance to assume that the founders of early communities on our remoter islands arrived there by some unhappy accident: in all probability the communities were started by people who, in their day, felt that the pressures of modern society and the moral decay among their children demanded some radical, Utopian solution. And if these various people were not quite like the others they left behind to battle it out on the mainland, that is not really very surprising.

Isolated communities are perpetually bedevilled by the problem of emigration. Essentially this means that the most talented, outward-looking members leave and the resident population suffers the consequences. Those that remain draw closer together, but tend to suffer a loss of confidence which can, and has, led eventually to the abandonment of their islands altogether. It happened on St Kilda, on the Blaskets off the west coast of Ireland, and to the first Viking community on Greenland. It explains the mounds and grass-covered humps of old settlements on all sorts of remote places. Not poverty, just the collapse of an ideal that was, sadly, going to be difficult to sustain

Soay Sheep — a Viking or Bronze Age survival found on St Kilda.

245

from the start, but an ideal that depended upon leaders of considerable intellectual integrity who could hold a community together during their own lifetime, and often substantially beyond that.

Despite such gloomy theorising, the romantic can still look for insular distinctions in Britain. The Norse element extends from the Orkneys and Shetlands down both the east and west coast, as many place names testify. Indeed, the indigenous population of the Hebrides would, presumably, be mainly composed of Viking, Celtic and Pictish elements. The Celts always constituted a culture rather than a distinctive race and ranged from the tall and fair to the short and dark. The origins of the Picts are mysterious, but they probably contained strong elements of the Bronze-Age people.

The Hebrides would originally have been colonised by the Picts or an earlier race. From about AD 500 Irish Celts started moving northwards and later the Vikings came south. The clash of cultures produced the Hebrideans of today, but it was the Irish Celtic language that prevailed. Indeed, it is curious that, of all the places conquered or colonised by the Vikings, only islands that they found uninhabited, like Iceland, have retained a Scandinavian language.

Leaving aside known historical fact, there are some entertaining speculations around, most of which are probably ill-founded or apocryphal. A number of guidebooks claim, for instance, that the villagers on Lindisfarne speak a dialect close to the Danish language (when I was there it sounded little different from any other 'Geordie' dialect); the people of Coningsburgh, near Lerwick in the Shetlands, are reputedly darker and quicker tempered than their neighbours and this has been ascribed to the shipwreck of a galleon of the Spanish Armada – one of many 'the Spanish navy was here' stories which can be garnered from around our coasts.

Amphibians and Reptiles

Among the very limited number of amphibians and reptiles resident in the British Isles, three are confined to the Channel Islands. The Agile Frog, *Rana dalmatina* – a good jumper on account of its particularly long legs – occurs on Jersey, Guernsey and Sark, the marbled brown and greenish-grey Common Wall Lizard, *Podarcis muralis*, only on cliffs in Jersey, and the brilliant emerald Green Lizard, *Lacerta viridis*, on this island and Guernsey also. Introduced examples of the Wall Lizard also flourish on the Isle of Wight and the same island has a colony of African Clawed Toads, *Xenopus laevis*; some were released at Brook in 1967.

Birds

Although far fewer birds breed on offshore islands than on the mainland – St Kilda has twenty-five species whereas central Scotland at the same latitude has sixty-five – there are special features about the islands that make ornithologists devote large amounts of effort to wondering how to get to some of the more remote. Remoteness does, of course, mean that the birds are relatively free from interferences, but islands are also important staging posts for migrants and, in some instances, have tiny populations of resident subspecies that are unique.

The ornithological glory of Britain's offshore islands is its sea-birds and the species that most symbolises this magnificent natural asset is the Gannet. Britain is the stronghold of this streamlined, creamy-coloured fishing bird that has only twenty-three breeding colonies in the world. The scientific name for the Gannet, *Sula bassana*, commemorates the Bass Rock where six thousand pairs breed today. Ten times as many are found on Boreray, part of the St Kilda group, and other noteworthy breeding grounds include Grassholme and Ailsa Craig. The Gannet has increased in numbers during the last century, probably as a result of its decline as an item of food (the people from Ness, in the Outer Hebrides, who take a regular harvest of birds from remote Sula Sgeir, are perhaps the only Gannet-hunters left), and it started colonising the Channel Islands only during the Second World War when some of the breeding pairs arrived on the small islands near Alderney where they have increased considerably.

Among gulls, Britain can boast Europe's largest ground-breeding colony of Lesser Black-backed Gulls and Herring Gulls on Walney Island, while no fewer than five species of gull breed on Horse Island, Strathclyde. Important research into gulls is done at a research station specially devoted to their study on Steep Holm. A number of islands hold important breeding colonies of terns. Foulney and Scolt Head have the Common, Sandwich, Arctic and Little Terns, while the Farnes have the rare Roseate as well.

Wading birds abound wherever there are sands or mud flats. One of the most important stations for them in Britain is the Hilbre Islands in the Dee Estuary and many thousands can often be seen in the area. With the waders come the romantic skeins of wild geese from the north. The little, dark Brent Goose winters in numbers down the east coast, particularly at Lindisfarne, around Osea Island and, of course, at Foulness, to the consternation of airport builders. Pink-footed Geese are also found on the east coast – Read's Island in the Humber can have up to ten thousand pairs. On the west there are the White-fronted Geese that regularly appear on Stert Island, while in Scotland one sixth of the world's population of Barnacle Geese, some ten thousand birds, visit Islay every winter and the species also winters on Eilean nan Ròn, off Oronsay.

Among wild swans, highlights include the Bewick's that winter on Havergate Island and the Whooper Swans on Mull's Loch Buie and on the Farnes – the latter has the largest flock in England. Britain is rich in duck and some island specialities include the Eider, or St Cuthbert's Duck, not surprisingly associated with the Farnes, the famous retreat of St Cuthbert. Eider have their most southerly British breeding station on Walney Island, Cumbria. Havergate Island is renowned for its Pintail, while Stert Island is unique in being the moulting ground for some three thousand Shelduck every autumn.

Islands make superb breeding grounds for members of the auk family and these are found from Scilly, with its colonies of Razorbills and Guillemots, to the northern isles, where the Tytsie or Black Guillemot has its strongholds. The comical and endearing Puffin still occurs on many islands, some of which bear its name (obviously in Puffin Island, but less obviously in Lundy, which is simply the Norse word for this particular bird). Some islands are named after birds, but one bird is named after an island: the Manx Shearwater. Known to the Bretons as 'souls of the damned', these birds congregate on the ocean and wait until night has fallen before flying to their nesting burrows. Their eerie night-time calls account for the French name. Famous breeding grounds for the Manx Shearwater include the Welsh islands of Skokholm and Skomer. Little Storm Petrels, or Mother Carey's Chickens as they used to be called, also breed on Skokholm, but a visit has to be made to the remoter parts of the Outer Hebrides to see breeding colonies of the mysterious Leach's Petrel. The Flannan Isles are amongst the best places.

No account of island seabirds would be complete without mentioning the Great Skuas or the Red-necked Phalaropes that nest on Foula and Shetland respectively, or the wonderfully delicate and graceful Avocet, with its up-curved bill, that returned to breed on Havergate Island in 1947 after an absence of many years.

The magnitude of the seabird colonies and the wealth of unusual species tend to obscure the fact that our islands have a number of very interesting landlubbers among their avian fauna.

Birds of prey always inspire awe, and one can watch Golden Eagles soaring in the up-currents from the cliffs of Gribun on Mull, Peregrine Falcons with their high-speed dive on to prey on Rhum, and Hen Harriers casting about for the local voles on Orkney. Orkney also has good stocks of Britain's smallest hawk,

Puffins by their nesting burrows scattered across Skomer Island.

248

(Above) *The Manx shearwater* (Procellaria puffinus) *sometimes hauntingly known as the 'souls of the damned'.*

(Opposite) *The graceful Avocet that breeds nowadays on Havergate Island.*

the Merlin, and is the only place in the country where Kestrels nest on the ground. Shetland's ornithological treasure is the Snowy Owl, which recently bred on Fetlar, while at the other end of the country strange things are happening among Channel Island Barn Owls. Like the rest of Britain, the Channel Islands had only the serenely pallid form of the Barn Owl until 1951, when swarthy, darker forms typical on the Continent started moving into the islands. Light and dark seem to live alongside each other happily enough and a mixed marriage was reported from Sark in 1971.

The elegant black Chough with its scarlet bill is nowhere common but occurs on some of our island cliffs – on the Calf of Man and Ramsey, for instance. Scotland has only two breeding colonies – on Islay and Jura. Snipe are widespread, both on the mainland and on islands, and Tiree used to have the reputation of offering the best Snipe-shooting in Europe. One cannot help wondering if the absence of rabbits had somehow helped the

birds flourish. Snipe breed even on remote St Kilda, where they are of the Faroese subspecies, *Gallinago gallinago faroeensis,* as they are on Orkney and Shetland. Corncrakes, once widespread in Britain, now breed regularly mainly on Scottish islands and it is good to know that their strange rasping call can still be heard somewhere.

To be able to see a myriad of Gannets or Golden Eagles wheeling untroubled in an island breeze would be nirvana for most ornithologists, but our offshore islands have some very special birds which, while they do not necessarily have the glamour of larger species, have a special importance. These are the birds that are found nowhere else but on their particular island, like the St Kilda Wren. These élite groups of birds, fascinating in themselves, have a disproportionate ecological significance. Everyone knows that the Theory of Evolution would not have come down to us in precisely the way that it has had it not been for Charles Darwin's understanding that there was something very significant about the finches on the Galapagos Islands. The Galapagos are what is known by ecologists as 'oceanic islands' – small bits of land that have been isolated so long that they are a living laboratory of adaptation. In Britain we do not have such islands. Even remote St Kilda has flora and fauna little different from those of the mainland. Nevertheless, the process of becoming an oceanic island has started: at some time, for instance, Wrens moved (or were pushed) out to these islands and they have subsequently changed sufficiently to constitute a recognisable subspecies. Wrens are essentially woodland birds on the mainland. They move little; they have no *rapport* with the sea – it is simply something to be avoided. But, perhaps millennia ago, some Wrens arrived at St Kilda. Now they live on the cliffs, a few hundred pairs, singing their hearts out at the vast Atlantic.

Because their wild song is distinctive, because they are slightly larger and brighter than mainland Wrens, they have been given subspecific status, *Troglodytes troglodytes hirtensis.* So small is the population that they have an entry in the Red Data Book of threatened fauna (the only British creature with this dubious distinction), but they are not really threatened. So long as St Kilda remains a protected archipelago with the huge Atlantic indifferently beating against its rocks, the special Wrens should survive. Most of us will never go there, but I like to think that there is some value for all of us in knowing a bold and unique song is being belted out by little brown birds all the way to America. If they can survive, surely humanity, for all its dangerous bickering, can do the same.

In a way the St Kilda Wren sums up what most naturalists feel about islands: that here we have things rare and strange that should be protected at all costs – not necessarily for us, but for our children and our children's children, and in the final analysis, because they simply are as they are.

The St Kilda Wren always steals the thunder of the Fair Isle Wren, *T. t. fridariensis*, but there we have another bright-songed bird unique to this particular habitat. On most of the Outer Hebrides there are Hedge Sparrows, *Prunella modularis hebridium*, and Song Thrushes, *Turdus philomelos hebridensis*, which are distinct from the mainland populations. The Channel Islands have the Continental form of the Tree Creeper, *Certhia familiaris*, and small flocks of unique Starlings, *Sturnus vulgaris zetlandicus*, have been thriving for centuries on places as remote as northern Rona.

Introductions are fewer among birds than among animals, but Budgerigars, *Melopsittacus undulatus*, and Bobwhite Quails, *Colinus virginianus*, have recently been established in the wild on Tresco in the Isles of Scilly.

Insects and Other Invertebrates

As any self-respecting producer of wildlife programmes for television will tell you, insects do not have the same appeal as animals and birds – they are, perhaps, too alien and too closely associated with summer stings and bites. They do, nevertheless, have their island forms that contribute to our understanding of evolution and represent an area where there is a great deal to be added to our knowledge by people who are prepared to do careful fieldwork. And surely there is some appeal in the prospect of sitting on a Hebridean hillside during a sunny summer afternoon watching butterflies and bumblebees.

Britain has comparatively few kinds of butterflies and, with changing agricultural practices, they have declined alarmingly during this century. Our islands have, perhaps, been less subject to the all-destroying insecticide, and island subspecies of butterfly still flourish. The Hebrides have unique forms of the Small Pearl-bordered Fritillary, the Grayling, the Small Heath, the Speckled Wood and the Meadow Brown. The last two also have subspecies on the Isles of Scilly. Common Blues on Scilly illustrate some of the difficulties in the way of understanding the development of island life. On the tiny island of Tean a distinctive race of the Common Blue has developed, but on neighbouring St Martin's, which at its closest is only 900 feet (274m) from Tean, the butterflies of this species are the same as the widespread typical form. Apart from anything else this would seem to indicate that the Common Blue rarely travels over the sea, which immediately raises the question of how they reached the Scillies in the first place. No account of island butterflies would be complete without mentioning the Glanville Fritillary, now confined to the Channel Islands and the Isle of Wight.

Among the moths, the attractive red and greeny-black, day-flying Burnets have some interesting island forms. The Narrow-bordered Five-spot Burnet, *Zygaena lonicerae,* has a subspecies, *Z. l. jocelynae,* found only on Skye, while several of the Inner Hebrides have the Scottish form, *caledonensis,* of the Transparent Burnet, *Zygaena viciae,* and the equally rare Slender Scotch Burnet, *Zygaena loti scotica.* Another moth that sometimes flies by day and very early in the year – it is out in March and April – is the Belted Beauty, *Lycia zonaria,* which has a subspecies, *L. z. atlantica,* peculiar to the Hebrides. For dramatic coloration it is hard to beat the Tiger Moths. One of these, the Jersey Tiger, *Euplagia quadripunctaria,* has its stronghold, as the name suggests, in the Channel Islands, though it also occurs in Devon. The smaller Wood Tiger, a declining species, has a form – *Parasemia plantaginis insularum* – that is commonest on our northern isles of Orkney and Shetland though it also occurs on the Scottish mainland.

At dusk the strange white Ghost Moths hover over meadows in many parts of Britain. Shetland has its own smaller, more strongly marked subspecies of this insect which has been named *Hepialus humuli thulensis.* A much scarcer relative of the Ghost, the Map-winged Swift, also has a Shetland subspecies, *H. fusconebulosa shetlandicus* (curious the names that taxonomists have used to indicate a Shetland provenance – *thulensis, thulei, thuleana, zetlandicus, hethlandica, shetlandicus*).

Typical of moths that come out at night to circle mindlessly round house lights with gleaming eyes are the Noctuids. Mostly greyish, greenish or brownish, their wings are endless subtle variations on a sombre theme – and watching them is not unlike looking at a selection of different tweeds. These wings are, of course, a cryptic camouflage designed to protect the moths against hungry birds during the daytime when they rest on tree trunks or rocks. On our islands some Noctuids are much darker than mainland forms and this is particularly so in Shetland. This variation was studied by entomologists during the sixties and it was shown that, in the case of the Autumnal Rustic, *Paradiarsia glareosa,* the Shetland form, *P. g. edda,* occurs primarily where there is dark, peaty soil. Similar factors operate with the Ingrailed Clay, *Diarsia mendica,* which has separate subspecies on both Shetland, *D. m. thulei,* and Orkney, *D. m. orkneyensis,* and the Square-spot Rustic, *Xestia xanthographa.* Another Noctuid, the Heath Rustic, has a Hebridean subspecies, *Xestia agathina hebridicola,* but this is paler than mainland forms. On the Isles of Scilly the local subspecies of the Shuttle-shaped Dart, *Agrotis puta insula,* varies in the same way, and the Scillies also have a unique

The Glanville Fritillary which breeds only in the Isle of Wight.

254

form of the coastal Feathered Ranunculus, *Eumichtis lichenea scillonea*. Also from the south is the grey form of the Square-spot Dart, *Euxoa obelisca grisea*, which is confined to the Isle of Wight.

Before leaving the Noctuids, it is worth considering some curious cases illustrating the complexity of wildlife distribution. In the British Isles the Grey Moth, *Hadena caesia*, is represented by the subspecies, *H. c. mananii*, first described from the Isle of Man but now known also to occur around the coast of south-west Ireland and in scattered localities between Islay and Skye in western Scotland. On the Continent the species occurs on mountains, but in Britain it is always found within about a hundred and fifty feet (50m) of high-watermark. One hypothesis for this peculiarly disjunctive distribution is that, as the ice rolled forward during the last glaciation, the Continental forms found refuge to the south and east while in the west refuges from the ice were exposed by the fall in sea level (the water was needed to make all that ice).

Other species of moth that may illustrate this aspect of post-glacial history are the Pod Lover (a subspecies of the Tawny Shears), *Hadena perplexa capsophila*, the Sheepsbit-eating race of Campanula Pug, known as the Jasione Pug, *Eupithecia denotata jasioneata*, and the Dew Moth, *Setina irrorella*. All these species are found on the Isle of Man, indicating that this is a particularly good place to study the phenomenon, but they are also found on other islands and here and there on the mainland.

A different kind of evolution is occurring in the case of the Small Ranunculus, *Hecatera dysodea*. Until the turn of the century this moth was not uncommon in south-east England, but it declined rapidly and disappeared altogether in the late thirties and early forties. In the last twenty years it has only been reported in Britain from Jersey. The species is still widespread on the Continent, but seemingly retracting in the north of its range. There is some reason to believe that decline in its food plants – various wild lettuces – has affected the moth, but more evidence is needed before definite conclusions can be drawn.

Numerous Carpet and Pug Moths have island forms, the most variable being those of the Netted Pug, *Eupithecia venosata*, with subspecies from the Hebrides, *E. v. hebridensis*; from Shetland, *E. v. fumosae*; from Orkney, *E. v. ochracae*; and even from the Blaskets off south-west Ireland, *E. v. plumbea*. The Arran Carpet, *Chloroclysta concinnata*, has its stronghold on the high moors of the Isle of Arran, but has also been found on the Scottish mainland, while the Isle of Wight Wave, *Scopula humiliata*, has its classic locations on the cliffs of the island whose name it bears.

It is well known that rare, vagrant birds settle during spring and autumn migrations on remote islands, but such places also attract long-haul moths (or those that have hitched a ride on a ship). *Utetheisa bella* from North America, a pretty relative of our own Crimson Speckled, is on the British list by virtue of one example caught on Skokholm in 1948. Similarly, one example of a moth of the Black Arches family, *Nola chlamitulalis*, from southern Europe, was found in a light trap in Jersey in 1963. Rather more dubious is the record of Gregson's Dart, *Agrotis spinifera*, from the Isle of Man in 1869. The charitable view of this report of a subtropical and Mediterranean moth so far off course is that the set example was muddled up in a Victorian collector's box; less charitably, it could be that the Victorian collector was trying to notch up a 'new' addition to the British list.

Among the smaller moths, the so-called 'micros', less popular in the past among collectors and therefore less well known, only two island subspecies have been described, both Tortrix moths from Shetland (*Eupoecilia angustana thuleana* and *Syndemis musculana musculinana*). No doubt many others remain to be found. Other invertebrates (which put together far outnumber all our animals, birds, butterflies, moths and plants) not surprisingly have some island specialities, and here again is a field in which the amateur worker can make an important contribution. The great Manx naturalist W. S. Cowin had one such invertebrate named after him: the Robber Fly, *Epitriptus cowini*, which was first described from the Isle of Man and has recently featured on one of their stamps. The Isle of Man also has a grasshopper, *Stenobothrus stigmaticus*, found nowhere else in Britain, while the Blue-winged Grasshopper, *Oedipoda caerulescens*, is confined to the Scillies and the Channel Islands. Other southern invertebrates right on the limit of their range in the Channel Islands are the famous Ormers, the Top Shell, *Gibbula pennanti*, and the Sandhill Snail, *Theba pisana*.

Most people seem to avoid spiders, which is a pity because they have a fascinating and intricate biology; those that do like them will be pleased to know that the marshes around Havergate Island have their own spider, discovered only in 1953 and named, quite delightfully, *Praestigia duffeyi*.

Plants

The northern isles of Shetland and Orkney have many Arctic plants and a sea-level flora of species found only on mountains further to the south. Shetland specialities include the Shetland Mouse-ear Chickweed, *Cerastium nigrescens*, which favours the serpentine rocks of Unst where it grows in the company of other very local plants such as Northern Rock-cress, *Cardaminopsis petraea*, and Scottish Sandwort, *Arenaria norvegica*. The Red

Campions that grow on Shetland cliffs show a number of distinctive characteristics and have been given subspecific status under the name of *Silene dioica zetlandica*. Cambridge ecologist H. C. Prentice has, however, recently subjected the Campions to multidimensional scaling and non-hierarchic cluster analysis, the upshot being that these plants lose their sub-specific status.

Shetland grasses include the scarce Northern Salt-marsh Grass, *Puccinellia capillaris*, also found in Orkney and on the northern Scottish mainland, and an alien Meadow Grass, *Poa flabellata*, which hails from the southern hemisphere.

Orkney has some fine colonies of Northern Shore-wort, *Mertensia maritima*, sometimes known as the Oyster Plant from the taste of its fleshy leaves, and the islands are one of the best places to see the purple-flowered Scots Primrose, *Primula scotica*, our smallest member of the Primula genus and unique to Britain.

The Hebrides are not so unremittingly northern in their floral constitution as Shetland and Orkney and, indeed, contain a mixture of fascinating elements. Northern plants are there, like the tiny Iceland Purslane, *Koenigia islandica*, found only on Mull and Skye, or the Shetland Pondweed, *Potamogeton rutilus*, from lakes in the Outer Hebrides and Shetland. The allied Leafy Pondweed, *Potamogeton epihydrus*, is a British native only in Outer Hebridean lakes, the remainder of the population being across the Atlantic in North America. Several other plants show this transatlantic distribution – Pipewort, *Eriocaulon septangulare*, for instance, is widespread in Ireland but otherwise grows only on Skye and Coll and in North America, while the Drooping Lady's Tresses Orchid, *Spiranthes romanzoffiana*, has a similar distribution: Ireland, Colonsay, Coll, North America and, in this case, the Far East as well. It is easy to infer that similar events, spread over millions of years, somehow caused the disjunct distributions of the Leafy Pondweed, Pipewort, Drooping Lady's Tresses and other plants in this category. Hypotheses ranging from continental drift to Atlantis disasters have been invoked, but the real explanation remains obscure.

Another floristic element represented in the Hebrides is the Lusitanian, a term used to describe species confined to the westernmost edge of Europe. Pale Butterwort, *Pinguicula lusitanica*, and Cornish Moneywort, *Sibthorpia europaea*, are examples. Most extraordinary, perhaps, is the distribution of the splendid moss, *Myurium hebridarum*, which grows only in the Western Isles, south-west Britain, the Azores and the Canaries and on St Helena: an excellent piece of ammunition for inventors of Atlantean mythologies.

The island of Rhum, which has been very carefully studied by naturalists, has a number of unique and interesting plants. There

The Drooping Lady's Tresses orchid, (Spiranthes romanzoffiana) which in Britain grows only on Coll and Colonsay.

258

are two endemic Eyebrights, *Euphrasia rhumica* and *E. eurycarpa* (Lewis also has an endemic Eyebright, *E. campbellae*), and two Sedges, *Carex glacialis* and *C. bicolor*, found nowhere else in Britain. Rhum also has its own special orchid, *Dactylorchis fuchsii* ssp. *rhumensis*, though another subspecies of the same plant – ssp. *hebridensis* – is more widespread in the Hebrides.

Other Hebridean specialities include two trees, halfway between Whitebeam and Rowan, *Sorbus arranensis* and *S. pseudofennica*, found only on Arran. On Mull there is a famous fossil tree, known as McCullock's Tree, embedded in columnar basalt lava. Thyme Broomrape, *Orobanche alba*, a plant of western coasts, reaches its greatest British concentration on Skye and Mull, and the sedge *Carex capitata* is on the British list by virtue of one tuft of the plant found on Lewis. Fuday in the Outer Hebrides is the sole habitat of a variety of the Fragrant Orchid, *Gymnadenia conopsea* var. *insulicola*, which, instead of having the delicious perfume of the typical form, smells unpleasantly of rubber. The plant is normally pollinated by moths: maybe those on Fuday have 'special requirements'.

Two interesting grasses occur in the Hebrides: Purple Marram, x *Ammocalamagrostis baltica*, an intergeneric hybrid between ordinary Marram and Wood Small Reed, grows on the cliffs of Handa, and Bristle or Black Oat, *Avena strigosa*, is still cultivated in some areas where conditions are unfavourable to normal oats. On Raasay the pretty Balearic Sandwort, *Arenaria balearica*, a popular rock-garden plant, has established itself. It hails originally from various islands in the Mediterranean and it is curious that it should only settle happily on a small British island when there would appear to be better opportunities on plenty of mainland sites.

At the southern extremes of Britain the mild, moist climate of the Isles of Scilly favours the growth of many subtropical plants, as the gardens of Tresco Abbey testify. The Channel Islands share one or two special native plants with Scilly, but their flora is essentially that of the Continent and they have thirteen native plants not found elsewhere in Britain.

The Orange Birdsfoot, *Ornithopus pinnatus*, is now confined to Scilly and the islands are the best British stations for Cornish Mallow, *Lavatera cretica*, and Shore Dock, *Rumex rupestris*. Scilly and the Channel Islands are the only British homes of two diminutive plants: the Early Adder's Tongue Fern, *Ophioglossum lusitanicum*, whose tiny leaf-blades, less than an inch tall, grow on grassy cliff tops, and the minute Dwarf Pansy, *Viola kitaibeliana*, that favours sandy ground near the sea. The Scillies are now the home of a number of alien plants, the daffodil fields being one of their favourite habitats. Among them are the Scilly Buttercup,

Early Adder's Tongue Fern (Ophioglossum lusitanicum); *this tiny plant grows only on the Scilly and the Channel Islands.*

Ranunculus muricatus, and *Gladiolus byzantinus,* locally called Whistling Jacks – a name that sounds as though it derives from the old Cornish language.

The more dramatic plants of the Channel Islands include the tall, purple-crimson Jersey Orchid, *Orchis laxiflora,* that grows in damp meadows, Jersey Thrift, *Armeria arenaria,* of stable dunes, a lilac-flowered Clary called *Salvia verbenaca,* and the violet and white Toadflax, *Linaria pelisseriana,* now sadly thought to be extinct in the heathy spots it prefers. The delightfully fragrant Western Pink, *Dianthus gallicus,* grows on grassy dunes in Jersey, and is considered to have been deliberately introduced. Less impressive, but fascinating to the botanist, are the little Annual Centaury, *Exaculum pusillum,* the Forget-me-not, *Myosotis sicula,* from damp spots on Jersey dunes, the Sea Lavender, *Limonium lychnidifolium,* which brightens rocks near the sea, and the Jersey Cudweed, *Gnaphalium luteo-album.* Another of the cudweeds, *Gnaphalium undulatum,* is an established alien in the Channel Islands. An interesting plant is the Sharp Bulrush, *Scirpus americanus,* which grows around the margins of Jersey ponds and, as well as occurring on the Continent, is found in America and Australia – a truly cosmopolitan distribution. The Branched Broomrape, *Orobanche ramosa,* is considered native on Jersey and Sark: it is one of those strange plants that contain no chlorophyll and derive sustenance by attaching themselves parasitically to the roots of other species. The Branched Broomrape has curiously narcotic predilections as its favourite hosts are cannabis and tobacco, though it will put up with tomato or potato plants.

Local grasses include the millet, *Milium scabrum,* from fixed dunes, and the pretty Hare's Tail Grass, *Lagurus ovatus.* Great Brome, *Bromus diandrus,* is naturalised, while a second species, *Bromus rigidus,* is considered native. In America *B. rigidus* is a troublesome weed commonly called Ripgut Grass from the damaging effect the sharply pointed seeds have on grazing cattle. Among the ferns the local speciality is the tiny, annual Jersey Fern, *Anogramma leptophylla,* which grows in shady hedge banks.

Although it is a South African plant from Table Mountain, the Guernsey Lily, *Nerine sarniensis,* is clearly associated with the Channel Islands. A beautiful, but not hardy, bulbous plant, it derives its name from the fact that a quantity of bulbs were washed up on a Guernsey beach after a shipwreck.

Islands outside the major groups also have their floral specialities, although in somewhat lesser number. The well-known rock-garden plant *Geranium sanguineum* var. *lancastriense* with its delicate pink flowers is a variant of the crude magenta-coloured Bloody Cranesbill and has been found only on Walney Island, Cumbria. The Isle of Man has the rare Dense-flowered

Orchid, *Neotinea intacta*, found there in 1965 and otherwise known only from south-west Ireland and the Mediterranean, and its own special cabbage. The Isle of Man Cabbage, *Rhynchosinapis monensis*, was described in 1660 from plants found at Ramsey, where it still grows, by the great botanist John Ray, but is now known to be quite widely distributed on western coasts. Another member of the same genus, the Lundy Cabbage, *Rhynchosinapis wrightii*, grows nowhere else in the world other than on the cliffs and slopes on the east of Lundy Island.

Anglesey has a unique Marsh Orchid, *Dactylorhiza majalis* ssp. *cambrensis*, and shares the Dune Helleborine, *Epipactis dunensis*, with Lindisfarne and Lancashire. South Stack, off Anglesey's Holy Island, has two plants – the Annual Rock-rose, *Tuberaria guttata*, and the euphoniously named Spathulate Fleawort, *Senecio spathulifolius* – that are both very rare on the mainland. In the Bristol Channel, Steep Holm has some flourishing colonies of Wild Leek, *Allium porrum*, as does (appropriately enough for a Welsh island) Flat Holm. Unique to Steep Holm are the Wild Peony, *Paeonia mascula*, a relic from the days when the island monks grew it for medicinal purposes, and a form of Sea Plantain, *Plantago maritima* var. *sabrinae*. The attractive Wood

Cornish mallow (Lavatera cretica), photographed on St Mary's, Isles of Scilly.

263

Calamint, *Calamintha sylvatica*, has its one British station on a chalky bank on the Isle of Wight.

As well as possessing rare and unique species, our islands have some special types of plant community which are of great interest to ecologists. The most extensive is the Hebridean machair, a kind of dune pasture created by sand being blown inland by the force of the Atlantic gales. Machair is rich in plants and other types of wildlife and is one of the most important nesting grounds for shore birds. The Monach Isles have notable stretches of uncultivated machair. Other communities are the peat mounds clothed in plants of the heather family found in Britain only on North Roe in the Shetlands and Hoy in the Orkneys, and a lichen heath above the cliffs at the north of Hoy. St Kilda and some other islands heavily subjected to salt spray have special turf called *Plantago* sward, composed mainly of Sea Plantain and Red Fescue grass, while the low-lying Fianuis peninsula on remote Rona has a *Stellaria* sward consisting of Chickweed and a number of other annual weeds whose growth is promoted by the seals that churn the ground into mud.

Discovery and Conservation

This brief review gives, I hope, an impression of the immense riches, in terms of wild animals and plants, that our offshore islands support. For the real enthusiast there are many discoveries to be made, particularly among lesser-known groups like insects and non-flowering plants. An instance is provided by the fact that no ants have so far been officially recorded either from Mull or Lewis, although it is almost certain that at least one or two species would occur there. The occasional naturalist and those who go with guided parties and tours will constantly wonder at the wilderness wealth of our islands. Anyone planning a holiday or visit is well advised to get in touch with the County Naturalists' Trust for the area in question before setting off. These organisations can give details of access to reserve areas and often have notes or other information on island wildlife. They do an immense amount of conservation work, mostly through volunteers, so if you enjoy one of the places they are looking after do try to remember to make some financial contribution so that future work can continue.

Finally, a word about conservation itself. Because our offshore islands are small, many of their special plants and animals exist only in tiny populations compared with those of the mainland. It is therefore even more important than on the mainland that any kind of disturbance or damage is kept to a minimum. Experienced naturalists should know how to behave themselves, but conservation problems can often be caused by simply not knowing what lies underfoot. The best way to feel at ease in an area of high wildlife interest is to have a chat with a nature-reserve warden, or similarly knowledgeable local person, before setting off to explore. The enjoyable and rewarding experiences in store can only be enhanced through the taking of this small precaution.

Index

N.B. 1. Illustrations are indicated by *italics*.
2. Islands are shown on maps at the beginning of each chapter.

A' Chùli 125–6
Ailsa Craig 98–9, 247
Alderney 17, 25–6, 27, 244
The Allans *see* Eileans, Inner and Outer
Am Fraoch Eilean 120
Anglesey 16, 78, 242, 263
Annet 54
Ardwall Island 98
Arran 102–7, *103–4*, 236, 244, 256, 260
Ascrib Islands 146
Asparagus Islands 16, 39, *42*
Auskerry 193

Badcall Group 182
Bait Island *see* St Mary's I. (Whitley Bay)
Balta 206
Bardsey *44*, 68, 77–8, *79*
Barlocco 98
Barra Group 149, 151–7 *see also* separate
    entries
Barra 115, 151, 152–4, *153*, 236
Barra Head Rock Lighthouse 151
Barry Island 235
Bass Rock 11, 99, 212–17, 247
Bearasay 167
Bell Rock 210
Benbecula 149, 157, 158
Berneray (Barra) 151
Berneray (Harris with Lewis) 166
Big Harcar 225
Bird Island (N. Ireland) 234
Bird Island *see* Mahee, Mingulay
Bishop and his Clerks *see* Bishops and Clerks
Bishop Rock (Scilly Is.) 52–5, *53*
Bishops and Clerks 76
Blaskets 256
Blockhouse Island 88
Boreray (Harris with Lewis) 166

Boreray (St Kilda) 171, 172, 173–5, 247
Borough *see* Burgh I.
Brecqhou 17, 23, *24*
Bressay 202
The Brisons 61
Brosdale Island 120
Brough of Birsay 190
Brownsea Island 34–6, *35*, 240
Brownsman 226
Bruray 206–7
Bryher 55, 57, 58
Burgh Island 37
Burhou 17, 26
Burial Island 90
Burra 198–200, 201
Burray 187
The Burroo 84–5
Burry Holms 69
Bute 15, *100*, 101–2, 237

Cairn na Burgh Beg 133
Cairn na Burgh More 133
Caldey Island 11, 68, 70, 72, *73*, 221
Calf Islands 16, 84–5
Calf of Bute *see* Inchmarnock
Calf of Eday 192
Calf of Man 84, *109*, 242
Calvay 157
Calve Island 126
Canna 135, 138–9, 140
Canvey Island 16
Cara 119, 242
Cardigan Island 76
Carn Islands 181
Carna 234
Carrey Rhoson 76
Carrick-a-Rede *94*, 95
Les Casquets 17, 26

Castle Island 95
Cava 188
Channel Islands *see* separate entries
Chapel Island 90
Chicken Rock 85
Chicken's Lighthouse 85
Chorrie Island *see* Eilean Choraidh
Churchill Causeways *see* Orkney
Cobmarsh 230
Cock Island 102
Cockle Island 92
Coll 113, 133, 134, 138, 258, *259*
Colonsay 121–3, *123*, *124*, 258, *259*
Coomb Island *see* Neave I.
Copeland Islands 90–92
Copinsay 190
Coquet 11, 227
Council Isle 116
Craigleith 217
Cramond Island *219*, 220
Crawlin Islands 147
The Crebawethans 54
The Crebinicks 54
Crevichon 17, 26
Crumstones 224
The Cumbraes 100–1

Danna Island 234
Davaar Island 107
Dee Island 235
Deer Island *see* Jura
Denny 67
The Dogs of Scilly 54
Drake's Island 37–8, *38*
Dubh Artach 126, 130
Dubh Heartach *see* Dubh Artach
Dun 171–5
Dùn Chonaill *see* Dùn Chonnuil
Dùn Chonnuil 126
Dunball *see* Dungball
Dungball 16, 67
Dunsey Rock 90
Dutchman's Cap 133

Easdale 124
Eastern Isles (Scilly Is.) 59–60
Les Ecréhous 17, 18
Eday 191–2
Egilsay 201
Eigg 135, 136, 137
Eikach an Naoimh 125
Eileans, Inner *and* Outer 101
Eilean Bàn 148
Eilean Chaluim Chille *see* St Columba's Isle
Eilean Choraidh 183

Eilean Mór (Crawlin Is.) 147
Eilean Mór (Islay) 116
Eilean Mór (Jura) 120
Eilean nan Ròn 183, 248
Eilean Trodday 146
Enchanted Isles *see* Shiant Is.
Ensay 167
Eorsa 132
Erisgeir 130
Eriskay 149, 154–7, 162
Erraid 130
Estholm *see* Hestan
Eynhallow 190

Fair Isle 197, *208*, 209, 239, 253
Far Isles 96, 108, 169–76 *see also* separate
  entries
Fara 188
Faray 191–2
Farne Island 226–7, 247, 248
Farne Islands 224–7 *see also* separate entries
Fetlur 197, 205–6
Fiaray Island 154
Fidra 217
Fladda 133
Fladday/Flodday/Floday 234
Flannan Islands 171, 248
Flannan I. Lighthouse 171
Flat Holm 68
Flory Island 234
Flotta 188, 189
Fort Island *see* St Michael's I.
Foula 197, 207–8, *214–15*, 239, 248
Foulney 86, 247
Fowley Island 234
Fuday 154, 260
Fuiary Island *see* Fiaray I.
Furzey 36

Gairsay 191–2
Gannet's Island *see* Boreray (St Kilda)
Garbh Eileach 126
Garvellachs 108, 124–6, *125*
Gateholm 72
Giant's Causeway 131
Gigga's Island 36
Gigha 118–19, *118*
Gilstone 54
Glims Holm 187–8
Glimpse Holm *see* Glims H.
Godrevy Islands 61, *65*
Gometra 133
Grassholme 72, 74, 247
Graemsay 188
Great Arthur 59

Great Bernera 167
Great Cumbrae 100–1
Great Ganilly 59–60
Great Mew Stone 37
Green Island (N. Ireland) 88
Green Island (Poole Harbour) 36
Greneze see Guernsey
Grim Rocks 52
Grimsay 158
Grove Island 36
Guernsey 17, 18, 24, 25, 26, 27–9, 28, 237,
    238, 239, 240
Gugh 16, 46, 50, 51–2, 52
Gull Rock 39
Gunna Mor 132
The Gunners 52
Guns Island 88
Gwales in Penfro see Grassholme
Gweal 57

Haaf Gruney 206
Hamford Water Islands 230
Handa 182–3, 183, 260
Harcar Island 226
Harris with Lewis 147, 149, 158, 160–6, 161,
    167, 177 see also Lewis
Haskier Islands 160
Havergate Island 228–30, 248, 252
Hayling Island 234
Hebrides 96, 108–48, 113, 119, 149–68, 236,
    246, 253, 256, 258 see also separate entries
Hellisay 154
The Hellweathers 54
Hen Island 90
Herm 17, 26–7, 41, 84, 240
Hermetray 167
Hestan 96–8
Hilbre 86, 87
Hilbre Islands 86, 247
Hildasay 201
Hirta 171–2, 172–3
Holy Island 16, 78, 107, 263 see also
    Anglesey, Lindisfarne
Horse of Copinsay 192
Horse Island (Strathclyde) 100, 247
Horse Island (Summer Is.) 181, 182
Horsey Island 230
Housay 206–7
Hoy 186, 187, 188–9, 264

Ile au Guerdain 22
Les Iles Normandes see Channel Is.
Inch Kenneth 128, 132
Inchcape Rock see Bell Rock

Inchcolm 217, 219–20
Inchkeith 217–19, 218
Inchmarnock 102
Inchmickery 217, 219
Inishanier 90
Inner Farne Light 227, 229
Inner Hebrides 108–48
Innis Bheag 235
Innis Mohr 235
Innis Patrick see St Patrick's Isle
Insh Island 235
Iona 85, 123, 125, 126, 127, 128–30, 129, 132,
    160, 221
Isinvrank 54
Island Magee 92
Island Taggart 90
Islandmore 90
Islands of Fleet 98
Islay 95, 108, 113, 116, 117, 119, 237, 239,
    240–2, 248, 256
Isle of Ewe 181
Isle of Grain see Tiree
Isle of May 16, 210, 211
Isle of Wight 11, 13, 15, 30–4, 31, 34, 83, 106,
    240, 242, 246, 254, 255, 256, 263–4
Isles of the Sea see Garvellachs
Isle Martin 181
Isle Ristol 181
L'Islet 21

Jane's Rock 90
Jersey 13, 15, 17, 18–22, 21, 22, 27, 239, 240,
    246, 254, 256, 257, 262
Jethou 17, 26–7
Jura 95, 108, 119–20, 120, 237, 240–2

Kerrera 135
Kishorn Island 235
Kitterland 84
Knivestone 225

Lady Isle 100
Lamb Holm 180, 187–8
Lamb Island see Craigleith
Lamb Islet 217
Lamba 202
Larry's Island see Ardwall
Lewis 149, 160, 161, 162–6, 163, 164, 167,
    169, 170, 178–9, 244, 260, 264 see also
    Harris with Lewis
Lighthouse Island 92
Lihou 17, 29
Lindisfarne 16, 216, 221–4, 226, 224, 246,
    247, 263

Linga 201
Lismore 135
Little Colonsay 132
Little Cumbrae 100–1
Little Eye 86
Little Hilbre 86
Little Ross 98
Little Shutter Rock 64
Llanddwyn 78
Long Island (N. Ireland) 90
Long Island (Poole Harbour) 36
Longa 181
Longay 235
Longstone 225
Looe Island see St George's Island
Luchruban 167
Luing 108
Lundy 51, 61, 62–6, 84, 237, 240, 242, 248, 263
Lunga (Luing) 123–4
Lunga (Treshnish Is.) 133

Mahee 90, 91
Maiden Bower 16, 57
Maiden Rocks/The Maidens 92, 93
Mainland (Orkney) 185, 188, 189–90
Mainland (Shetland) 194, 197–207
Man 11, 13, 15, 81–4, 83, 84, 119, 198, 242, 248, 256, 257, 262–3
Medway Islands 234
Megstones 224
Melledgan 54
Men-a-Vaur 58, 59
Mersea Island 230
Mew Island 92
Mew Stone 72
Middleholm see Midland Isle
Middle Island see Midland Isle
Midland Isle 72
The Minaltos 57
Mincarlo 57
Mingulay 151–2
Les Minquiers 17, 18, 20
Mochras see Shell Island
Monach Islands 160, 244, 264
La Motte 22
The Mouls 61–2
Mousa 204
Mouse Island (Lundy) 16, 66
Mouse Islands (Skerries) 80
Muck 16, 92, 92, 135–6
Muckle Flugga 206, 207
Muckle Rae 201
Muckle Skerry Lighthouse 185
Mugdrum 210

Muic see Muck
Mull 95, 108, 126–8, 127, 129, 130, 132, 133, 237, 248, 258, 260, 264
Mullion Island 39
Murray's Isles 98

Nave Island 235
Neave Island 183
Newland 61
Nornour 59–60
The Norrads 57
North Islands (Shetland) 197
North Roe 264
North Ronaldsay 180, 184, 191, 193
North Stack 78
North Uist 149, 157, 158–60, 159
Northey Island 234
Northwethal 57–8
Noss 202

Oigh-sgeir 138
Oldany 182
Orkney 11, 96, 184–93, 194, 190, 191, 237, 238–9, 248–50, 254, 256, 258 see also separate entries
Ornsay (Sound of Sleat) 148
Oronsay (Eilean nan Ròn) 248
Oronsay (Inner Hebrides) 121, 122
Oronsay (Loch Sunart) 235
Oronsay (Uist) 160
Ortac 17
Osea Island 68, 230–1, 247
Out Skerries 206
Out Stack 202
Outer Hebrides 149–68
Oxna 200

Pabay (Inner Hebrides) 147
Pabbay (Barra) 151, 152
Pabbay (Sound of Harris) 147, 152, 166–7, 166
Papa 200
Papa Little 201
Papa Stour 201, 213
Papa Stronsay 191, 193
Papa Westray 193
Parton 90
Peggy's Island 90
Pentland Skerries 186
Pergin's Island 36
Piel Island 86–7
Pig Island 90
Pladda 11, 107
Pladda Lighthouse 107

'Plenty-to-come-yet' Reef 61
Pomona 189–90
Priest Island 181
Priestholm *see* Puffin Island
Puffin Island 80, 248
Isle of Purbeck 234

Raasay 146–7, *148*, 239, 260
Rabbit Islands 183
Ragged Island 59
Raghery *see* Rathlin I.
Ramsey 68, 76
Rat Island 66
Rathlin Island 93–5, *110–11*, 131, 243
Raz 17, 26
Read's Island 228, 247
Rechra *see* Rathlin I.
Reogh Island 90
Rhum 135, 136–8, *139*, 248, 258–60
Roa Island 86
Rockall 11, 108, 169, *175*, 176
Rona (Inner Hebrides) 16, 113, 146, 147, 169
Rona Lighthouse 146
Rona (Far Isles) 146, 169, 171, 264
Ronay 160
Rosevear 54
Rough Island 96
Round Island (N. Ireland) 90
Round Island (Poole Harbour) 36
Round Island (Scilly Is.) 58
Round I. Lighthouse 58–9
Rousay 190
Rum *see* Rhum
Rumblings 206
Rysa Little 188

St Agnes' Island 50–1, *51*, 52
St Aubin's Fort 22
St Catherine's Island 69–72, *69*
St Clement's Island 40
St Columba's Isle 168
St Cuthbert's Island 224
St George's Island 38–9
St Helen's 58
St Kilda Group *ii*, 11–12, 96, 108, 169, 171–6, *173*, *174*, 208, 236, 237, 239, 244, 247, 252–3, 264
St Margaret's Island 72
St Martin's Island 59, *60*, 253
St Mary's Island (Scilly Is.) 48–50, 54, 56, 59, *48*, *50*, *60*, *261*
St Mary's Island (Whitley Bay) 227–8
St Michael's Island (Fort Island) 85–6
St Michael's Mount 16, 30, 39–40, *40*, 221

St Ninian's Island 198
St Patrick's Causeway 77
St Patrick's Isle (Man) 85, *85*
St Tudwal's Islands 11, 77
Samson 57
Sanda 107
Sanda Lighthouse 107
Sanday (Inner Hebrides) 138
Sanday (Orkney) 193
Sandray 151, 152
Sark 17, 22–4, *23*, *24*, 27, *125*, 240, 246
Sarn Badrig *see* St Patrick's Causeway
Scalpey (Inner Hebrides) 147
Scalpey (Outer Hebrides) 147, 168
Scarba 123, 237
Scarp 167
Scilly Isles *see* separate entries
Scilly Rock 57
Scolt Head 228, 247
Seil 124, 237
Sgeir an Fheòir 133
Shapinsay 191–2
Sheelah's Island 90
Sheep Island (Mull of Kintyre) 107
Sheep Island (N. Ireland) 95
Sheep Island (Wales) 72
Shell Island 77
Sheppey 16
Shetland 11, 194, *197*, *203*, 242, 248, 254, 256, 257–8 *see also* separate entries
Shiant Islands 11, 167–8, *168*
Shieldaig Island 148
Shillay 167
Shoan Island 90
Shuna 123–4, 240
The Skerries (Anglesey) 78–80
Skerry Islands (N. Ireland) 95
Skerryvore Lighthouse 130
Skipper's Island 230
Skokholm 72–4, *75*, 238–9, 248, 257
Skomer Island 72, 74, *74*, 239, 248, *249*,
Skye 108, *112*, 113, *113*, 126, 134, 136, 139–44, *141*, *142–3*, *145*, 146, 147, *147*, 148, 157, 254, 256, 258, 260
Small Islands (Jura) 120
The Small Isles (Inner Hebrides) 135–40 *see also* separate entries
The Smalls (Wales) 74–6
Soay (St Kilda) 144, 171, 175–6, 242, 243
Soay (Skye) 144–6
South Bishop Lighthouse 76
South Havra 198
South Ronaldsay 186, 187, 188
South Stack 78

South Uist 115, 149, 154, 155, 157, 158, 159, 173, 236
Stac Lee 175
The Stack (Calf Islands) 84–5
Stack Island (Uist) 157
Stack Skerry 190–1, *192*
Staffa 11, 51, 95, 130–2, *131*, 201
Staple Island 226, *226*
Steep Holm *66*, 237, 247, 263
Stert Island 248
Strangford Lough Island 88
Strona 185–6
Stronsay 191, 193
Sula Sgeir, 113, 162, 170, 247
Sule Skerry 190–1
Sully Island 235
The Summer Isles 182–2 *see also* separate entries
Sunken Island 230
Swona 186

Tanera Beg 181
Tanera Mór 181
Taransay 167
Tean 59, 253
Texa 118
Thorn Island 72
Tipta 206
Tiree 113, 133–4, 242
Toll's Island 60
Torran Rocks 126
Trainor Island 90
Tresco *43*, 46, *52*, 54, 55–7, *56*, 59, 253, 260
Treshnish Islands 133 *see also* separate entries
Trondra 200–1

Tyree *see* Tiree

Uist Islands 149, *156 see also* separate entries
Ulva 132–3
Unst 197, 204–5, 206
Uyea 206

Vaila 201
Vatersay 151, 152
Vementray 201

Walney 86, 87, 247, 248, 262
The Wamses 226
Western Isles 113, 149, 258
Western Rocks (Scilly Is.) 46, 52–3
Whalsay 202, 206
White Island *see* Eilean Bàn
White Island (St Martin's, Scilly Is.) 59, *60*
White Island (Samson) 59
Wiay 146, 158
Wolf Island *see* Ulva
Worms Head 16, 69
Wyre 190

Yell 16, 197, 204–5
Ynys Bery 76
Ynys Dewi *see* Ramsey
Ynys Dulas 80
Ynys Eilun 76
Ynys Enlli *see* Bardsey
Ynys Gwylan 77
Ynys Pyr *see* Caldey I.
Ynys Seiriol *see* Puffin I.
Ynyscantwr 76
Ynys-Lochtin 77

Illustration Acknowledgements

Colour
Peter Baker, Crewkerne 41, 112 top, 177; British Tourist Authority, London 109, 180 bottom, 216; John Bulmer, London 44, 180 top, 213 top, 214–15; John Green, London 178–9; A. Hamilton, Pinner 43; Kenneth McNally, Belfast 110–11; Spectrum Colour Library, London 112 bottom; Bob and Sheila Thomlinson, Carlisle 213 bottom; Judy Todd, London 42

Black and White
Aerofilms, Borehamwood 34, 40, 185, 211, 218, 219, 225; K. M. Andrew, Prestwick 2; Avon County Library, Weston-Super-Mare 66; Peter Baker, Crewkerne 24; British Petroleum, London 195; British Tourist Authority, London 25, 28, 56, 73, 85, 187, 199; John Bulmer, London 79, 200; Clyde River Steamer Club, Glasgow 100; B. C. Crichton, Edinburgh 104–5; Crown copyright – reproduced with permission of the Controller of Her Majesty's Stationery Office 31; M. Dent, London 183; The Distiller's Company Limited, London 117; F. E. Gibson, Scilly Isles 51, 52, 53, 55, 60; Fay Godwin Photo Files, London 50, 58, 164, 191; Michael Hales, Exeter 127; A. Hamilton, Pinner 23, 48–9; Hebridean Press Service, Stornoway 166; Eric Hosking, London 74, 75, 87, 207, 243, 249, 250; Imperial War Museum, London 188; Geoffrey Kinns, London 241, 245, 251; John Lewis Partnership, London 35; Loganair, Glasgow 153; Kenneth McNally, Belfast 91, 92, 93, 94; Mansell Collection, London 22, 69, 99, 131; Mansell Collection–British Tourist Authority 21; National Trust, London 224; National Trust for Scotland, Edinburgh 103, 208; National History Photographic Agency, Saltwood 255; A. P. Paterson, London 259; Press Association, London 84; Gordon Ridley, Glasgow 125, 192; Scottish Tourist Board, Edinburgh 120, 159, 190, 197; J. Small, London 261, 263; Spectrum Colour Library, London 65, 142–3, 204–5; Bob and Sheila Thomlinson, Carlisle 226, 229; Pamla Toler, London 168; John Topham Picture Library, Edenbridge 27, 83, 139, 145, 156, 173, 175, 203; John Topham–Keystone Press Agency 20; Tom Weir, Gartocharn 118, 122, 123, 137, 148, 155, 174; Western Morning News, Plymouth 38; Gus Wylie, St Albans 124, 129, 141, 147, 161, 163